Curbing the spread of nuclear weapons

Manchester University Press

Curbing the spread of nuclear weapons

Ian Bellany

Manchester University Press
Manchester and New York
distributed exclusively in the USA by Palgrave

Copyright © Ian Bellany 2005

The right of Ian Bellany to be identified as the author of this work has been asserted by him in accordance with the Copyright, Designs and Patents Act 1988.

Published by Manchester University Press
Oxford Road, Manchester M13 9NR, UK
and Room 400, 175 Fifth Avenue, New York, NY 10010, USA
www.manchesteruniversitypress.co.uk

Distributed in the United States exclusively by
Palgrave Macmillan, 175 Fifth Avenue,
New York, NY 10010, USA

Distributed in Canada exclusively by
UBC Press, University of British Columbia, 2029 West Mall,
Vancouver, BC, Canada V6T 1Z2

British Library Cataloguing-in-Publication Data is available

Library of Congress Cataloging-in-Publication Data is available

ISBN 978 0 7190 6797 6 paperback

First published by Manchester University Press in hardback 2005

This paperback edition first published 2013

The publisher has no responsibility for the persistence or accuracy of URLs for any external or third-party internet websites referred to in this book, and does not guarantee that any content on such websites is, or will remain, accurate or appropriate.

Printed by Lightning Source

Contents

List of figures	*page* vi
List of tables	vii
Preface	viii
List of abbreviations	ix
Introduction	1
1 Nuclear weapons and nuclear energy	4
2 Nuclear weapons and international security	48
3 The International Atomic Energy Agency and safeguards	76
4 Understanding nuclear-free zones	104
5 United States policy on non-proliferation and the Nuclear Non-proliferation Treaty	126
6 Bargaining for test ban treaties	160
Appendices	
A The Baruch Plan	173
B Atoms for Peace	181
C Treaty on the Non-proliferation of Nuclear Weapons	187
D Treaty of Tlatelolco documentation and texts	198
E Joint Declaration on the Denuclearization of the Korean Peninsula	221
Index	223

Figures

1.1 Schematic representation of the nuclear fuel cycle   13

2.1 International security in a complex as a function of nuclear spread: case 1, C_0 equals A_1 56

2.2 International security in a complex as a function of nuclear spread: case 2, C_0 is greater than A_1 57

2.3 International security in a complex as a function of nuclear spread: case 3, C_0 is less than A_1 57

2.4 International security in a complex as a function of nuclear spread: case 4, C_0 is much greater than A_1 58

2.5 Risk of accidental nuclear war as a function of nuclear spread, plotted as the number of years before an accidental nuclear strike may be expected to occur   61

2.6 International security in a complex as a function of nuclear spread: k-value   71

3.1 Intrusiveness of inspections versus frequency   84

Tables

2.1	Deadlock game	54
2.2	Prisoner's dilemma game	54
2.3	Acute prisoner's dilemma game	54
2.4	Multilateral prisoner's dilemma game	55
2.5	Security values for a 10-state complex	73
3.1	Inspection game with qualitative payoffs for the state	79
3.2	Inspection game with quantitative payoffs for the state	79
3.3	Inspection game with imperfect technique	82
4.1	Defence expenditure as percentage of gross domestic product within nuclear-free zones	113
A.1	Signatories and parties to the Treaty on the Non-proliferation of Nuclear Weapons	193
A.2	Status of signatures and ratifications of the Treaty for the Prohibition of Nuclear Weapons in Latin America and the Caribbean	220

Preface

The author's professional life began with the Nuclear Non-proliferation Treaty, when during the 1960s he was, at the public expense, learning something about the non-physical world from his brilliant colleagues at the Arms Control and Disarmament Research Unit in Whitehall. He has continued to benefit from the generosity of others, and would like to take this opportunity to thank all who have given him a hand in the production of this book. Chief among these is the Leverhulme Trust, without one of whose fellowships in 2003–4 it would have scarcely been possible to complete this work, given the present harsh climate of overstretch facing staff even in the best of British universities.

Indispensable help with the book of a different kind has come from a large number of individuals both in Britain and in the United States, in the public service and outside, who will understand if I do not attempt to name them all individually.

Finally, thanks are due to Manchester University Press, one of the few remaining academic presses in the country deserving of the name, without whose original interest in the project it would never have got off the ground, and their anonymous reader, whose name should be added to the large list of those of whose help these few words are a poor acknowledgement.

Lancaster, 2005

Abbreviations

ABACC	Brazilian–Argentine Agency for Accounting and Control of Nuclear Materials
ABM	Anti-Ballistic Missile (Treaty)
AFCONE	African Commission on Nuclear Energy
AGR	advanced gas-cooled reactor
ASEAN	Association of Southeast Asian Nations
CTBT	Comprehensive Test Ban Treaty
EMIS	electromagnetic isotope separation
EU	European Union
IAEA	International Atomic Energy Agency
ICBMs	intercontinental ballistic missiles
INFCE	International Nuclear Fuel Cycle Evaluation (conference)
KEDO	Korean Peninsula Energy Development Organisation
MTCR	Missile Technology Control Regime
MUF	material unaccounted for
NATO	North Atlantic Treaty Organisation
NPT	(Nuclear) Non-proliferation Treaty
NSG	Nuclear Suppliers' Group
OPANAL	Agency for the Prohibition of Nuclear Weapons in Latin America
PNE	Peaceful Nuclear Explosions (Treaty)
PTBT	Partial Test Ban Treaty
PWR	pressurised water reactor
SEANWFZ	South East Asia Nuclear Weapon-Free Zone
TTBT	Threshold Test Ban Treaty
UN	United Nations

Introduction

This book is made up of a series of partially self-contained, partially overlapping chapters, each looking at an aspect of the question at hand. Each chapter attempts to illuminate the whole or a goodly part of the spread of nuclear weapons and how to curb it, but from a particular perspective. The chapters are like a series of photographs of a particular three-dimensional object taken from different angles. In one way this should make the book easier to read, in that it can be dipped into piecemeal. Even so, a reader encountering an unsupported assertion in one chapter should be aware of the possibility that justification for the point will be found in another.

Each chapter, moreover, has been written to a plan. What has to be said is said as far as possible in plain-language but the argument is normally underpinned by a theoretical treatment, without which it would be incomplete. A particularly straightforward example is Chapter 6, where elementary bargaining theory is used to throw light on the long international history of attempts to secure a ban on the testing of nuclear weapons. But even there, the plain-language statement will usually be sufficient to allow a reader in a hurry in good conscience to take the theoretical adjunct on trust.

One thing each chapter has in common is a reference, often lengthy, to the Nuclear Non-proliferation Treaty (NPT), the chief global political instrument operating to restrain the spread of nuclear weapons, first opened for signature in 1968 and to which every member state of the United Nations (UN) is party, bar India, Israel and Pakistan. Thus, in the first chapter, the NPT appears in the context of the uptake of nuclear energy for commercial reasons. In the second chapter the context is that of international relations theory, with special reference to rational-choice approaches. In the third the context is the inspection procedures adopted by the International Atomic Energy Agency (IAEA), an essential prop to the effectiveness of the NPT. In the fourth chapter the context is that of regional nuclear-free zones, a phenomenon both influencing the NPT and influenced by it, and on the whole beneficially. The fifth chapter places the NPT in the context of US non-proliferation policy, and vice versa. The final chapter is about the main missing prop of the NPT, an international agreement to ban all testing of nuclear weapons, which remains just out of reach. The concluding section of the book is a series of appendices (broadly in chronological order) which aims to fill in the documentational background. Aside from the texts of the NPT and the Latin American nuclear-free zone, its earliest entry is the speech given by US delegate Bernard Baruch to the UN Atomic Energy Commission in 1946, and the latest the Joint Declaration by the governments of each half of Korea on the denuclearisation of the peninsula.

Since the structure of the book does not naturally lend itself to one, there is no concluding chapter. This does not mean that no conclusions are reached. One concerns the IAEA, whose safeguard activities are at the heart of the NPT. It seems likely that the Agency, to some extent abetted by vigorous state campaigners against proliferation such as the USA, originally became rather fixated on plutonium as the critical precursor of nuclear weapons and for too long gave too little attention to highly enriched uranium.

Another is more theoretical. Traditionally, the neo-realist laissez-faire view of Waltz that nuclear proliferation can be beneficial to international security has been regarded as standing in opposition to the liberal institutionalist view that collective action to prevent proliferation is a better guarantee of international security. The conclusion reached here is that much depends on how far proliferation may have progressed within a given security complex. The practical relevance of this point chiefly relates to the status of the 'big power' nuclear weapons states (the Permanent Five of the Security Council) and possible future additions to their ranks.

A third conclusion concerns nuclear-free zones. These are seen as both less significant and more significant than is often assumed. Sometimes they do not especially resemble security complexes and either for that reason or because they are not doing any particular job of work in holding back pressures to go nuclear (e.g. the South Pacific Nuclear Free Zone) they should not automatically be seen as a good thing. But when they do not clearly fail such tests, their potential contribution as major building blocks of a relatively unproliferated world should not be underestimated.

A fourth conclusion relates to the structure of international institutional approaches to securing a public good like a relatively unproliferated world for member states. Because the more powerful states would be better able than the remaining parties to the arrangement to tolerate a world where the institutional arrangement collapsed, the powerful states can normally expect to obtain privileges for themselves within the context of the institutional bargain. The Comprehensive Test Ban Treaty, an adjunct arrangement to the NPT, has been stalled for a decade chiefly because, on the present analysis, of its excessively democratic structure, where all states are treated alike.

A fifth conclusion concerns nuclear disarmament in the sense of the abolition of nuclear weapons. It is out of the question, partly for the same sort of reason that the Comprehensive Test Ban Treaty has run into the sand, and partly because it would place an impossibly large task on any inspectorate required to verify that no state had secretly hidden away a few warheads out of an original stockpile of thousands.

A final conclusion relates to the NPT itself. Like all good arms control treaties, it should be at constant risk of failure since, like a good nuclear-free zone, it is doing a job of work. Its success as an international arrangement is not therefore to be judged by occasional failures as such (which simply demonstrate the fact that it is needed) but by how well its chief backers react and adapt to these emerging realities.

1
Nuclear weapons and nuclear energy

This chapter is about nuclear technology and the technical interconnections between commercial and military nuclear programmes. It is also about the spread of nuclear technology and the use to which it has been put by a number of states, both inside and outside the NPT, to bring them close to or even take them over the nuclear weapons threshold.

The scope of nuclear energy

Nuclear energy has peaceful applications and non-peaceful applications. The centrepiece of all political efforts to curb the spread of nuclear weapons lies in attempting to harmonise the proliferation of nuclear reactors with the non-proliferation of nuclear weapons. Nuclear reactors for peaceful uses are constructed in the main for the power they produce, as alternatives to fossil fuels for the generation of electricity on an industrial scale, but in some cases for other peaceful purposes, such as the production of isotopes (normally radioactive versions of common chemicals), for use in, for example, medical diagnostic imaging.

What all nuclear reactors have in common is nuclear fuel, which must contain at least some uranium in the form of the isotope uranium-235 (or very much more rarely 233), or plutonium, or both. This is usually described as 'fissile material'. Additionally, reactors normally contain so-called 'fertile material', which is nearly always the common uranium isotope uranium-238 (or more rarely thorium – see below). Finally, as soon as a reactor begins to operate, the original fissile material is gradually used up as energy is produced (it is converted into 'fission products', a process that is accompanied by heat and the emission of neutrons), and some of the fertile material is converted to new fissile material (by the absorption of neutrons). The latter process is an untidy one in as much as the creation of new fissile material is accompanied by the creation of numerous other products, many of which are highly radioactive, and these gradually and unproductively begin to compete with the original fertile material for the capture of valuable neutrons emitted by the fissile material. Periodically, therefore, a reactor has to be refuelled to remove the unwanted fission products and to insert fresh fuel.

Some of the original engineering appeal of nuclear reactors lay in the economies of fuel use promised by the possibility of using the new fissile material produced in the reactor itself to refuel the reactor, or more usually a different reactor, next time around. The new fissile material – plutonium – can be separated from the other fission products using chemical processing. Once separated, it can be incorporated more or less directly into the fuel elements of the sort of reactor that produced it in the first place. Indeed, it is possible to design reactors – so-called 'fast breeders' – that produce a net gain in the amount of fissile material involved. Prototype fast breeders have been developed in France and Japan.

Where thorium is used as the fertile material, the story is similar. Thorium, though less widely found in natural deposits than uranium, occurs in particularly high concentrations in India and Brazil. Unlike uranium, thorium is fertile without having a fissile component and would need to be mixed with plutonium or uranium-235 to provide an initial charge of fuel for a reactor. But during the operation of the reactor, as a fertile material, some thorium will be converted into uranium-233, a uranium isotope similar in properties to uranium-235, which, after chemical separation, could be used mixed with fresh thorium to form the next batch of fuel.

Peaceful and non-peaceful applications of nuclear energy intersect in three places (see Figure 1.1, p. 13): uranium-235, plutonium-239 and, less markedly, radioactive waste (the last is considered in some detail under a separate heading, below). One fissile isotope of uranium, uranium-235, can be extracted directly from (or more commonly made more concentrated within) natural uranium, of which it comprises about one part in 140. This may be achieved by a variety of so-called 'enrichment' techniques. Unlike plutonium separation, which in spite of the hazardous radioactivity involved is a variant of well understood chemical engineering processes, uranium enrichment was at first, in the middle of the twentieth century, as unfamiliar as an industrial undertaking as were nuclear reactors themselves. Enrichment to low levels, such that 2–4 per cent of the material is uranium-235, is increasingly seen as commercially sensible, partly because reactors fuelled with slightly enriched uranium as opposed to natural uranium can squeeze more power out of each tonne of fuel.

Uranium, provided it consists almost exclusively of the 235 isotope, can be used directly for the manufacture of a nuclear weapon. The amount needed depends on the design of the weapon. Crude designs which demand a minimum of specialist knowledge from the designer and a minimum of engineering ingenuity perhaps require 50 kg. Sophisticated designs probably make do with half as much or less.[1] Similarly, plutonium can also be used directly for the manufacture of a nuclear weapon. But there are a number of important differences between the two routes. First, plutonium is a more difficult metal to handle and work – for one thing it is highly poisonous. Secondly, care has to be taken over its composition. Like uranium, plutonium occurs in a number of isotopic forms, of which plutonium-239 is the best suited to bomb manufacture. Plutonium produced in reactors fuelled with natural uranium contains fewer of the other, unwanted, isotopes (mainly because it is not left inside the reactor for as long) that reduce its value for bomb purposes. Thirdly, designing a plutonium bomb is intrinsically more demanding of engineering expertise than is the case with uranium. The problem is one of critical mass.

Critical mass and nuclear bombs

Any quantity of fissile material will produce neutrons spontaneously. The neutrons are a form of radioactive emission. Each of these neutrons, on colliding with intact fissile material, will stimulate new fission and cause further neutrons to be released virtually instantaneously, perhaps two on each occasion, and so forth in a chain reaction. If the original quantity of fissile material is small, neutron production does not get very far – most simply escape into the surroundings. But if there is just enough fissile material so that only half the neutrons escape while the other half all produce two others, a critical mass is said to be present.[2] A mass slightly greater than this ensures an avalanche of neutrons and a rapid chain reaction of successive fissions, accompanied by an enormous release of energy.

Because of detailed differences between the two nuclides – in fact the fissile uranium-235 nucleus liberates about two and a half neutrons (on average) per fission and plutonium-239 nearer three – a critical mass of plutonium is smaller, but at the same time harder to assemble. A simple uranium-based bomb can be made by assembling two subcritical, shaped masses of uranium, at either end of what is essentially a stout gun barrel, and detonated by firing one mass at the other. A plutonium bomb cannot be made as simply and normally requires the pre-forming of plutonium into two slightly hollowed out metal hemispheres, which when mated together form a sphere with a hollow centre (supposing the critical mass to be 6 kg, which will depend on the bomb's design, the diameter of the sphere must be about 8 cm). The sphere is encased in a jacket of conventional explosives, whose effect on detonation is to drive it inwards at every point, compressing the plutonium (both the shape to a solid sphere and the metal itself) to turn it from sub-critical to super-critical. The US codename for the first plutonium bomb was the descriptive 'Fat Man'; the uranium bomb developed at the same time was more whimsically named 'Little Boy'.

Plutonium bombs require that the neutron chain reaction is started at just the right time through the presence of a carefully designed neutron trigger at the centre; uranium bombs do not require a trigger but produce an explosion closer to the theoretical maximum if they do use one. The trigger is a source of neutrons that are produced only once the sphere of plutonium (or uranium-235) has been compressed. A radioactive isotope of polonium (polonium-210) produces charged nuclear particles (alpha particles) spontaneously and these produce neutrons if they impact on a relatively common substance, beryllium; in a bomb this is achieved by removing a screen between the two. In the first plutonium bomb, the trigger was a small amount of polonium and beryllium separated by a thin barrier that would itself collapse under the compression of the sphere. The polonium has to be produced in a nuclear reactor (from the more common element bismuth); it is very difficult to handle and has such a short half-life (138 days) that fresh supplies need to be on hand constantly.[3]

In both sorts of bomb, the fissile material is surrounded by a heavy metallic casing (or 'tamper', as opposed to being left 'bare'), in order to improve neutron economy (some escaping neutrons are reflected back in) and therefore reduce the critical mass. At the same time, by virtue of its inertia, the tamper ensures the critical mass, once formed, holds together long enough for the chain reaction to proceed far enough for the nuclear explosion to be effective.

Thermonuclear bombs (also termed hydrogen bombs) have been tested that give explosive yields a thousand times greater than the sorts of fission (or atom) bomb just described. They employ plutonium or uranium bombs as igniters, usually in the form of two separate critical masses, to bring about the fusion of light elements, deuterium (also know as 'heavy hydrogen') and tritium (the latter another hydrogen isotope, usually manufactured in nuclear reactors).[4] These light elements can be assembled in any quantity, since fusion requires no critical mass of material, although the geometry of the whole assembly must be consistent with the requirement that the ignition of the fusion reaction by a fission bomb should not simultaneously blow apart the fusion section of the device.

Reactors

In some respects a nuclear reactor is only a tamed or slowed down version of a fission bomb (reactors based on fusion seem to be theoretically possible but a fully working prototype has yet to be demonstrated). Inside a reactor, fissile material is not normally present in the same concentrations that are common in bombs. In a reactor, the very small proportion of uranium-235 in natural uranium can be enough under the right circumstances, although 100 tonnes or more of fuel may have to be assembled. These right circumstances include careful choice and positioning of component parts to make maximum use of the comparatively small number of neutrons produced. This involves minimising losses by avoiding the use of constructional and cladding materials (including the 'fuel elements' – the containers that hold the fuel) known to absorb neutrons. It also involves introducing into the reactor so-called 'moderating materials', which reduce the speed of the neutrons to improve the productivity of their interactions with the comparatively small amount of fissile material actually present.

Since nuclear reactors produce heat and drawing this heat off through the use of coolants for power production is how electricity is produced, the coolants too have to pass the 'neutron economy test'. The best understood and cheapest coolant is water, and it can also be used as a moderator, provided it is combined with reactor fuel that is at least slightly enriched in uranium-235 (e.g. to 3 per cent). Where natural uranium is the only fuel available, neutron economy is more critical. Water would absorb too many neutrons unless it were in the form of heavy water, where the ordinary hydrogen of water is replaced by heavy hydrogen, as in the Canadian CANDU design. An alternative is to use graphite as a moderator and a fast flow of gas (carbon dioxide) as coolant,[5] as in most British designs of reactor, beginning with the Magnox.

The heat or power rating of a nuclear reactor can give an approximate indication of its plutonium-producing capacity using a simple rule of thumb. The reason is again critical mass. When a reactor is operating normally, the rate of production of neutrons as a result of fissions of uranium-235 will equal the rate at which they are 'lost'. Some are lost by being absorbed in the concrete shielding that is usually part of the reactor structure, and some are absorbed by 'control rods', which are inserted to keep the reactor running at just a little above the level of criticality.[6] A more or less fixed proportion of the neutrons will be absorbed in the fertile material present, usually uranium-238, which produces plutonium. So, the rate of plutonium production will depend on the rate of neutron production, which depends on the rate of fissions, which is also the rate at which power is produced. For earlier reactor designs, such as the British Magnox, which relied on natural uranium as fuel and used graphite as a moderator, the rule of thumb formula is that about 1 g of plutonium is produced for 1 MW of total (thermal) power produced. A Magnox reactor rated at 500 MW electrical power (that which it contributes every day to the national grid) has a thermal power three times that much, since the efficiency with which the total power produced can be converted into electrical energy in this type of reactor is only one-third (to be exact, 32 per cent). By the formula, then, a 500 MW(e) Magnox reactor produces 1,500 g of plutonium a day and 450 kg a year (taken as 300 days, to allow for reactor shut-downs). This formula is very rough and more closely applicable to the maximum rate of plutonium production possible than an average rate (plutonium production rates can be boosted by somewhat more frequent refuellings than would normally be dictated by commercial considerations, i.e. where efficient power production was the priority, since in normal operation some plutonium produced is used up in the reactor itself and contributes to the power produced).[7] The same formula can be applied pretty well unchanged to other reactors fuelled with natural uranium, such as the Canadian CANDU design. With other designs of power reactor, the difference between the average rate and the maximum rate of plutonium production is more marked. When run for efficient power production, more modern designs of reactor with slightly enriched uranium as fuel will produce plutonium at a rate perhaps only half that given by the formula. Furthermore, the quality of the plutonium they produce is less suitable for weapons because of the presence of fairly large amounts of isotopes of plutonium other than 239. Whereas a Magnox reactor run normally for power production might produce plutonium that is between 70 and 80 per cent isotope 239, a pressurised water reactor (PWR), the most commercially successful modern design, will produce plutonium not only in half the quantities (megawatt for megawatt) but also comprising only 50 to 60 per cent the 239 isotope. Such plutonium is not absolutely useless for bomb production but it is not accorded the description 'weapons-grade', since the design of an effective bomb becomes much more difficult, partly because the presence of other plutonium isotopes increases the risk of premature detonation.[8] While there does not exist such a thing as a 'proliferation-proof' design of reactor, diverting a PWR type from its normal operating (i.e. electricity-producing) mode to produce weapons-grade plutonium would mean a very considerable and virtually self-evident (to any inspector) departure from normal refuelling schedules. That it needs to be shut down to accommodate refuelling, moreover, makes it more inspection-friendly than most alternative designs, which can be refuelled while running ('on load').

Where commercial pressures to generate electricity from nuclear power as cheaply as possible have been strong, PWRs have come to dominate. The fact that a PWR requires fuel that has been enriched (an added cost) is more than compensated for by its greater fuel 'mileage'. A single charge of fuel of 35 tonnes produces the same amount of energy as 255 tonnes does in a Magnox reactor, partly because plutonium produced in the PWR contributes significantly, through fission, to the production of power, while still in the reactor. Also, enriched fuel has a smaller critical mass and this allows for a more compact reactor structure (megawatt for megawatt, a Magnox requires 10 times the initial weight of fuel loading of a PWR). Had technology moved in the opposite direction, and cost and commercial considerations begun to favour reactor designs that used natural uranium over PWR types, then it is much less likely that, in over 30 years of inspections under the NPT, there would have been no single instance of plutonium being diverted from a power reactor.

This does not exhaust possible designs of reactor. Physically very compact designs are possible when highly enriched uranium is available as fuel, as is normally the case with reactors designed for naval propulsion, or in any instance where the production of power at low cost is not an issue (enriching uranium is itself a costly exercise). From the perspective of nuclear non-proliferation, such reactors present a particular difficulty. Their original charge of fuel, as uranium already enriched, say, to 50 per cent uranium-235, is almost as useful for bomb purposes as any plutonium produced, provided some means of further enriching the uranium is at hand. However, any diversion of enriched uranium from a compact reactor would be a 'one-off' operation, when the reactor was first fuelled, because the reactor would have to be shut down in order to divert fuel already within it and this would be most unlikely to escape the notice of inspectors. Nor would they be likely to overlook a comparable diversion from refuelling stocks. But in either case the time between the inspectors giving the alarm and the state in question obtaining a significant amount of highly enriched uranium could be very short indeed. Moreover, if there was in any case a supply of enriched fuel for the compact reactor, there would be no reason to divert the fuel from that reactor for military purposes.

One drawback of the commercial success of the PWR design is the incentive it has given to importing states with their own stocks of natural uranium to take an interest in methods of enriching uranium. It is sometimes difficult to gainsay an official justification for this along the lines of wanting security in fuel supplies, but it adds to the opportunities for the diversion of fissile material away from peaceful uses. Oppositely, where the types of reactor that are fuelled with natural uranium have retained a foothold, as in Britain, Canada and eastern Europe and in their nuclear export markets, a different consideration arises, in that their large fuel throughput encourages recycling of spent fuel. Eking out fuel supplies in this way inevitably means an interest in fuel reprocessing and hence the separation of plutonium; opportunities then arise for the diversion of plutonium away from peaceful uses. Additionally, these reactors produce a relatively large quantity of radioactive waste, which needs to be safely stored so as to prevent its accidental or deliberate introduction into the human environment (see below).

Peaceful and military uses of nuclear energy

The choice between reactors based on natural uranium and those based on slightly enriched uranium as fuel has political implications, and these run all the way up the supply chain. The original development of nuclear reactors in Britain was shaped by two considerations that pointed in the same direction. One was the possibility of using essentially the same design of reactor to produce both plutonium for the British nuclear weapons programme and electricity for the national grid. So the Magnox design was a direct descendant of the plutonium-producing military reactors at Windscale. Like all reactors fuelled by natural uranium, the Magnox types were efficient plutonium producers. The other consideration was economy in the use of uranium, since Britain had no supplies of its own and hence a strong interest in reprocessing spent fuel to extract plutonium for eventual recycling.

In the USA, reasoning was similar but led to very different conclusions. There, a proven capacity for enriching uranium for the military programme had eventually emerged from the Manhattan Project in the form of a large gas diffusion plant, and using some of that same capacity to provide enriched uranium for reactor fuel for military (naval propulsion) and civilian uses seemed logical. The Americans were not initially sanguine over the question of uranium supplies, although later it became clear that domestic sources of uranium ore were comparatively plentiful. Their choice of lightly enriched uranium as fuel for power-producing reactors (ultimately for the pressurised water design) could be seen as consistent with uranium economy, in that their mode of operation permitted a larger portion of the plutonium produced in operation to be consumed inside the reactor, without active recycling.

Only if uranium were to become extremely scarce does it seem that the British preference for overt recycling would make complete economic sense, although the break-even point requires certain assumptions to be made about the real cost of enriching uranium. Accordingly, Britain's original interest in enriching uranium was essentially military, since enriched uranium allows a certain flexibility in the design of bombs, especially of the thermonuclear variety, not permitted by plutonium alone. It was also a hedge against wartime nuclear cooperation with the United States, which had been suspended in 1946, failing to restart even in the rapidly deteriorating international climate of the Cold War. A gas diffusion plant was built at Capenhurst in Cheshire that produced highly enriched uranium between 1954 and 1961, but it was too small to reproduce the economies of scale available to the Americans. When the USA resumed close nuclear collaboration at the end of the 1950s, Britain took advantage of this to shut down Capenhurst and to meet its military requirements for highly enriched uranium, which by now was needed for naval propulsion reactors as well as for bombs, by obtaining it from the USA in exchange for surplus plutonium. A hiccough in this arrangement occurred in the context of the attack on the plutonium fuel cycle in the name of nuclear non-proliferation by the US Carter administration in the 1970s, which led to the suspension of the barter deal. To meet the gap, the British built a centrifuge plant, at Capenhurst again, at the end of the 1970s, named A3, but were soon able to save at least 50 per cent on capital costs when the USA agreed (in the context of a worsening of the Cold War) to enrich the output from A3 up to military levels (from 4.5 per cent to 90 per cent or more). After the end of the Cold War, in 1993 the A3 plant was made part of a purely peaceful tripartite uranium enrichment programme called Urenco, a joint venture with the Dutch and German governments, and was placed under the safeguards of both the IAEA and Euratom (on the latter, see the Annex to Chapter 4).[9]

This tripartite arrangement dated back to 1970 and coincided not only with Britain's successful approach to join the European Community but also with a decision to base Britain's next generation of nuclear power reactors on a design – the advanced gas-cooled reactor (AGR) – that required slightly enriched uranium as fuel. As the name suggests, these were updated versions of the Magnox design (fuelled with natural uranium), but they proved less successful. Even so, seven two-unit stations with each pair having a combined output of 1300 MW(e) were built, the last coming on stream in 1986.

The conversion of Britain to the idea that reactors should be fuelled using enriched uranium did nothing to persuade it to abandon the plutonium economy or the plutonium reprocessing fuel cycle (Figure 1.1), which the Carter administration had concluded was a threat to the objectives of the NPT. Technically, the new reactors did offer an opportunity to do so, since it had become an article of faith in Britain (probably wrongly) that the spent fuel elements from Magnox power stations could not safely be kept in store for any length of time (and so they were chemically reprocessed), but other considerations proved overwhelming. In this Britain found allies in Western Europe, especially France, which had gone even further by adopting wholesale the US-designed PWR type of reactor for its own very extensive nuclear power programme. In a national context, plutonium reprocessing now offered a way of extending uranium supplies by creating a stockpile of fuel for the expected new generation of fast-breeder nuclear reactors. It also meant an opportunity in the short term to economise on enriched uranium both by salvaging uranium (still slightly enriched from an AGR or PWR) at the same time as plutonium and reincorporating plutonium in the fuel elements of current reactor types (as mixed oxide or 'MOX' fuel). Internationally, it meant contracts to reprocess spent fuel for overseas

Nuclear weapons and nuclear energy

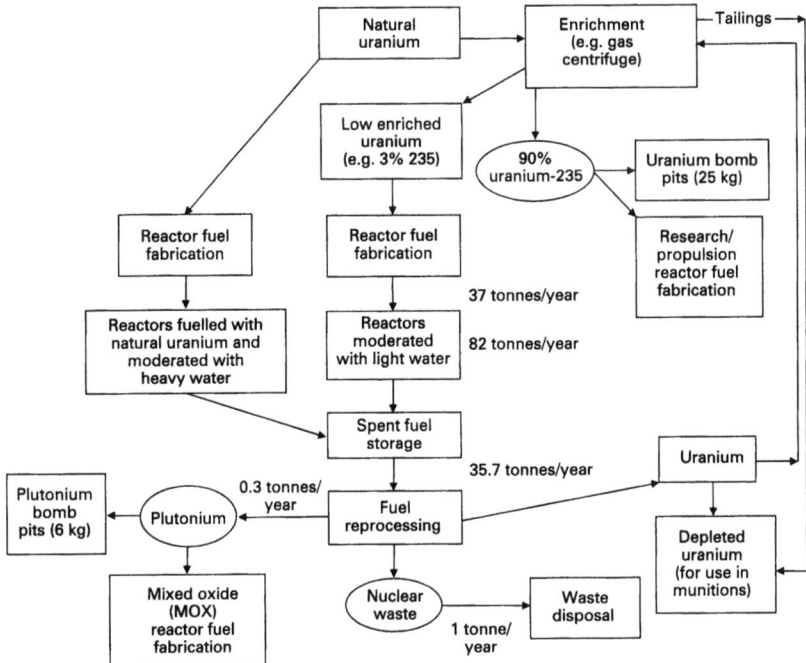

Figure 1.1. Schematic representation of the nuclear fuel cycle. Numbers refer to tonnes or tonnes per year for a 1,000 MW(e) PWR. 'Pits' are the critical mass assemblies. Based, with permission, on a diagram that first appeared in T. Greenwood, G.W. Rathjens and J. Ruino, *Nuclear Power and Weapons Proliferation*, Adelphi Paper No. 130 (London, International Institute for Strategic Studies, 1977), p. 7.

customers who also saw a commercial future in plutonium but lacked a plutonium reprocessing capability of their own.

The differences between the United States and its natural allies over nuclear proliferation were not about strategy. All – even France and the Soviet Union it would seem – were essentially agreed on the wisdom of combating the spread of nuclear weapons or at worst agnostic in this regard. The differences were about tactics, and especially engagement as opposed to restrictiveness. Restrictiveness meant the US plan to put an end to all fuel reprocessing anywhere; the policy was given initial impetus by the Carter administration and was essentially adhered to by all its successors. Engagement meant the Europeans providing countries with reprocessing services so that they would have no excuse for developing their own. Restrictiveness also meant so-called 'full-scope safeguards' on all nuclear exports (see Chapter 3). Engagement meant safeguards only on what was exported, for fear of driving importers to the black market, where they could import with no safeguards at all. But as in war itself, intra-allied disagreement over tactics was only partly about disagreements over the means to a common end. Also present were transatlantic economic jealousies. The cooperation that was key to preventing nuclear proliferation lay uncomfortably alongside the competitiveness that characterised the approach of the same countries to the economic exploitation of nuclear power. And imponderables such as national pride in a distinctive technical approach to nuclear power also played a part.

The attempt by the Carter administration to bridge these differences in 1980 under the International Nuclear Fuel Cycle Evaluation (INFCE) conference succeeded only in as much as it did nothing to make the situation worse. After the end of the Cold War, some of the old problems died away. With virtually every country in the world now party to the NPT, the argument about full-scope safeguards lost its relevance. But the essential differences remained. The restrictive USA now sought to hold back on exports of nuclear materials and technology even to member states of the NPT, if, in the US view at least, the states in question were of doubtful character. The engagement view was that such exports should continue, under safeguards, which might be strengthened where necessary. This was not only out of respect for the bargain implicit in the treaty (unhindered access to peaceful technology in exchange for a forswearing of nuclear weapons – see Chapter 3) but also out of the old worry that denying exports will encourage domestic programmes or a delving into the black market, leaving supplier states with very diminished leverage.

Radioactive waste and nuclear accidents

While enriched uranium and plutonium have peaceful uses (well established in the case of enriched uranium, but in practice less well established in the case of plutonium), the same is not true for radioactive waste – the name usually given to the by-products of the extraction of plutonium from used reactor fuel (plutonium separation or plutonium reprocessing), although strictly speaking spent fuel elements that are simply stored without reprocessing are also a form of waste. The permanent isolation of the fission products left over from reprocessing in such a way as to prevent any uptake into the human food chain of radioactive materials dangerous to health *and* at the same time to give the public assurance that this is the case has often proved very difficult. The scale of the problem naturally increases with the amounts of waste involved. Any nuclear programme will create a certain amount of waste, but a 'once-through' fuel strategy, which sees spent fuel elements permanently stored in an intact form, produces smaller quantities of waste per megawatt than a fuel recycling strategy, which involves separation of plutonium from the spent fuel. Both methods leave behind a core of waste – in one case spent fuel elements, in the other highly radioactive fission products packaged in glass cylinders. But in the recycling case the core of waste is not the only waste produced.

A direct reading of the public attitude to the dangers implicit in nuclear waste comes from British experience. The British nuclear power programme, partly because of its original close attachment to reactors fuelled with natural uranium, has long had an interest in the reprocessing of spent fuel. The total volume of waste simply in the form of spent fuel elements arising in one year from a 1 GW(e) PWR is about 40 tonnes. If the fuel were to be reprocessed, plutonium and residual enriched uranium extracted, and the most highly radioactive parts of residual waste segregated from the rest, the segregated part would amount to about one tonne. In practice it has to be encased in about 10 times its own weight of glass blocks to provide long-term insulation from the environment. Reprocessing also produces a species of less radioactive waste, 'intermediate waste' in British parlance, which also requires insulation from the environment. Perhaps 200 tonnes are produced from 1 GW(e) of power production.

Thus there is about a fivefold difference between a reprocessing policy and a once-through policy in terms of the volume of radioactive waste. This large volume of intermediate waste can theoretically be disposed of immediately by burial in geologically suitable sites in such a way as to isolate it from natural environmental processes and hence from the food chain. Such sites exist in Britain, but intense public suspicion concerning the safety of disposal has forced governments to abandon the search for physically suitable disposal sites of a 'natural harbour' kind in favour of a very expensive and elaborate arrangement, using land at Drigg adjacent to the main reprocessing plant at Sellafield.

The public sensitivity concerning the safety of nuclear waste and, as we shall see below, actual accidents at nuclear reactors have simply added to the non-peaceful potential of radioactive waste. In those parts of the world where environmental protection is lower on the political agenda than is the case in most Western industrialised states, the absence of value attached to waste, and the fact that it has until recently tended to fall outside the remit of international agreements on the use of fissile materials, can mean that it is more vulnerable to theft than any other product of the nuclear fuel cycle. A threat from irregular forces to contaminate public water supplies with it, or to spread it in dry form in a built-up area, will make up in psychological impact for what it may lack in real menace to life. In defence of the reprocessing approach, the once-through strategy leaves plutonium inside fuel elements whose radioactivity is decreasing rapidly (and hence increasing their vulnerability to theft), whereas reprocessing (at least in theory) removes plutonium to the comparative safety of the interior of a reactor, as fuel. No actual use of radioactive waste for warlike purposes has ever been recorded, although there is evidence that US commanders gave serious thought to spreading waste along the border between China and North Korea during the Korean War (1950–53).[10]

Radioactive waste has, however, been spread over inhabited areas, on more than one occasion, as a result of accidents during the operation of nuclear reactors. In spite of the presence of critical masses of fissile materials in both bombs and reactors, when reactors go wrong they do not behave like bombs and explode but tend to overheat through some failure of the cooling system, and catch fire as a result. Indeed, overheating adversely affects the neutron economy of the reactor and will tend to move it away from criticality (especially in water-cooled designs). But with a fire in the reactor, radioactive materials from the core can be ejected into the atmosphere and can carry for hundreds of kilometres downwind, should the fire be accompanied by, or by itself be the cause of, failure in the containment shell most modern power reactors are equipped with.[11]

The Swedes voted to abandon nuclear power in the aftermath of the notorious but technically quite trivial accident at the PWR at Three Mile Island near Harrisburg in Pennsylvania. In March 1979 one of the reactors at this two-unit station accidentally lost some of the cooling water that normally circulates around the fuel elements and conveys the heat produced within the elements to the steam-generating plant. This exposed the tops of some of the fuel elements. At the high temperatures prevailing, the metal cladding of the fuel elements (a zirconium alloy) chemically reacted with steam. This naturally dissolved the fuel cladding, allowing volatile (meaning compounds usually solid or liquid but easily capable of becoming gaseous) and gaseous radioactive fission products normally contained within the fuel elements to escape. These escaping fission products were almost wholly contained within the structure of the plant. The most immediately dangerous of these products is the volatile solid iodine-131, which is a reactive element readily taken up by the human body, where it concentrates (alongside natural iodine) in the thyroid gland. It is in fact customary to measure the size of a nuclear reactor accident by the amount of radioactivity released as iodine-131 into the locality. The amount of radioactivity released as iodine-131 at Three Mile Island seems to have been about 10 curies (Ci).[12] The total radioactive content of the reactor was about 10,000 MCi.

In April 1986 a considerably more serious accident occurred at Chernobyl in the Ukraine (then part of the Soviet Union), when one reactor of a four-unit nuclear power station caught fire and burned for 10 days.[13] Fission products were released into the atmosphere and deposited downwind, to the north and west, as radioactive fallout. The reactor had little or nothing by way of a containment outer shell. Iodine-131 (along with other radioactive substances) was released in large quantities – 10 MCi, approximately. This may be compared with the Windscale fire of 1957, when 20,000 Ci of iodine was released as a result of an accident at one of the reactors designed to produce plutonium specifically for the British nuclear weapons programme. As with the very much smaller Windscale reactor, graphite – a common moderator material for reactors fuelled with natural uranium – was implicated in the fire at Chernobyl. Exposure in the Chernobyl case was again chiefly a matter for the nearby population, some of whom were evacuated, but some of the escaping radioactivity crossed international boundaries. Ten years later the consequences of iodine began to show up as an increased incidence of thyroid cancers among the surrounding population, particularly in children. There are indications that this increased incidence (and likely subsequent deaths) may be both more widespread (reaching into Belarus and Russia) and appearing sooner than current scientific understanding would seem to predict.[14] The Chernobyl accident, with the several thousand persons affected by its release of iodine-131, is a reasonable guide to the sort of thing that could happen were a nuclear power reactor anywhere to be deliberately attacked with the aim of breaching its containment shell and causing a fire.

The correspondence between reactor accidents and the scale of public apprehension concerning nuclear waste is very crude. The very small accident at Three Mile Island may have had a larger psychological impact on Western publics than the very much more serious accident at Chernobyl because the setting and circumstances were more familiar. The impact of the Windscale accident was considerably muted by the official secrecy surrounding the event and the deliberate construction of the plant in an area of low population density.

At the physical level, radioactive iodine is the most dangerous substance released in nuclear reactor accidents, whereas stockpiles of nuclear waste will contain none of this, since it has a half-life of only eight days (spent fuel elements being cooled at the reactor site automatically see their radioactive iodine content reduced by a factor of 1,000,000 in six months). But all longer-lived radioactive substances present within an operating reactor are present in nuclear waste (with the exception of plutonium if the waste has been reprocessed), with the most dangerous of these to health after plutonium probably being caesium-137 and strontium-90, with their awkwardly long half-lives (of around 30 years). Whereas plutonium is most dangerous to health when breathed in, perhaps in the form of smoke from a deliberately ignited fire involving unreprocessed waste, caesium-137 mimics potassium and strontium-90 mimics calcium, in a physiological sense. Both can enter the food chain, and strontium-90 for instance concentrates in the bones, where its radioactivity can produce cancers. Again, the quantities of materials capable of being ejected in the course of a reactor accident are potentially very great, whereas the deliberate diversion of nuclear waste to non-peaceful ends will involve relatively small amounts, especially if the diversion is being done by sub-state groups. But even a small quantity of nuclear waste deliberately dispersed near the centre of a large city with a high population density will expose a large number of persons to the fear of radioactive contamination, if not the reality. Some indication of the psychological multiplication factor at work where radioactivity is concerned comes from the Three Mile Island accident. Great disruption of normal life was created in the vicinity of the reactor, but the 10 Ci of radiation released was the equivalent (averaged over the population affected) of only about one month's exposure to natural background radiation. That the people living near Three Mile Island were alarmed because they were given poor or misleading information about what was happening is precisely the point: uncertainty among the public if they were ever deliberately subjected to a radioactive release by a terrorist group is likely to be at least as great.

Uranium enrichment

While it is reasonable to say that technological progress in the design of nuclear reactors has raised the barriers between the peaceful and non-peaceful uses of nuclear energy – from the reduced quantities and suitability for weapons of the plutonium produced by PWRs, to the weaker commercial and technical arguments for fuel recycling when such reactors are in use rather than the types fuelled with natural uranium – the opposite is true for uranium enrichment.

Of the first five nuclear weapons states – the acknowledged nuclear powers within the terms of the NPT – only one, China, seems to have based its military programme on enriched uranium. Of the following 11 states thought to have at least flirted with manufacturing nuclear weapons – Algeria, Argentina, Brazil, India, Iran, Iraq, Israel, Libya, North Korea, Pakistan and South Africa – seven did so. And of the four that based their programmes on plutonium, two, India and Israel, began their programmes before the NPT came into being, in 1968. While this is not cast iron evidence – the first nuclear power, the USA, had an interest in the military potential of enriched uranium from the start, and the next three soon discovered its military uses for themselves and began enrichment programmes – the broad trend suggests that both the political and technical obstacles to a bomb programme based on enriched uranium have reduced compared with the obstacles to a programme based on plutonium.

The unprecedented problems presented by the requirement to enrich uranium on an industrial scale originally faced by the managers of the Manhattan Project saw them adopt a worst-case analysis approach. This meant not only a programme for the production of plutonium as well as enriched uranium, but also a simultaneous assault on a variety of potential industrial methods for uranium enrichment, with the risk that none of these would work hedged against by the pursuit of a method that was guaranteed to work, if only laboriously and inefficiently. This was a variant on the well established laboratory instrument known as a mass spectrometer. In this instrument, an orderly stream of atoms or molecules of the substance in question is first given an electrical charge and then fired through a vacuum chamber under the influence of an electrical voltage and an applied magnetic field. The molecules are speeded up by the voltage and their trajectories bent by the magnetic field (into the curve of a D-shape). The path of lighter molecules is bent more than the path of heavier ones, and in the instrument the two separate currents produced can be detected and distinguished electrically. To adapt the instrument to isotope separation and collection, it is necessary to place a collector in the appropriate place within the vacuum chamber and the lighter isotope can then be physically extracted from the feed of natural uranium. The process is essentially a small-scale one. To apply it to the extraction of uranium-235 in kilogram amounts from natural uranium, where it is present as one part in 140, it has rather to be duplicated on a large scale, since it cannot be scaled up without disrupting the physical principles the method relies on. In the Manhattan Project the D-shaped units ('dees') were paired back to back and then sandwiched together with the dees upright between the poles of a smaller number of magnets, in groups of about 100. The rear face of the last sandwich was made the leading face of the first, so that the whole assembly was in the shape of a running track. This adaptation of the mass spectrometer was given the name calutron, after the home base of its inventor, Ernest Lawrence, of the University of California, and this method of enrichment was called EMIS (electromagnetic isotope separation).

To obtain 150 kg of uranium in the pure form of the 235 isotope, at a minimum 140 times that quantity of natural uranium has to be used as feed, or just over 20 tonnes. Using Lawrence's calutron set-up this took one year. If feed at a higher level of enrichment were available – say 3 per cent – only about five tonnes would be needed and the bomb material could be extracted in three months. In actual fact this feature, which is a characteristic of all enrichment processes, was taken advantage of during the Manhattan Project. Two sorts of running tracks of calutrons were made. One, the Alpha, using big dees, with a radius of just under 1.5 m, enriched the feed of natural uranium up to 15 per cent, and a smaller, Beta complex (4 tracks to the Alpha's 10), using dees half the size, completed the task, taking enrichment to 90 per cent.[15] The bigger machines had a bigger throughput (a feed of 100 kg of natural uranium would produce 0.5 kg of 15 per cent enriched feed for the smaller machines), but simply because they were so large they had a poorer ability to separate the isotopes cleanly than the smaller machines, in a striking confirmation of the 'scaling up' problems mentioned above.

These inefficiencies could probably have been reduced somewhat in time, but post-war interest in the calutron faded rapidly (although it sputtered into life again briefly in the Soviet Union after the war).[16] It not only suffered from being a batch process, as opposed to the possibility of continuous operation offered by some alternatives, but it was also exceptionally costly to run in terms of electricity consumption to power the magnets, the accelerating voltage and the vacuum pumps. The calutron would indeed have been forgotten had it not been resurrected in the 1980s as part of the secret Iraqi bomb programme.

Two other methods of enriching uranium on an industrial scale for military or for civil use quickly became of more interest (both had actually been explored extensively during the Manhattan Project). One was gas diffusion, which was brought into practical operation in the USA just before the end of the war. The other was the centrifuge method, which had to wait another 20 years in the West for it to become practicable on an industrial scale, although there is good evidence that it had started to displace gas diffusion in the Soviet Union from an earlier date.[17] Both work in a continuous mode and both use a series of interconnected discrete stages for isotopic separation. Both use uranium in the form of the molecule uranium hexafluoride ('hex'), which has good thermal properties, does not add to isotopic variety (fluorine is monoisotopic) and, very importantly for the diffusion method, does not add too greatly to the mass of the molecules. The separation is not clean at each stage but rather each stage of separation increases the concentration of uranium-235 over its concentration in the gas that is fed in from the previous stage. Flows of hex depleted in uranium-235 are not discarded (as 'tailings') until the concentration of uranium-235 drops below 0.2 per cent.

The principles of separation are different in each case. In gas diffusion (or more correctly 'effusion'), separation is passive, in that the gas is pumped through porous barriers which the faster-moving (because lighter) uranium-235 hex molecule penetrates more easily than the commoner uranium-238 hex. The gas on the other side of the barrier is enriched in the lighter isotope as a result, but only very slightly. The reason is that the separation power of each stage depends on the ratio of the masses of the two isotopic molecules involved, which is only 1.009.[18] Accordingly, a very large number of enrichment stages and barriers are needed to produce worthwhile levels of enrichment on a continuous process. About 1,000 stages are required for 3 per cent enrichment and about 4,000 for enrichment to the 90 per cent level nominally required for a bomb (see the four-to-one ratio established in relation to Lawrence's calutron set-up, above). On the other hand, there seems to be no limit to the size of the individual separation stages. A diffuser unit (enrichment stage) can reach the size of a double-decker bus.[19]

In the centrifuge method, separation is achieved by rotating the gas in a vertical cylinder (a rotor) at very high speeds, causing the heavier isotope preferentially to be concentrated on the periphery and the lighter towards the centre of the rotor. The relatively lighter component is then fed into the next centrifuge stage, and so forth. Again, it is a continuous process, but here the amount of separation at each stage depends on the *difference* between the masses of the two component molecules, rather than the *ratio*. This means that 3 per cent enriched uranium can be achieved after only 10 stages and weapons-grade uranium after 35 stages.[20] But the individual stages are required to be physically small. A typical centrifuge of basic design might be only 1 m high and 20 cm across so as to be able to withstand the high stresses caused by the very rapid rotation speeds (exceeding the velocity of sound at the periphery). So, in turn, the actual gross amounts of material in any given period of time processed in a cascade of 35 units will be rather small. Increasing the rotational speed can reduce the number of stages required for a given degree of enrichment, although it forces designers to explore alternatives to the aluminium alloy rotors used in earlier designs[21] and it does nothing for the volume of flow. Increased rotational speed is a feature of more advanced designs, as are longer (i.e. taller) rotors, which also increase efficiency of operation. But taller rotors can vibrate awkwardly with increased rotational speeds unless carefully designed. Machines with tall rotors (up to 3 m in some cases) and capable of overcoming vibrational problems are usually termed 'supercritical'. In practice, short cascades are the norm but material throughput is brought up to industrial quantities by harnessing a large number of units in parallel.

The economic and to some extent political differences between the two methods are related to the technical differences. The first important difference concerns size. A small gas diffusion plant is possible but very uneconomic to run and impossible to scale up (the only alternative is to build a larger one). And yet even a small plant will be difficult to disguise because of its size and its requirement for unusually large amounts of electrical power. The power is needed for the pumps and to keep the whole warm enough so that the hex, under pressure, remains in the gaseous form. Centrifuges are more concealable. A comparatively small centrifuge plant does not inflict great penalties of cost per unit of output and it is easily expanded by building copies, which can be plumbed so as to run in parallel with the original. And for a given level of output it requires less than a twentieth of the electricity of a diffusion plant. The one advantage of gas diffusion seems to be a long, trouble-free operating life, provided the difficult technology of mass producing suitable porous barriers can be mastered initially, but this is not a sufficient advantage over the centrifuge where a secret or semi-secret bomb programme is concerned.

There are other established ways of enriching uranium, including chemical methods (used in the Manhattan Project), which have cost advantages where low enriched uranium for reactor fuel is a genuine priority. These have been explored extensively in France and Japan, where demand for such fuel is relatively high, although even in these countries the advantages of the centrifuge (including the further development potential inherent in a comparatively recently proven technology, in contrast with the technical plateau reached by chemical methods and gas diffusion) are beginning to be understood and acted on. Politically, the immediate potential of chemical methods for producing highly enriched uranium seems to be limited, however. Their relevance where the proliferation of nuclear weapons is concerned is that the construction of such plant and the chemical compounds involved need not involve 'trigger list' components – and may therefore fail to attract the attention of exporters alert to the need to attach safeguards (IAEA inspections) to certain materials. And, as we have seen, having a feed of uranium enriched to 3 per cent makes the further enrichment up to 90 per cent a relatively easy task, using small and concealable supplementary enrichment techniques.

All of the enrichment methods so far mentioned have been known and explored to greater or lesser extents for at least 50 years. While concealability, in terms of both the physical dimensions of the plant and its requirement for electrical power, is probably the principal determinant of the suitability of an enrichment technique for a secret programme, its popularity among states at or near the top of the cascade of potential suppliers is another factor. This increases the chances of being able to import components in secret, from suppliers with the weakest safeguards. Gas diffusion has in only one case (Argentina) disseminated in this sense beyond the five acknowledged nuclear weapons states and its limited spread may have something to do with the military standards of secrecy that will have applied to the technique, at least in its earlier phases. It is now used in France and Russia to enrich uranium for reactor fuel. In contrast, the centrifuge has been openly explored more widely beyond the nuclear weapons states, both in its basic form and in variants using the 'stationary wall' technique, where a high-speed jet of gas is directed at a curved wall. Germany has explored both the traditional method and the less economically promising stationary wall, the Netherlands collaborates with the UK and Germany in the multinational Urenco centrifuge plant, and apartheid South Africa openly worked on the stationary wall method.

Legitimate interest in uranium enrichment can be found in places where: enriched uranium is the preferred reactor fuel, and that is now almost everywhere that has a nuclear power programme; the total installed nuclear capacity is high; and national reliance on nuclear power is great enough for considerations of reliability of fuel supply to be prominent. Elsewhere, considerations of the advantage enjoyed by the established large-scale producers of enriched uranium and the absence (possibly temporary) of any cartel among suppliers almost certainly mean it is very much cheaper to import enriched uranium fuel. The one important exception to this rule are states with large reserves of uranium ore that are aiming to improve the profitability of exploiting these reserves by enriching uranium before export. This explains the stated interest of Australia and Canada, and probably Brazil too, in enrichment techniques, in addition to the continued interest of South Africa after apartheid.[22] A similar template can be drawn for plutonium separation plant (leaving to one side the US position that there is never any justification, commercial or otherwise, for such a facility). Legitimate interest can be suggested by similar criteria to those set out for uranium enrichment, as it will normally be much cheaper to have spent fuel reprocessed overseas, even if the spread of providers of reprocessing services is rather narrower that would seem ideal from the perspective of the operation of a free market.

Non-nuclear weapons states that do not fit the template but that nonetheless have an interest in the military applications of enriched uranium or plutonium will normally aim to pursue this interest in secret. A secret plutonium separation plant normally means a secret reactor too, unless there is a large reactor already openly present, some of whose output of spent fuel can be diverted without attracting attention.

As we have seen, among the proven methods of enrichment, concealment is easier with centrifuge technology than with gas diffusion. The same trend towards concealability is continued with the more recent laser methods, which were given a boost in the mid-1990s by the decision of the US government to fund commercialisation of the process, which until that time had been proven only on a laboratory scale. It has some similarities with the calutron in that enrichment can be virtually 100 per cent in a single stage, but without the drawback of enormous electricity consumption (it requires only 1 per cent of the power for the same output). It is based on the principle that atoms and molecules resonate (to use a mechanical analogy) when bathed in light of a particular frequency (or colour). Different atoms have different resonant frequencies, although with isotopes of the same element this difference is very small. The development of powerful lasers which can be tuned to emit light at the precise frequency desired (and only this frequency) allows the uranium-235 in a vapour of natural uranium atoms to be preferentially 'excited' (made to resonate) while the uranium-238 is unaffected. With further manipulation these excited atoms can, for instance, be relatively easily ionised (made to shed an electron), and the ionised atoms can then be collected as in the calutron. Obstacles to scaling up to an industrial level might be those essentially to do with obtaining continuous operation from what has every appearance of being a natural batch process. That making the transition from laboratory to the factory may not be straightforward is illustrated by the 1994 decision by the transnational European enrichment consortium Urenco to abandon the laser enrichment possibility in favour of new (supercritical) generations of centrifuge design.

Even so, the attraction of the laser method for states wishing to pursue a secret enrichment programme for military purposes, where the requirement for highly enriched uranium may not be very large, is undeniable. Interest in developing the method must have been taken by each of the acknowledged nuclear weapons states.[23] And every state mentioned above in connection with the centrifuge method, plus Australia, Brazil, Canada and Japan, have also taken an active interest in the laser method.[24]

Two factors may inhibit the inadvertent cascading downwards of this technology, at least in the short term. One is the ending of the Cold War, which has allowed the output of very large, formerly military plant to be placed on a rather flat international market for enriched uranium. This plainly discourages commercially motivated investment in new processes, however promising. The other is the very newness or unproven aspect of the method. While it is still in the development phase, the desire for commercial confidentiality will limit dissemination of the technology horizontally and vertically, and the track record of the dissemination of enrichment technology indicates that the very latest techniques are often of less interest than something proven, provided it has the attributes of concealability. Even so, the IAEA has uncovered evidence that Iran has explored laser enrichment techniques. And the South Korean authorities have admitted to the IAEA that small (gram) amounts of uranium-235 were produced there by the laser technique in 2000.[25]

States at the margin

Background

The oil crisis years of the mid-1970s stimulated interest in nuclear power over a broad spectrum and proved an early test of the NPT. Among states with a strong dependence on oil but no domestic supplies, nuclear energy began to be seen as a cost-effective alternative. Since the oil crisis had been brought about by a deliberate restriction on supplies by producers, the nuclear alternative was seen as especially attractive as it promised self-sufficiency in energy. This tended to mean that not only were nuclear reactors in demand but there was demand too for reactors to be accompanied by key components of the fuel cycle, especially means for enriching uranium (because of the economic advantages of reactors fuelled with slightly enriched uranium, as indicated above). Even among states with oil supplies of their own, gloomy projections before and after the crisis concerning the all too finite nature of oil reserves encouraged thinking along conservationist lines and investment in alternative energy sources. Finally, potential suppliers of nuclear energy plant were themselves often states that had been hit hardest by the sudden upward shift in oil prices and that were therefore anxious to exploit nuclear energy export markets.

The seemingly impending widespread dissemination of full-cycle nuclear energy programmes never in fact came about. As stated above, the US Carter administration took a restrictive line concerning transfers of uranium enrichment or plutonium separation plant, especially to states not then party to the NPT, but to member states as well, arguing that no transfers should be made. At the time, one principal potential exporter, France, was not itself party to the NPT. European supplier states were more for engagement, that is to say meeting export demand but attaching safeguards to transfers of sensitive items, arguing that a restrictive line would be self-defeating in as much as disappointed importers would look elsewhere, possibly covertly (to domestic resources or the black market), for the technology they needed. The transatlantic division never became critical, since demand for nuclear energy subsided in the wake of the slump in the international economy brought on by the oil crisis but, without conceding the principle, European suppliers generally bowed to US pressure.

Four important 1970s deals were disrupted in the process. A sale to Pakistan of a French-supplied reprocessing plant did not in the end occur, but Pakistan built its own (unsafeguarded, as Pakistan then, as now, was not a party to the NPT). A sale to South Korea of a reprocessing plant was cancelled as a result of US pressure. A German sale of reactors and uranium enrichment plant to Brazil appeared to survive US hostility, but eventually fell through on grounds of cost. Brazil subsequently explored uranium enrichment (originally unsafeguarded). German and French sales of nuclear technology to Iran were restricted to one PWR plant plus some laboratory-scale nuclear technology. Iran subsequently developed a uranium enrichment facility while keeping the IAEA inspectorate largely in the dark.

A fifth deal in the 1970s was of a different character. The French sale of a PWR to South Africa was dependent on sales of slightly enriched uranium as fuel from the USA, which cut off the supply in 1977, citing non-proliferation concerns in partial justification. This gave South Africa a further incentive to develop its own, unsafeguarded, uranium enrichment programme.

Leaving the South African case to one side, even if the other four cases were a fair sample, the disruption of these deals tells us very little about whether the restrictive approach is better than the engagement alternative, but it underlines a difficulty. For member states of the NPT in good standing as far as the IAEA inspectorate is concerned, and this was the case with South Korea and Iran, to be denied transfers of nuclear plant connected with fuel reprocessing or fuel enrichment decreases confidence that contracts for the supply of reactor fuel from outside suppliers will themselves be adhered to. A new incentive is therefore created to pursue the same goals domestically or by black market operations, and with any sense of obligation to notify the IAEA weakened by the failure of bona fide supplier states to live up to their side of the original NPT bargain. After all, despite their signing the NPT, South Korea and Iran seemed in this matter to be treated no differently from Brazil, Pakistan and South Africa, which were all at the time a long way from doing so.

Since the coming into force of the NPT in 1970, a rather large number of states, some at the time party to the treaty and some not, have attracted reasonable suspicion, as we have already seen, that they were working towards the acquisition of nuclear weapons based on a domestic programme of manufacture, usually supplemented by imports of materials, equipment or know-how. These programmes have sometimes taken the plutonium route of reactors and plutonium separation plant, sometimes the uranium enrichment route, and occasionally both. Those that got furthest without drawing attention to themselves, in the sense of causing surprise when the programmes were discovered or admitted to, have all followed the uranium enrichment route.

In chronological order of disclosure we have Argentina, Brazil, Iraq, South Africa, North Korea, Iran and Libya. Of these states, at the time of disclosure three – Iraq, Iran and Libya – were fully party to the NPT and subject to regular IAEA inspection. North Korea was in an anomalous position of threatening to withdraw from the treaty. The other three were outside the treaty entirely; South Africa was totally unbound by any international commitment to stay non-nuclear and so is not much further discussed here, whereas Argentina and Brazil were to a greater or lesser extent party to the Latin American nuclear-free zone agreement. Since the disclosures were made, with the exception at the time of writing of North Korea and Iraq, all the states concerned have either signed up, or reaffirmed their adherence, to the treaty and submitted all their nuclear programmes to IAEA inspection. Unfortunately, the confidentiality that attaches to the outcomes of IAEA inspections for states in good standing with the treaty or in IAEA eyes working earnestly to achieve that status, while understandable up to a point, means that details of states' formerly secret nuclear programmes, now in the hands of the IAEA, are covered in the same blanket of secrecy.

Argentina and Brazil

In 1983, Argentina admitted that it had been building a gas diffusion plant for uranium enrichment in the Rio Negro province since 1978. The explanation officially proffered – that the plant was to service power reactors and to provide enriched uranium for export – was punctured by the small size of the plant, as the technology used makes economies of scale predominant: the Rio Negro plant when operating would have only about one-tenth the capacity of the original British gas diffusion plant at Capenhurst and about one-fiftieth the size of the modern French Tricastin plant, whose output it would need to match in price. But had it operated as designed – which it seems to have failed to do – it might have produced enough highly enriched uranium for two or three bombs a year. Earlier, in 1978, Argentina had announced its intention to build a plutonium reprocessing plant near Buenos Aires. The plan seems never to have been fully carried through. In spite of its intended capacity to separate up to 15 kg of plutonium annually, there was no obvious source of unsafeguarded spent reactor fuel which it could reprocess to produce plutonium for weapons.

In 1990, the newly elected Brazilian President Fernando Collor de Mello announced the decommissioning of a nuclear weapons testing site in the Amazon basin and the cancellation of an equally secret bomb project, called Solimoes, which had been in existence since 1975. At the heart of that project was a centrifuge-based uranium enrichment plant run semi-openly by the Brazilian navy in the state of Sao Paulo. Civilian work on centrifuges had begun in Brazil in 1982; in 1988, in the new climate of mutual candour concerning both the Brazilian and the Argentine nuclear programmes (see Chapter 4), it was announced that the Brazilian navy plant had centrifuge rotors made out of maraging steel, which, with twice the tensile strength of normal steel, permits higher rotor speeds and more effective isotope separation per rotor than the aluminium alloy of more basic designs. Nonetheless, progress was slow and in the mid-1990s the plant, along with Argentina's Rio Negro plant, was put under IAEA safeguards. In different circumstances, put to military ends without further expansion, the plant might have produced enough highly enriched uranium for a bomb to be produced every two or three years. And in a curious parallel with Argentina, in 1991 the Brazilian army announced it had carried out research and development work on a Magnox-type reactor fuelled with natural uranium, with a view to having the reactor begin operation by the mid-1990s. Plutonium separation techniques had been explored on a laboratory scale in the civilian sector, in the same institute at Sao Paulo University that had made the original investigations into centrifuge technology before handing things over to the navy. And plans existed for this work to be taken to the stage of an operating separation plant, until these affairs were overtaken or at least placed on an entirely different footing, like the plan for a reactor, by the decision of Brazil and Argentina to sign up to the NPT (in force from 1998 and 1995 for these states, respectively).

Iraq

The case of Iraq is well known. In the aftermath of the Gulf War of 1990–91, a special inspection team from the IAEA and mandated by the UN uncovered a secret bomb programme. This was only months after Iraq had received a clean bill of health from the IAEA inspectorate on completing a regular inspection of the declared Al Tuwaitha nuclear complex (or rather declared *buildings* on the complex) under the rubric of Iraq's membership of the NPT. The bomb programme was based on an Iraqi version of the calutron method of enriching uranium and was to be based at a two separate undeclared locations, Al Tarmiya and Ash Sharqat, each with a racetrack containing 90 dees. Preliminary design work, however, had been carried out at the Al Tuwaitha site. In careful imitation of the original US (and probably Soviet) programmes, 70 of these were to be large dees for preliminary enrichment purposes and 20 were to be smaller dees to take enrichment up to that required for a bomb. Further, the sizes of the large and small dees were exactly those used by the American programme, namely 240 cm and 120 cm in diameter. It seems that the Iraqis were able to use a more sophisticated system of magnets than had been available during the Manhattan Project some 50 years before, and there is every reason to think that they were expecting to replicate the output, in proportion, achieved by the USA, which was about 500 g a day of weapons-grade uranium-235 for the US Alpha/Beta calutron system 10 times the size of the Al Tarmiya plant. This equates with about 15 kg a year from each Iraqi racetrack. This is broadly in line with the estimate made after the war by IAEA inspectors, who placed the probable annual output of Al Tarmiya at 12–15 kg of weapons-grade uranium.[26] Evidence from weapons testing facilities, furthermore, indicates that this quantity might have sufficed for one bomb a year since, rather than the crude gun barrel device of the Manhattan Project, the plan was to design a uranium bomb using the compression method originally developed for plutonium.[27]

Reminiscent of the Manhattan Project, the Iraqis had planned to develop a gas diffusion plant to supply low enriched uranium as feed for the calutrons but, as with the Argentines, developing a suitable material for the barriers proved too difficult, and they explored the chemical enrichment methods developed in France and Japan instead, with the same purpose in view. In addition, the transfer of work on gas diffusion from the Al Tuwaitha site to a purpose-built but undeclared site at Rashdiya, near Baghdad, was accompanied by a new programme for enrichment based on the centrifuge method. While this parallel pursuit of a range of enrichment techniques might have represented a sort of insurance against failure, it may be wondered whether the dilution of scientific and engineering effort it involved (to say nothing of the plan for an implosion-type uranium bomb as opposed to the simpler gun barrel device) and the sheer proliferation of activity were consistent with a secret programme quickly executed. However, it seems that the centrifuge programme was surprisingly successful, in part because of the greater ease in obtaining crucial imports, including know-how, than had been the case with the gas diffusion project, chiefly from German firms.[28] In particular, the Iraqis had got well beyond elementary aluminium alloy rotors and had begun to work with rotors made of maraging steel and carbon fibre. The German firm involved was MAN, a centrifuge-manufacturing subcontractor to the German branch of Urenco. Two ex-employees of MAN, Karl Heinz Schaab and Bruno Stemmler, set up on their own account to provide centrifuge parts and technology to Iraq, based on Urenco designs, up to and including the design of the supercritical TC-11 centrifuge, 3 m long. Their motives appear to have been purely financial. The connection was brief but intensive. It began in the late 1980s and continued until shortly after the 1990 UN embargo on trade with Iraq, which they at first were able to circumvent using an intermediary front company in Singapore called Mitramas.[29]

Independent estimates indicate that, without the war, the single calutron racetrack at Al Tarmiya could have produced enough uranium for a bomb by 1995, and the projected centrifuge plant at Rashdiya could have matched it, before reaching an annual output of four or five times as much before the turn of the century.[30] It seems that the second calutron racetrack, planned for Ash Sharqat, 200 km north-west of Baghdad (while still within Sunni heartlands), was a shadow plant, held in reserve, and was never in fact used.

Unlike the Manhattan Project, plutonium scarcely featured in the Iraqi bomb programme, except at the fringes. The largest nuclear reactor in Iraq was a 5 MW (thermal) research reactor at Al Tuwaitha, supplied by the Soviet Union, called the IRT-5000, fuelled with highly enriched uranium, and under IAEA safeguards. Between regular visits from IAEA inspectors, before the war the Iraqis had secretly irradiated three home-made fuel elements containing natural uranium at the reactor and had subsequently extracted from them 3 g of plutonium in total. The extraction was carried out at a 'hot cell' (a laboratory-scale plutonium separation facility) of Italian origin known to the IAEA and within the Al Tuwaitha complex, alongside the reactor and the fuel element fabrication plant, but not legally subject to inspection until it started accepting irradiated fuel. That fuel had begun to be processed there was also kept secret by Iraq. Risking detection for such a painfully slow method of accumulating plutonium makes little obvious sense.[31]

The IRT-5000 reactor played one final part in the Iraqi bomb campaign. In what Albright *et al.* call the 'crash programme',[32] immediately after the invasion of Kuwait a decision was taken to commandeer the fuel for this reactor and replacement stocks, together with those of another small research reactor supplied by France at the same time as its sale to Iraq of the larger Osirak reactor, which was bombed by the Israelis while still under construction in 1981. This fuel was all in the form of highly enriched uranium (to about 84 per cent) and amounted to about 40 kg in total. The plan was to enrich it rapidly to weapons-grade using the centrifuges at Rashdiya, but it was overtaken by events. The allied bombing campaign of the first Gulf War and the freezing of relations between Iraq and the outside world put an end to the scheme.

If lessons were to be looked for from the perspective of the NPT from the Iraqi example, there are perhaps four. One is that states may be willing to run greater risks of detection than seem prudent in order to achieve a goal as important as a nuclear weapons capability. Linked to this, states working on a covert bomb programme cannot be relied upon to do so in such a way as to maximise the chances of success in the eyes of a neutral observer. Some allowance has to be made for imponderables: national prestige may be an important motive for the acquisition of nuclear weapons, and pride of achievement may be inferred where an unnecessarily difficult or circuitous route to the bomb has been taken, for example. Both risk taking and national pride work in the favour of IAEA inspectors, provided they do not dismiss as an absurd rumour the fact that, for example, Iraqi agents are looking for maraging steel or carbon fibre winding machines, on the grounds that they would draw far less attention to themselves if they focused on the much more widely available aluminium alloy instead, even if it meant a slightly longer cascade of centrifuges.[33]

In fact, Iraqi weapons scientists seem to have begun logically enough, by making exact copies of the American calutron, but even here, with a quaint pride, they chose to call them Baghdadtrons. However, they soon branched off in directions which seemed to have more to do with scientific curiosity than was fully compatible with a covert and presumably urgent weapons programme. The decisions to rely on an implosion design for a uranium bomb and to procure the latest designs of centrifuge while dabbling with other methods of enrichment seem to put scientific curiosity or perhaps prestige first and matters of state second.

Thirdly, the requirement for deception was not forgotten, and two routes were followed. One consisted in hiding irregular activities by carrying them out within the same nuclear complex that housed acknowledged activities, as it was believed that additional movements of people and material would scarcely be noticeable to a casual observer. The other consisted simply in hiding away in a remote part of the country that which it was wished to keep hidden.

Lastly, there may be a lesson concerning the supply side. The European Urenco consortium, perhaps because it is quite clearly not attached to any state's nuclear weapons programme and is multilateral, may police itself and more importantly its large number of suppliers against making questionable transfers of technology and know-how less well than equivalent national programmes.

North Korea

North Korea did not become a party to the NPT until 1985. The delay could have been a reflection of the then hostile attitude to the treaty of China, North Korea's influential neighbour. There was then a further delay between the country signing the treaty and its entry into the required safeguards agreement with the IAEA. This did not occur until 1992. The length of this delay was not unusual for safeguards agreements in general but was unusually long when there was general agreement that the country concerned had embarked on a substantial nuclear programme. The log jam was broken in 1992 as a result of steps taken the previous year to denuclearise the Korean peninsula. The USA withdrew its nuclear weapons from South Korean soil in 1991, which was followed by an agreement between the two constituent parts of Korea to make the whole a nuclear-free zone. Attempts to operationalise the nuclear-free zone agreement on the part of the South in 1992 were rebuffed, but the IAEA fared better.

North Korea's nuclear programme had originated with a small Soviet-supplied research reactor, and since 1977 it had been under the IAEA safeguards that apply to notified transfers from a member state to any recipient. But it had grown to include three other, much larger reactors in varying degrees of completion, although with only one, the smallest, in operation, and a partially built and partially operational plutonium separation plant. When the inspectors arrived at the main nuclear complex at Yongbyon, 100 km north-west of Pyongyang, to verify the substance and accuracy of the North Korean declarations to the IAEA, their main object of interest was the operational 5 MW(e) reactor claimed by the North Koreans to be part of an electrical power programme. Also part of the programme at the same site was a 50 MW(e) reactor under construction and a new nuclear waste storage facility. The inspectors were also shown a 200 MW(e) reactor under construction at Taechon, in the north of the country.

All three reactors were of the Magnox type, fuelled with natural uranium, and were inefficient by modern standards, but were good plutonium producers and were normally dependent on there being plutonium reprocessing available, as in the original British programme.

The IAEA inspectors did a 'swipe' environmental sample at the reprocessing and waste plants; these samples would be able to indicate not only whether reprocessing had occurred but also when (using a similar principle to carbon dating) and to a certain extent how much. The findings did not square with the North Korean claim that they had separated 100 g of plutonium in 1990 but nothing else apart from a few grams in 1975 from the research reactor. Had all the plutonium that could have been produced by the 5 MW(e) reactor, equivalent to 15 MW(th), which had started operating in 1986, been reprocessed, this would have amounted to about 30 kg by 1992.[34] But the possibility that some reprocessing had involved the research reactor prevented a certain diagnosis being made.

An opportunity to do this quickly arose when the IAEA was given what appears to be US intelligence based on satellite reconnaissance concerning two further, undeclared, structures on the Pyongyang site. One appeared to be a nuclear waste site of a sort normally used for research reactors of the kind supplied by the Soviets, and the other, probably under military control according to the IAEA's own information, was suspected of housing waste from the reprocessing of fuel from the 5MW(e) reactor. The climate created by the discovery of the extent of Iraq's deceptions emboldened the IAEA to activate a clause in its inspection agreement with North Korea that allowed a special inspection – that is to say, a visit to a site that the state in question had omitted to declare. This clause was in all Agency inspection agreements under classical safeguards but had been allowed to become a dead letter. The invocation of the clause at this time in respect of the nuclear waste facilities got a hostile response and North Korea threatened to withdraw from the treaty. The country then withdrew that threat and invited the IAEA back in to verify the refuelling procedure at the 5 MW(e) reactor. But the North Koreans played cat and mouse with the IAEA and refused to coordinate refuelling with the inspectors' requirements, thus denying the latter the opportunity to reconstruct the fuelling/refuelling history of the reactor.

By mid-1994, the US government had started diplomatic manoeuvring at the UN in an attempt to impose sanctions on North Korea. But a visit to Pyongyang by former US President Jimmy Carter, at the behest of ailing North Korean leader Kim Il Sung, allowed a face-saving outcome. In exchange for an IAEA-monitored freeze on all its nuclear activities – the 5 MW(e) reactor shut down, no reprocessing of fuel, construction of the other reactors halted – North Korea receives at minimal cost to itself two PWRs of about 1,000 MW(e) each, and deliveries of heating oil while the new reactors are built. But only when the new reactors are near to completion does the agreement ask for greater North Korean openness about the past history of operation of the 5 MW(e) reactor.[35] As the new reactors are built, the deal allows for the partially built Magnox-type reactors to be dismantled, along with the operating 5 MW(e) reactor and the plutonium separation plant. The fuel elements from the 5 MW(e) reactor were to be made safe and eventually removed from the country.

The deal survived the death of Kim Il Sung within weeks of his discussions with Carter and was embodied in the so-called Agreed Framework of 1994. The tasks of putting the agreements into operation and providing the finance were given to the multilateral Korean Peninsula Energy Development Organisation (KEDO) in 1995. Financing the deal would be organised by the USA but it would be paid for by others, with large contributions from Japan and South Korea, and a smaller one from the European Union (EU).

From the perspective of containing proliferation, the deal had substituted proliferation-resistant reactors for the Magnox types under construction, although no guarantees seem to have been given the North Koreans concerning the future supplies of fuel for the new reactors. North Korea had its own natural uranium supplies for the Magnox scheme, but the PWRs need enriched uranium. In the light of the North Koreans' economic doctrine of *juche* (self-sufficiency), this seems a curious omission. There also remained some vagueness about IAEA verification of North Korea's original declarations, including special inspections of the two nuclear waste sites at Yongbyon, and the matching of the timetable for this with the construction schedule of the PWRs.

The subsequent progress of the deal has been turbulent. The signing of the Agreed Framework seems to have meant not the sealing of a bargain but the signal for the start of bargaining by other means. Delays in the construction of the new reactors of at least three years have themselves added to disagreements over the meeting of the cost of the interim supplies of oil as questions arose about whether the North Koreans were really using the oil as agreed, to generate power. The delays also postpone IAEA scrutiny of Pyongyang's past record of plutonium reprocessing. Second thoughts have also been expressed within KEDO over whether Pyongyang really needs two reactors.

Further alarm was created by North Korea's missile development programme, which culminated in the very public firing in 1998 of a three-stage stretched version of the *No-dong* ('Labour') missile, which has a 1,000 km range with a one-tonne payload. There is a very long developmental path between the untested plutonium-based devices that may have emerged from Yongbyon before 1992 and a warhead light enough and reliable enough to be deliverable over long ranges by missile,[36] but even if, consequently, the programme is dismissed as being merely a bargaining counter in connection with the implementation of the Agreed Framework, other problems soon emerged.

On 18 August 1998 leaks from US intelligence agencies appeared in the *New York Times* and the *Washington Post* to the effect that North Korea had begun to construct a nuclear installation, underground, at Kumchangri, 40 km north of Yongbyon, with work on the site having started at least as early as 1996. The US government negotiated access to the site in 1999 and 2000 in exchange for a further delivery of food aid to North Korea. US inspectors found no evidence of anything untoward, although suspicion remained. In March 2000, US President Bill Clinton notified Congress (as required by US domestic anti-proliferation legislation) that he was unable to certify that North Korea was not 'seeking to develop or acquire a capability to enrich uranium, or any additional capability to reprocess spent fuel'.

In August 2002, at the ceremony attending the beginning of work on the PWRs, the US special envoy to North Korea, Jack Pritchard, repeated the warning of the Bush administration that the USA would suspend the Agreed Framework if Pyongyang did not cooperate with the IAEA over the matter of the 5 MW(e) reactor and the undeclared nuclear waste sites. In fact a year before, the new US Bush administration unilaterally interpreted the Agreed Framework on this matter to mean that, while it was understood that the full coming into operation of the PWRs would have to wait until the Yongbyon matter was cleared up, the IAEA would have to start work at Yongbyon almost immediately, since it would take years for its inspectors to be able to certify fully that Pyongyang was in good standing with the NPT. In fact, the date for nuclear components to arrive at the PWR sites was set at 2005, and Washington was demanding that the 'special inspections' should therefore begin at once. In March 2002, Bush refused to certify to Congress that North Korea was in compliance with the Agreed Framework.

Shortly after work had begun on constructing the PWRs, a meeting in Pyongyang in October 2002 between US and North Korean officials saw, or allegedly saw, a surprisingly frank exchange of views. During the meeting, US Assistant Secretary of State James Kelly raised US suspicions concerning a secret North Korean bomb programme. Astonishingly, at the same meeting North Korean officials apparently admitted to a uranium enrichment programme, which admission they have since denied making.

Not long afterwards, in November, the KEDO suspended deliveries of fuel oil, which had reached 500,000 tonnes annually and whose alleged diversion away from electrical power production had itself become another bone of contention, while the following month North Korea responded by saying it would restart the 5 MW(e) reactor to produce electricity (the amount of electricity produced by it is trivial and it seems to be used essentially to meet the needs of the Yongbyon nuclear complex itself).[37] IAEA seals and monitoring equipment at Yongbyon were removed and the inspectors from the IAEA expelled. In January 2003 Pyongyang announced that it was withdrawing from the NPT.

With the withdrawal of the inspectors and the earlier completion of the US programme for 'canning' the spent fuel elements at Yongbyon, to allow their indefinite future storage without reprocessing, a window to the outside world closed on North Korean nuclear activities. Without that, there is no hard information – only that communicated between the two sides, and that information is not guaranteed to be free from misapprehension, on either side.[38] More, with no one 'on the ground' in North Korea, apart from a possible presence at the construction sites for the PWRs (although here the lead contractor is South Korea), information on what might be happening within Pyongyang's nuclear programme became more dependent on US intelligence gathering, whose reputation for accuracy, even within Washington, has not been enhanced by the Iraq war of 2003.

The initial US reaction was to suggest bringing North Korea before the UN Security Council with a view to obtaining a condemnatory resolution, but this met with opposition from the Chinese delegate. Perhaps as a compromise, China agreed instead to host a resumption of Washington–Pyongyang discussions in Beijing in April. This met a minimum US position that it was no longer prepared to have bilateral discussions with Pyongyang and forced North Korea to retreat from its position that only bilateral talks would be good enough. The meeting, which took place on 23–25 April 2003, saw the North Koreans admit that they possessed nuclear weapons. They also claimed that they had begun reprocessing fuel from the 5 MW(e) reactor, although the canning of the fuel elements done in 1997 would have complicated the chemistry of the plutonium extraction process, since the canning material was stainless steel and the original casing a magnesium alloy. US Secretary of State Colin Powell cast some doubt on the reprocessing claim by saying immediately after the talks that there was no US intelligence confirmation of this. North Korean statements after the talks spoke of a willingness to discuss 'verification and the dismantlement of physical deterrent force' in exchange for a non-aggression treaty with the USA – a long-standing request given obvious new urgency by the 2003 Iraq war.[39]

The 'bargaining by other means' has continued until the present day. The North Korean admission that it possessed centrifuges and nuclear weapons may have been an attempt to improve its bargaining position vis-à-vis the United States and, possibly, China. There has certainly been no slackening in the dependence of the North Korean economy on food and energy aid from outside. While it is by no means certain Pyongyang does actually possess nuclear weapons, any that it has will almost certainly be based on plutonium extracted from the 5 MW(e) reactor at some stage in its history. On the other hand, it does seem certain that North Korea possesses some sort of centrifuge programme, dating from the late 1990s and built with assistance, at governmental or sub-governmental level, from Pakistan, with centrifuges being bartered for North Korean missile technology.[40] The extent and even location of this programme remain unknown, although educated guesses seem to place its output at enough enriched uranium for one or two bombs a year by 2005.[41]

Roundtable discussions have continued. China brokered six-sided talks at Beijing in August 2003, with Japan, South Korea and Russia also present, along with the principals. The chief tangible outcome, however, appears to have been the US decision in December 2003 to halt the construction of the PWRs. As Pyongyang appeared to be extending its collection of bargaining chips, the USA was moving in the opposite direction, or at least dispensing with carrots in favour of sticks.

Or rather, this seemed to have been the case until June 2004, when the USA put forward new proposals at the talks, in the latest indication of a possible shift in the internal balance of power within the US administration towards an appreciation of the usefulness of diplomatic and multilateral approaches to proliferation questions. Indeed, citing allied pressure as the reason for its shift, the USA offered Pyongyang a new two-phase process, in which carrots once more replaced sticks. North Korea would have to freeze its nuclear programmes and then dismantle them under international supervision (it is not clear whether this includes the half-built PWRs, although it is reasonable to speculate that, under the new softer line taken by Washington, work on these will go ahead). In return it would receive immediate shipments of fuel oil from China, Russia and South Korea. In addition the USA, together with the other five powers, would draw up a multilateral security guarantee for Pyongyang, and undertake a broad survey of North Korean energy needs. More, if all of this were to unfold as planned, the USA offered bilateral talks with North Korea on the removal of US economic sanctions. A game theorist would immediately recognise in the new US position the old truth that where one wishes to compel an adversary to alter course this is more easily done through a process of withholdable rewards than through threats.

By the end of 2004 the North Koreans had not reacted to the new US proposals, presumably because they were awaiting the outcome of the November presidential elections and the prospect of an even better offer. When this was not forthcoming, they indicated that the June 2004 offer was not good enough and said they would in fact withdraw from the six-power talks, perhaps seeing their own position as having strengthened in proportion to how far the USA had become bogged down in Iraq.

Iran

As we have already seen, Iran's first steps in nuclear energy involved the purchase of a PWR. This actually comprised two units of 1,300 MW(e) each, which came from Germany and which were to be built at Bushehr, on the Gulf coast. Construction began in 1974 but was stopped by the Iranian revolution in 1979. The site was damaged by bombing during the Iran–Iraq war. After the war, the USA put pressure on the western European suppliers to boycott the Iranian plan, alleging it was cover for a secret weapons programme. In 1995 US Secretary of State Warren Christopher publicly claimed that Iran had had a programme for the acquisition of nuclear weapons in existence since the mid-1980s.[42] This was part of a diplomatic drive aimed at reining in a Russian deal made with Iran in 1992 to complete the Bushehr installation with Russian-designed reactors, which included a further understanding that additional nuclear facilities would be provided, including a centrifuge enrichment plant. While it is difficult to see the Iranian case for haste over the Bushehr plant to the extent of being willing to contemplate, in Russian replacement reactors, a poor second-best solution to the problem, both technically and commercially, it is easy to understand, by contrast, a heightened Iranian interest in a means to acquire nuclear weapons, given the recent discoveries in Iraq. The extent of the Iraqi bomb programme presumably surprised Iranian observers as much as it had anyone else.

The US diplomatic offensive met with some success, at least initially, in that Moscow was persuaded to back down on the centrifuge part of the deal and the Chinese government – suppliers of nuclear equipment on a small scale to Iran since 1985 (under IAEA safeguards, although China acceded to the NPT only in 1992) – sharply to limit to more or less laboratory scale what it was prepared to transfer. However, the USA experienced problems in getting the agreement with Moscow to stick. In 2000 the Russians officially renounced the 1995 restrictions, having earlier tested their limits by trading heavy-water technology with Iran. It was now preparing to sell Iran further power reactors and apparently seriously entertained a request for the transfer of laser enrichment technology, which the USA eventually succeeded in blocking.[43]

While with hindsight it is clear that Iran had begun overstepping the limitations on its nuclear activities agreed under the NPT from at least 1995, the fact that the USA was the chief prosecutor and judge, together with Iran's long-held status as a bête noire of US foreign policy, added to the fact that there was no evidence that Iran had contravened any of its undertakings within the NPT, meant that an impartial outside observer even by 2000 would not have known what to think. But in August 2002, independent confirmation emerged when an Iranian group of opponents to the regime in exile abroad, the National Council of Resistance of

Iran, claimed the existence of undeclared (to the IAEA) nuclear facilities, and of 'front companies' for the procurement from overseas of nuclear equipment, materials and know-how. One of the two undeclared facilities was a plant for the production of heavy water, near Arak, about 240 km south-west of Tehran, and the other, it later emerged, was a gas centrifuge plant built underground at Natanz, at the southerly corner of an approximately equilateral triangle between Arak and Tehran. Tehran itself housed a third undeclared facility, the JHL facility, where natural uranium (in three forms – see below), whose importation (from Russia or China) had not been notified to the IAEA, was stored and processed.[44]

The reaction of the Iranian authorities was initially to aim to explain the extent of this activity in broad terms by announcing the existence of a long-term plan to add a further 6,000 MW to their nuclear energy programme by 2020. They then issued an invitation to the IAEA to visit Iran, scheduled originally for October 2002 but later rescheduled to the following February. The IAEA Director General, Mohamed ElBaradei, led the party.

The IAEA sought confirmation of and explanation for three pieces of information. One was its own information (belatedly supplied by the exporting state) that Iran had imported in 1991 about a tonne and a half of natural uranium in forms suitable for more or less immediate use as reactor fuel or enrichment plant feed (1,000 kg of hex; 400 kg of uranium tetrafluoride, an intermediate compound involved in either the production of uranium metal or hex; and 400 kg of uranium dioxide, a common form of reactor fuel when enriched). The other information was that released by the National Council of Resistance, supplemented by further claims concerning a Tehran facility (the Kalaye Electric Company) for the manufacture of centrifuges. These details were said by the IAEA to have been made public.

The Iranians admitted or half-admitted to everything and volunteered additional information to the effect that they were about to start work at Arak – the site of the heavy-water plant – on a new 40 MW(th) reactor that would use heavy water as moderator and natural uranium as fuel. They denied, however, that they had contravened the letter of their safeguards agreements with the IAEA. They claimed that heavy-water plants were specifically excluded from the list of things the inspectors interest themselves in (see Chapter 3); they also claimed that the small quantities of natural uranium they had imported in 1991 were below the threshold for notification to the IAEA; and finally they denied that any of their centrifuge work had involved any testing of the machines, through a trial feed of hex or otherwise.

The credibility of these denials is unequal. Heavy-water manufacturing plants are outwith the remit of the IAEA and in this the Iranians were correct.[45] But the rationale for building a research reactor fuelled with natural uranium simply as a research reactor while incurring the considerable costs of design and construction (compared with the costs of importing) not only of the reactor but of the heavy-water plant too is obscure. This is especially so when it is recalled that such reactors are very efficient plutonium producers, even if there is no evidence of Iranian work on plutonium separation. Even so, no safeguarding rules had been broken.

The failure to notify the IAEA of the importation of the natural uranium in a ready-for-use form the Iranians put down to an innocent misunderstanding of the rules. Since the rules have been in existence since 1971, in the form of INFCIRC/153,[46] their interpretation cannot presumably be in doubt, however imprecise the wording to a lay eye.[47] Importation of uranium in any of the finished forms in question, in any quantity, is meant to come under safeguards (INFCIRC/153, paragraph 34c). Where the quantity of natural uranium is below 10 tonnes, as in this case, it can be exempted from safeguards entirely, but the importer has to enter a request with the Agency to this effect (paragraph 37). Iran had not done this and the initial findings of the Director General's visit concentrated on this failure and on other failures directly arising. For instance, some of the material was handled and processed in new or substantially modified facilities in Tehran, and waste products were stored at sites elsewhere. Had the material been under safeguards, Iran would have been required to keep the inspectors abreast of these changes and of additions to facilities for handling material. Where there are nuclear material flows, so there is created an IAEA right of access to a facility. As it was, the IAEA knew nothing about them. Contritely, the Iranians undertook to reconstruct a record of what had been done with the materials, and what had been transferred between sites. And as a confidence-building measure they agreed to a 10-year-old request that they should supply early (that is to say before operation) design information on new plant to the Agency as well as notify it of new centres of nuclear activity.

The third issue – that concerning Iranian work on centrifuge methods for enriching uranium – was left unresolved at this visit. The IAEA party visited the pilot enrichment plant at Natanz and took environmental samples there in May 2003, having been told that the plant was due to start operating the following month. More difficulties were experienced with obtaining access to the Kalaye Electric Company in Tehran, and although the entire premises were eventually made available to the visitors, environmental sampling was not allowed, although a promise was made that this might be possible on a subsequent visit.

Iran could again claim that no rules had been broken. The pilot centrifuge plant would have become notifiable to the IAEA only after it started processing nuclear material or some little time before. And the Kalaye Electric Company could be described as a strictly research and development facility and hence off limits to the IAEA (except for states that had signed up to the Additional Protocol, but at this time Iran had not done so). Reading between the lines of the Agency's official report on the visit, there was at the least a puzzle that Iran had nearly completed a pilot centrifuge plant and was starting to build a full-scale plant alongside it but had never, apparently, checked on the operation of the centrifuges by feeding in even trial amounts of hex. Of course, had they done so, which they denied, the existence of the plant would have become notifiable to the Agency, whereas the Agency had received no official notice at all.

The pressure on Iran to conform to NPT norms was increased in October 2003 as a result of an initiative by the EU, perhaps taking advantage of a lull in US concern due to distractions elsewhere and a desire not to alienate Iran at a difficult stage in the United States' attempts to reach a post-war settlement in Iraq. In exchange for an Iranian promise to open up everything to IAEA inspection and to freeze all activity on centrifuges, the EU group (Britain, France and Germany – the EU Three) pledged a willingness to cooperate with the Iranian peaceful nuclear programme. The Iranians also got a guarantee, to which the USA gave its backing, that, provided the deal was adhered to, Iran would not be reported to the Security Council as being in breach of the NPT and so risk becoming subject to economic sanctions, certainly from the West and probably from Russia and China too.

Progress was still of the 'two steps forward, one step back' variety. In October 2003, Iran passed the IAEA documentation that amounted, it was said by Iran, to a full disclosure of its past nuclear activities, against a background of continuing IAEA inspections. In that November, Iran indicated that it would sign the Additional Protocol to its existing safeguards arrangements with the IAEA. It also confirmed suspension of all uranium enrichment and reprocessing activities.

Against this, inspectors in the field reported discrepancies between the official Iranian statement of activities on the one hand and on the other the story told by their close professional study of Iranian records and swipe sampling at the centrifuge plants. The main discrepancies pertained to the centrifuge programme. Sampling had shown the inspectors that centrifuges at Natanz and Kalaye had, on a small scale presumably, been operated with a feed of hex, which had left behind microscopic traces of enriched uranium. The Iranians denied doing any enriching themselves and explained the environmental samples by claiming that they had imported the centrifuges or major components thereof and that these had already been used for enrichment by the previous owners (Pakistan). If true, it was the first indication the IAEA had been given that Iran had imported centrifuges. But the inspectors had difficulty in believing this explanation, since it was hard to reconcile with the various degrees of enrichment found in the environmental samples. Secondly, inspectors found evidence that Iran had carried out work on so-called P2 (presumably supercritical) centrifuge designs, and this had been omitted from the October report. The reason given by the Iranians for the omission was pressure of time. Finally, away from the centrifuges, the inspectors found written evidence that Iran had been working on polonium for the period 1989–93. The Iranian explanation for this was that they were interested in it as a miniature power source. But it is a very difficult and dangerous substance to handle, with a short half-life, whose only *known* application is as an initiator at the core of a nuclear explosive (see above).[48] Interestingly, documents uncovered in the IAEA's 'sixth inspection' of Iraq, in September 1991, included a description of the manufacture of polonium there to act as a nuclear initiator. Some 6 mg was produced by irradiating 15 kg of bismuth in a reactor.[49]

The year 2004 began with a further set of two steps forward, one step back, when Tehran told the IAEA that it intended to restart the conversion of uranium into hex – the feed material for enrichment plant. The IAEA made an official protest, to which Iran responded by saying it intended to go further and resume work on its centrifuges, including testing. This was too much for the EU Three, which had negotiated the deal in 2003, and their response was to threaten Iran with reference to the Security Council unless it restored the freeze agreed the previous November. The deterrent threat worked since, unlike North Korea, Iran is singularly short of friends in the Security Council (or indeed anywhere else), and the 2003 freeze agreement was reaffirmed in Paris in November 2004. What may be different about the Paris agreement is its embedding of a new cluster of incentives for Iran, provided it sticks to the agreement. In this case, now oddly reminiscent of North Korea, the EU Three are holding out the prospect of guaranteed fuel supplies (lightly enriched uranium for Iran's power reactors), concessions on trade and, interestingly, positive and negative security assurances. If, on the other hand, the IAEA were to report a failure to abide by the freeze terms, the threat of a report to the Security Council remains.

It remains a moot point whether Iran will continue to hold on to 'nurse' in the shape of its deal with the EU Three in order to avoid something 'worse' – the wrath of a USA still professing scepticism at European efforts – or will find a way before long to exploit the differences between Brussels and Washington.

Libya

The Libyan government announced in December 2003 that it would dismantle its programmes for the production of weapons of mass destruction (biological, chemical and nuclear) and allow inspections to verify that it was in compliance with its undertakings under the NPT and the biological weapons convention of 1975 (which has no inspection procedures) as well as sign up to the chemical weapons convention (which does have inspection procedures), in force since 1997. It also volunteered to sign up to the Additional Protocol further to its existing safeguards arrangements with the IAEA, which allows inspectors to verify not only that declared facilities are being used solely for peaceful purposes but also that there are no undeclared facilities in existence. The British government on the same day said that Libya had approached Britain in March 2003 about making a clean breast of things and that the December announcement was the product of tripartite discussions also involving the USA. During these discussions it had emerged, among other things, that Libya had centrifuges for uranium enrichment and components for many more, although no actual plant in operation.

Towards the end of December, Mohamed ElBaradei indicated that the IAEA had not known about the enrichment programme, which included a now dismantled pilot centrifuge plant. He added that Libya had imported centrifuge components and natural uranium and had been in breach of IAEA safeguards.[50]

At the time of writing, the closest analogy with the Libyan case seems to be South Africa. Both had been pariah states and subject to economic sanctions and both voluntarily owned up to a nuclear weapons programme and sought to gain credit internationally for doing so. One difference is that it is possible Libya went into the centrifuge business simply in order to be able to 'own up' to something substantial, whereas the South Africans had a definite strategic rationale for the bombs they manufactured during the 1970s and 1980s.

Coda: some reasons why

We have discussed how states acquire nuclear weapons, and identified which states appear to be on the borderline of joining the nuclear club, but we have yet to say why.

A Baconian might hope that the five acknowledged nuclear states, plus India and Pakistan, as well as the borderline states looked at, would all have in common something amounting to a self-evident motive. But the best that can be said probably is that states 'go nuclear' or seriously consider doing so when the alternatives are unattractive.

What normally are the alternatives? Firm attachment to a non-proliferation arrangement (the NPT and/or a regional nuclear-free zone) is now chief among them, but this will not appeal to states (even should they be formally attached to such an arrangement) that tend to feel themselves cold-shouldered in comparable associations of states and whose international relations in general (along political or economic dimensions) are apt to be abnormal. China from the death of Stalin to the formal recognition by the USA of the Mao government, Israel since its foundation, Libya since Gaddafi, North Korea with its *juche* philosophy (especially idiosyncratic since the end of the Cold War), apartheid South Africa, Iraq between the 1991 and 2003 Gulf Wars, and perhaps revolutionary Iran fall into this category.

Consistent with the alternative of forswearing nuclear weapons is reliance on conventional armaments. But this is obviously problematical for a state that finds itself with a nuclear armed neighbour with which it is not on good terms. India, Iraq, Iran, Pakistan and to a lesser degree Libya fit here. It might be thought that the alternative option of a satisfactory external alliance has been overlooked. But in the case of states with nuclear-armed enemies on their doorstep, external guarantees have a poor reputation: the USA struggled for years during the Cold War to find a means of reassuring its European allies without allowing them actual access to nuclear weapons. And in the case of pariah states (they are pariahs not because they refuse to conform to NPT norms – they refuse to conform to non-proliferation norms because they are pariahs) their bad international relations mean at best a very restricted choice of allies and at worst none at all. To complete the circle, poor access to allies increasingly means poor access too to the most effective kinds of conventional weapons. At one time what is true about access to the most effective sorts of conventional weapons (i.e. the fact they are obtainable from only a few Western states) would also have been true of nuclear weapons technology; now, with the extensive black market in the latter, especially centrifuge technology, this no longer applies.

Not so well explained so far are the cases of Argentina and Brazil. Perhaps there is less to be explained, in that both states dallied with the idea of nuclear weapons rather than gave it their full attention. Even so, the question here seems to be not quite one of pariahdom, but one of military governments at a time when the fashion for military governments in Latin America, and indeed anywhere else, was starting rapidly to pass. The collapse of the military governments in both states certainly coincided with an outbreak of candour about their past nuclear programmes and a burst of enthusiasm for their participation in the NPT and the Latin American nuclear-free zone arrangement.

Notes

1 Flowers indicates that the critical mass of a bare sphere of 100 per cent uranium-235 is 25 kg; the critical mass of a bare sphere of 80 per cent enriched uranium will weigh half as much again. See R.H. Flowers, 'How

reactors work', in W. Marshall (ed.), *Nuclear Power Technology. Volume 1: Reactor Technology* (Oxford, Clarendon Press, 1983), p. 17.

2 Of course, if each fission produces three neutrons, two-thirds of those produced can now escape and we can still have a critical mass, but smaller in dimensions because the number escaping depends on the surface area of the mass while the production rate depends on the volume. This intuitively appealing interpretation of the concept of critical mass is due to T.C. Schelling, *Micromotives and Macrobehavior* (New York, W.W. Norton, 1978), p. 94.

3 Richard Rhodes, *The Making of the Atomic Bomb* (New York, Touchstone Books, 1988), pp. 578–9.

4 Fusion of two lighter elements to produce a heavier one is difficult to arrange since the nuclei in question electrically repel each other. But once this repulsion is overcome by injecting sufficient energy, the act of fusion then releases energy in even greater quantities.

5 Early graphite-moderated reactors were built as a pile of graphite bricks, with fuel elements inserted at regular intervals: hence the name 'pile' for a nuclear reactor.

6 A small contribution (circa 1 per cent) of neutrons to the neutron economy of a reactor comes in the form of 'delayed neutrons' from fission. Without this, reactors would have to be run on more of a knife edge between supercriticality and subcriticality, which would be problematical.

7 For a more precisely detailed plutonium calculation see David Albright, Frans Berkhout and William Walker, *Plutonium and Highly Enriched Uranium 1996: World Inventories, Capabilities and Policies* (New York, Oxford University Press for the Stockholm International Peace Research Institute, 1997), pp. 472–8.

8 That this matters is illustrated by the US Defense Department's plan in 1986 to use an enrichment process to convert plutonium rich in the 240 isotope to weapons-grade, where the isotope can be tolerated only to the extent of 6 per cent or less. The ending of the Cold War saw the scheme dropped. See Richard Kokoski, *Technology and the Proliferation of Nuclear Weapons* (Oxford, Oxford University Press for the Stockholm International Peace Research Institute, 1995), p. 54.

9 Albright *et al.*, *Plutonium and Highly Enriched Uranium 1996*, p. 118.

10 In March 1951, during the Korean War, General Douglas MacArthur suggested in Tokyo that as an alternative to extending the war into China he might 'sever Korea from Manchuria by laying a field of radioactive wastes – the by-products of atomic manufacture – across all major lines of enemy supply'. After he had been sacked he repeated the idea to President-elect Eisenhower in December 1952, who rejected it. See 'Korean war at 50', *Army Magazine* (of the Association of the US Army), December 2002.

11 The early British Magnox design, being comparatively massive, has built-in safety from this factor alone, as the structure has a large thermal inertia.

12 Hans A. Bethe, *The Road from Los Alamos* (New York, American Institute of Physics, 1991), p. 216, implies rather than states that about 10 Ci of iodine-131 was released, but says that no caesium-137 was released.

13 L.A. Ilyin and O.A. Pavlovskij, 'Radiological consequences of the Chernobyl

accident in the Soviet Union and measures taken to mitigate their impact', *IAEA Bulletin*, Vol. 29, No. 4, 1987, p. 17.
14 F-N. Flakus, 'Radiation in perspective: improving comprehension of risks', *IAEA Bulletin*, Vol. 37, No. 2, 1995, p. 11.
15 Rhodes, *The Making of the Atomic Bomb*, pp. 489–92.
16 David Holloway, *Stalin and the Bomb* (New Haven, Yale University Press, 1994), pp. 190–1.
17 Holloway, *Stalin and the Bomb*, p. 222, tells of the Soviets using the centrifuge on an industrial scale from the late 1950s.
18 Separation is even poorer than this suggests, since it is the square root of the ratio of the masses that is involved, which is 1.0043.
19 Judging by a scale drawing in J.H. Tait, 'Uranium enrichment', in W. Marshall (ed.), *Nuclear Power Technology. Volume 2: Fuel Cycle* (Oxford, Clarendon Press, 1983), p. 123.
20 Kokoski, *Technology and the Proliferation of Nuclear Weapons*, p. 63.
21 Thereby making it more difficult to keep the activity secret, as attempts to import more exotic materials will draw attention to themselves.
22 Australia and Canada have about 40 per cent of the commercially interesting (i.e. low-cost) uranium in the world. South Africa and Namibia taken together account for a further 18 per cent. The other member of the top five is Kazakhstan, with 15 per cent. Brazil is the next biggest, with 6 per cent. Source: Uranium Information Centre, Submission to Senate (Australia) Inquiry on Uranium Mining, August 2002.
23 The reason is partly that the laser method works almost as well with feed in the form of the otherwise discarded tailings of depleted uranium, which are produced in large amounts wherever gas diffusion or centrifuge plants have been operating.
24 Kokoski, *Technology and the Proliferation of Nuclear Weapons*, pp. 57–63.
25 *Economist*, 2 September 2004.
26 Albright *et al.*, *Plutonium and Highly Enriched Uranium 1996*, p. 325.
27 Kokoski, *Technology and the Proliferation of Nuclear Weapons*, pp. 124–8.
28 The first laboratory test centrifuge operated successfully in 1990, with hex feed. At this point the IAEA should have been informed, under the terms of the NPT.
29 See www.exportcontrols.org (site of the Institute for Science and International Security, last accessed 4 April 2005).
30 Albright *et al.*, *Plutonium and Highly Enriched Uranium 1996*, p. 341.
31 Even if there had been no need to dodge the inspectors, it seems that the procedure could have produced only 100 g of plutonium a year. See Kokoski, *Technology and the Proliferation of Nuclear Weapons*, p. 122.
32 Albright *et al.*, *Plutonium and Highly Enriched Uranium 1996*, p. 344.
33 Amusingly, before the second Gulf War in 2003, British intelligence became much exercised over Iraqi attempts to import aluminium tubes for what the British took to be a new centrifuge programme. The tubes as it turned out were for missile fuselages. See *Review of Intelligence on Weapons of Mass Destruction*, Report of a Committee of Privy Councillors, Chairman Lord Butler, HC 898 (London, The Stationery Office, 2004) (henceforth the Butler report), p. 130.

34 Albright *et al.*, *Plutonium and Highly Enriched Uranium 1996*, who make careful allowance for probable shut-downs and teething troubles at the reactor, put the figure at 25–30 kg. British intelligence is more cautious and describes the amount of plutonium as sufficient to make at least one weapon. Butler report, p. 24.
35 Larry A. Niksch, *North Korea's Nuclear Weapons Program* (Washington, DC, Congressional Research Service: Library of Congress, Issue Brief for Congress IB91141, October 2002).
36 For use in missiles, warheads have to be light enough not to compromise range and efficient enough to ensure a large yield to compensate for missile inaccuracy.
37 Robert Alvarez, 'North Korea: no bygones at Yongbyon', *Bulletin of the Atomic Scientists*, Vol. 59, No. 4, July/August 2003, pp. 39–45. The power produced from this reactor is the equivalent of 5,000 tonnes of fuel oil a year.
38 For US misreading of North Korea, mainly due to language and ideological barriers (which are likely to be two-way), see Daniel A. Pinkston and Phillip C. Saunders, 'Seeing North Korea clearly', *Survival*, Vol. 45, No. 3, autumn 2003, pp. 79–101.
39 Paul Kerr, 'North Korea, US meet: Pyongyang said to claim nukes', *Arms Control Today*, Vol. 33, No. 4, May 2003.
40 Possibly with cash adjustments. See 'Pakistan and North Korea', *Strategic Comments*, Vol. 8, No. 9, November 2002.
41 Averaging estimates from the US Central Intelligence Agency, as reported by Paul Kerr, 'Deconstructed: North Korea's nuclear programs', *Arms Control Today*, Vol. 34, No. 1, January/February 2004, and the estimate of Alvarez in 'North Korea: no bygones'.
42 'Press Briefing by Secretary of State Warren Christopher on the President's Executive Order on Iran', US Department of State, 1 May 1995.
43 'Iran's nuclear ambitions: full steam ahead?', *Strategic Comments*, Vol. 9, No. 2, March 2003, and 'Iran's nuclear programme: suspended animation', *Strategic Comments*, Vol. 10, No. 9, November 2004.
44 'Implementation of the NPT Safeguards Agreement in the Islamic Republic of Iran', Report by the Director General, IAEA, GOV/2003/40, June 2003.
45 Were this not so, the IAEA would also, by parity of reasoning, need to interest itself in other moderator materials too, including ordinary water! But, importantly, since heavy water in bulk has few other uses, exporter states that are members of the Nuclear Suppliers Group add it and heavy-water plant to their trigger list.
46 For the text of INFCIRC/153 and INFCIRC/66/Re. 2, see David Fischer, Paul Szasz and Jozef Goldblat (eds), *Safeguarding the Atom: A Critical Appraisal* (London, Taylor and Francis for the Stockholm International Peace Research Institute, 1985).
47 Misunderstanding is not impossible. Luxembourg failed to have safeguards imposed on a transfer of depleted uranium to Israel on the grounds that this was not intended for nuclear uses. Under INFCIRC/153 this would have been correct, but since Israel was not a party to the NPT, INFCIRC/66 should have applied, and this does not make an exception for non-nuclear use.

48 'UN inspectors find secret Iran experiments', *Financial Times*, 24 February 2004, and 'Iran faulted on nuclear declaration', *Washington Post*, 25 February 2004, p. A18.
49 Kokoski, *Technology and the Proliferation of Nuclear Weapons*, p. 125.
50 Paul Kerr, 'Libya vows to dismantle WMD program', *Arms Control Today*, Vol. 34, No. 2, January/February 2004.

2

Nuclear weapons and international security

In 2000, almost every state in the world (all except Cuba, India, Israel and Pakistan) publicly subscribed once again to the principle that the spread of nuclear weapons to states not already possessing them is dangerous to international security and that it should therefore be energetically discouraged.[1] The occasion was the latest review conference of the 30-year-old NPT, the chief international instrument for restricting nuclear proliferation, and for reversing such proliferation as has occurred, if its Article 6 – which amounts to a promise by the countries already with nuclear weapons in their possession to disarm themselves of them – is taken seriously.

But the correctness of this principle is not self-evident. An important intellectual challenge comes from Kenneth Waltz, writing most recently in 2003.[2] The basis of his challenge is a generalisation of what he regards as a significant lesson of the Cold War years. Then, the presence and possession of nuclear weapons seemed to prevent serious wars breaking out, when these might otherwise very easily have done so (e.g. between the USA and the Soviet Union, or China and the Soviet Union during the period of the Sino-Soviet dispute). His conclusion is that, under certain not very restrictive conditions chiefly to do with what he seems to think are the possible dangers of very rapid spread, the further proliferation of nuclear weapons might have the same 'fire-blanket' effect on other international quarrels, or, in other words, might promote international security. Yet it may be the case that Waltz's challenge, when examined carefully, does not take great issue with the conventional wisdom about the unmitigated dangers of nuclear spread.

Overview

We start with Barry Buzan's concept of a 'security complex' to describe a grouping of states whose calculations concerning their security must take into account the others in the group, and the security calculations of these others.[3] This is a more compact term than, but essentially means the same as, 'geopolitical system' in the sense used by Bruce Bueno de Mesquita and William Riker.[4] It is usually possible to say which states are definitely within a complex and which definitely outside, but the definition of the boundaries of a complex will never be completely precise.

A state contemplating acquiring nuclear weapons normally needs to consider the impact of a decision to do so on other states in the complex. If no other state acquires nuclear weapons, it makes sense for the first state to do so, as its security level will rise. The danger of serious attack will be very much smaller than before. But if other states think the same and do likewise, it will still have made sense for the first state to have acquired nuclear weapons, since if it had not its security level would have been poorer. Ultimately, then, all states in the system acquire nuclear weapons. This is common ground between the conventional wisdom and the Waltzian position.

International security – a phrase widely used without always receiving a definition – if it is to mean anything, must have something to do with the security of not just one or a few states but of all the states in the security complex. A simple working definition might make it equivalent to the 'total' or average (average simply being the total divided by the number of states in the complex) security of states within the system. What can we say about what happens to total security in a security complex as nuclear weapons spread?

Jon Elster hints at a possible way of tackling this question by his brief suggestion that (in an imaginary non-nuclear world) a unilateral act of comprehensive disarmament by a state in a security complex might actually reduce international security within the complex.[5]

We can modify the Elster example slightly to consider a situation, again in an imaginary non-nuclear world, where the states in question are armed, but in a defensive manner, corresponding to a world where defensive military technology had the upper hand (at least for the time being). With all states in the complex thus armed, international security is obviously at a relatively high level. However, should one state disarm, its security will drop, since even defensive arms can easily be used for offensive purposes against a completely disarmed opponent. The security of other states in the system, because of the defensive bias of the armaments in question, will not itself rise by very much at all (they have lost a potential attacker but only in the abstract, given the presumed dominance of the defensive) and indeed may fall, since exploitation of the disarmed state may become a reason for rivalry between them. Thus on average we may expect international security to fall with the disarming of one state. And any subsequent further disarming by other states will, up to a certain point, similarly lead to further reductions in international security. But only up to a certain point. This is because international security in a totally disarmed complex must surely be at a higher level than international security in a wholly armed one, even when the wholly armed one comprises states equipped only with defensive weapons. The reason is that in the latter case a war resulting from a miscalculation or even accident is always possible. In addition, even defensive arms may be costly to procure and maintain and while precision in the specification of the 'exchange rate' cannot be looked for, most states would prefer a given level of security obtained cheaply to one obtained only at considerable cost to the public.

From this analysis a very important conclusion may be drawn. If international security is at a higher level when no state is armed compared with the situation where they are all armed, and if nonetheless international security begins to decrease as states individually disarm from the fully armed condition, then there must be a point in the disarming process where the decline in international security reverses itself. Or to word the same point differently, starting from a completely disarmed world, states rearming themselves defensively always benefit as individual states but cause international security to deteriorate until, beyond a certain point in the spreading of the arming tendency, it begins to improve again.

It is suggested here that, for Waltz, a security complex in which all states possessed nuclear weapons would be closely comparable to the above situation of a complex where every state was armed but in a very (virtually impregnable) defensive way. None would then have much reason to fear an attack of any kind, although in the Waltz case the mediating influence would be nuclear deterrence, perhaps as sure as classical defence or even more so, but on the whole less well tried and partly in consequence less well understood. Waltz's view in effect is that states with nuclear weapons are not only virtually immune from nuclear war but immune from all but relatively trivial conventional war too. So for Waltz a completely nuclearised security complex would enjoy a very high level of security by historical standards. However, Waltz concedes that international security would be at an even higher level if nuclear weapons simply did not exist: 'one may prefer a world of conventional great powers having a higher probability of fighting less-destructive wars to a world of nuclear great powers having a lower probability of fighting more-destructive wars'.[6] We might additionally observe that, in a completely nuclearised complex, an unprecedentedly destructive war is always a possibility at any moment, something that is not true of a denuclearised complex. And again, it is far from clear empirically that maintaining nuclear weapons in quantities and to a quality sufficient to deter is particularly affordable (although the same may be said about maintaining the effectiveness of defensive conventional weaponry). Of the five 'legally recognised' nuclear powers, the USA and the USSR engaged during the Cold War in a sometimes deterrence-threatening arms race in terms of the quantity and quality of their nuclear weapons; the other three, however, for the most part were able to maintain forces nearer a minimum deterrent level.

So, to re-run our version of Elster's argument in a Waltzian setting, within a completely nuclearised complex, one state deciding on nuclear disarmament will lose its ability to deter attack. Its security level will diminish as it may become prey to other members of the complex. The security of the remaining members of the complex will not rise significantly with the denuclearisation of one of their number since they already were virtually immune to deliberate attack (on accidental nuclear war, see Annex A to this chapter). Moreover, in a large complex, the denuclearisation of one among many will not significantly reduce the risk to the others of embroilment in an accidental nuclear war. As further states denuclearise we would expect average security in the complex to decrease until a certain point is reached when it must rise again with further denuclearisation as the condition of complete denuclearisation is reached, this condition being one of greater average security even (Waltz seems to be saying) than the one of complete nuclearisation. If, on the other hand, the risk of accidental nuclear war within a completely nuclearised complex was comparatively high and the complex small, one state disarming itself of nuclear weapons would still add to its own insecurity (mitigated by a somewhat reduced exposure to the risk of accidental nuclear war) but this might be compensated by the increase in security felt by the remaining nuclear powers now that one centre of nuclear decision making had been removed and with it a small portion of the risk of an accidental nuclear war (small because while the likelihood of an accidental launch would drop, there would now be one fewer candidate for the position at the receiving end of an accidental missile launch, say). Of course, a high risk of accidental nuclear war would place international security in a completely nuclearised complex at a particularly low level compared with that in a denuclearised complex. But as far as can imperfectly be judged, within the great power complex the risk of accidental nuclear war is significantly lower than would have been the risk of conventional war between them (see Annex A).

Considerations of accidental nuclear war to one side (for the present), we have seen that as proliferation proceeds international security at first declines until some minimum value is reached, after which it increases again with further proliferation.

The obvious question now to ask is where in the progressive nuclearisation of a security complex this point of minimum international security is reached. If the answer should be half-way, which as we shall see below will not often be far from the truth, collective political attempts to slow down nuclear spread, even after some nuclear proliferation may have already occurred in a large complex, will be plainly sensible, even in the absence of any likelihood of reversing such proliferation as may have occurred.

In practice there are two senses in which we can speak of security complexes in the present discussion. The simplest can be a geographical region housing an ideal type of nuclear-free zone (see Chapter 4). Here the striking feature is the absence of nuclear weapons, mainly created by reciprocated abstinence within the zone or complex itself, coupled with its relative isolation from the security concerns of the great powers. The benefit to international security of non-proliferation in such a region is obvious and even limiting proliferation short of the half-way point among states capable of obtaining such weapons will normally pay in terms of the international security of the zone. At the opposite end of the spectrum we may equally speak of a security complex comprising only the great powers and emerging great powers (great powers actual or emergent, meaning states recognised *de facto* by other great powers as great powers or emerging great powers). The striking feature here is the nuclearised condition of the complex, where nuclearisation is essentially a result of and a response to such nuclearisation as was already present within it. Most states in this complex (which we may take to include the five nuclear weapons states officially acknowledged by the NPT) are already nuclear powers and the logic of our analysis would suggest that it is at least possible that international security in such a complex (which perhaps already includes India) would benefit more from further incremental nuclear proliferation (e.g. to Germany or Japan) than from incremental nuclear disarmament. Of course, it would also benefit from a complete reversal of such proliferation as has already occurred, but that might be difficult to achieve if only because it will be nearly impossible to verify to mutual satisfaction that states which once possessed perhaps thousands of nuclear warheads may not have secretly retained a few.

Both classes of security complex are specifically identified in the text of the NPT. The remaining targets of the treaty might be described both as preventive and pre-emptive. First, they are pre-emptive in that encouraging nuclear restraint in the round increases the prospects for the emergence of new nuclear-free zones, as existing nuclear powers may decrease their security involvement in the areas concerned. An example of what is meant here is the emergence of the South East Asian, African and the (failed) Korean nuclear-free zones in the half decade after the ending of the Cold War. Secondly, preventive is about discouraging nuclear additions to the complex of great powers. The logic here, as we

Nuclear weapons and international security

have seen, may be dubious in its own terms but, in conjunction with the pre-emptive objective, the fewer the nuclearised great powers, the smaller will be the degree of unavoidable security involvement outside their complex of mutual interaction.

Encouraging nuclear restraint on a global scale was once an easier task than it now is, given that most states lacked the technical and managerial expertise necessary to run a national programme for the exploitation of nuclear energy. This is now changing, partly as the 'secrets' of nuclear energy have become widely disseminated and partly because the taboo (encapsulated in the NPT itself) against states with nuclear weapons technology and components making these available to other states for payment at a state-to-state or other level has eroded. Even so, the dissemination of expertise in nuclear technology has not gone much further than the 37 non-nuclear weapons states (counting Israel as a non-nuclear weapons state) identified in the text of an adjoint treaty to the NPT, the Comprehensive Test Ban Treaty (Article 14 and Annex 2), opened for signature in 1996, as comprising (together with the nuclear weapons states) all those whose ratifications are required before that treaty can enter into force (which had not happened as of early 2005 – see Chapter 6).[7] Of the 37, only 13 are not member states of recognised nuclear-free zones or Euratom.

Before attempting a fuller formal demonstration of the chief points assumed above without proof, a useful introduction can be obtained from the simple case where a security complex consists of only two states. We draw three matrices representing the choices available in three sets of circumstances. The payoffs for these choices are in every case consistent with the plain-language analysis above.

Two-state case

Table 2.1 sets out the 'Waltz-plus situation', in which general nuclear proliferation is better for both states than a non-nuclear world; this is an example of a 'deadlock game'.[8] Table 2.2 shows the 'Waltz situation', in which general nuclear proliferation is slightly worse for both than a non-nuclear world; this is an example of prisoner's dilemma game. Lastly, the 'Waltz-minus situation' is shown in Table 2.3, and this results from a comparatively high risk of accidental nuclear war; it forms another (acute) example of a prisoner's dilemma game.

For convenience we focus on the situation illustrated in Table 2.2. From the perspective of State A considering whether or not to acquire nuclear weapons, it has to take into account what choices may be made by State B, the only other state in this security complex of two. If State B chooses not to acquire nuclear weapons, State A does better by choosing

Table 2.1. Deadlock game

	State B	
	Acquire nuclear weapons	Stay non-nuclear
State A		
Acquire nuclear weapons	4.5, 4.5	5, 0
Stay non-nuclear	0, 5	4, 4

Table 2.2. Prisoner's dilemma game

	State B	
	Acquire nuclear weapons	Stay non-nuclear
State A		
Acquire nuclear weapons	3, 3	5, 0
Stay non-nuclear	0, 5	4, 4

Table 2.3. Acute prisoner's dilemma game

	State B	
	Acquire nuclear weapons	Stay non-nuclear
State A		
Acquire nuclear weapons	2, 2	5, 0
Stay non-nuclear	0, 5	4, 4

to go nuclear, since it gets a payoff of 5 compared with the alternative of 4. If State B, on the other hand, does choose to go nuclear, State A is better off doing likewise, since it gets a payoff of 3 as opposed to the alternative of 0. So we can see that State A always has an incentive to go nuclear. And what is true of State A is true of State B, so the outcome is that both states go nuclear. When this happens we can see that they finish up with payoffs of 3 each, compared with the 4 each they would have obtained had they stayed non-nuclear. This is why the situation faced by the two players is an example of the security dilemma. The pursuit of national security means less international security in the end. A functioning arms control agreement in this case would attempt to restrict the two states to the bottom right-hand corner of the matrix. It would be worthwhile because both states would be better off than in a state of nature. But the arrangement would be in constant danger of failing because it pays both to cheat on the arrangement if they feel they can manage to do this without being detected.

Nuclear weapons and international security

We can also use this simple two-state case to illustrate some of the ideas already introduced. In explicit terms of international security as defined above, where neither state has nuclear weapons average security rates at 4 units. When both states have nuclear weapons the average security is 3 units. When only one state has them, average security is 2.5 units. So in the case shown in Table 2.2, international security reaches a minimum when only one of the two states has nuclear weapons and further spread would actually improve the situation, as would a retreat to a non-nuclear condition for both. Interestingly, no actual prisoner's dilemma need be involved for the same point to hold. In Table 2.1, where total proliferation produces a higher (average) level of international security than none, perhaps because of a particularly low risk of accidental war, average security still declines as nuclearisation proceeds only to rise again as nuclearisation becomes complete.

In Table 2.3 a slight change has been made to the payoffs to reflect the possibility that there is a relatively high risk of accidental nuclear war. When neither state has nuclear weapons, average security is 4 units, as before. When both states have nuclear weapons the level of international security is now put at 2 units. When only one state has them average security is 2.5 units, as before. But now there is no minimum. As nuclear spread proceeds average security declines from 4, to 2.5, to 2.

None of this really answers the question we set ourselves concerning the point at which a minimum in average security within a complex would be reached as nuclear proliferation proceeded, since the two-state complex is obviously rather artificial.

As a first step towards making the argument more general, we can illustrate what happens to the level of security (as the y-axis) enjoyed by states within a complex of moderate size as the proportion of nuclear states in addition to the state under discussion increases from zero to one. While the actual calculations involved have been reserved for Annex B to this chapter, their gist is easily seen and understood using a series of graphs.

These are best introduced by a modification of the two-by-two matrices employed above. Table 2.4 shows the payoff to one state, Z,

Table 2.4. Multilateral prisoner's dilemma game

	Rest	
	Acquire nuclear weapons (p)	Stay non-nuclear ($1 - p$)
State Z		
Acquire nuclear weapons	A_1	A_0
Stay non-nuclear	0	C_0

in a complex, according both to whether it goes nuclear itself and to whether other states go nuclear, which they do in proportion p, or stay non-nuclear in proportion $(1-p)$.

Each resulting graph (see Figures 2.1 to 2.4) shows three lines. The top line in each case is the trend in the security of a *nuclear* state in the complex as the number of other nuclear states in the complex increases. This trend is assumed for simplicity to be in the form of a straight line, running from a security value of A_0, when it is the only nuclear state in the complex, to A_1, when all states are nuclear. It is obvious from first principles that this trend is downwards. For instance, a state with a nuclear monopoly has extensive coercive and deterrent powers vis-à-vis every other state in the complex and no fear of accidental nuclear attack. The bottom line in each case shows the trend in the security of a *non-nuclear* state, again as the number of other states in the complex going nuclear increases. It is at its maximum (C_0) when no other states are nuclear and reaches a minimum (put at 0 for convenience) when every other remaining state has gone nuclear. Again the trend is downwards and assumed to be linear, for simplicity. Note that the security of a state that has decided to go nuclear is always greater than that of a state that has decided to stay non-nuclear, by the margin separating the top line from the bottom. The third line in the graphs intermediate between the two straight lines is normally curved and this is the line of average security (i.e. international security) in the complex.

We can see readily that when all states are non-nuclear, their average security is C_0; when all states are nuclear, their average security is A_1.

Figure 2.1 illustrates the case when $C_0 = A_1$. This is a special case chosen for illustrative purposes but perhaps corresponding to a Waltzian world with an unusually low risk of accidental nuclear war. And in this

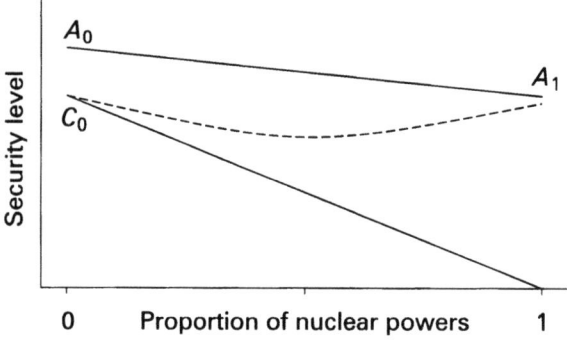

Figure 2.1. International security in a complex as a function of nuclear spread: case 1, C_0 equals A_1.

Nuclear weapons and international security

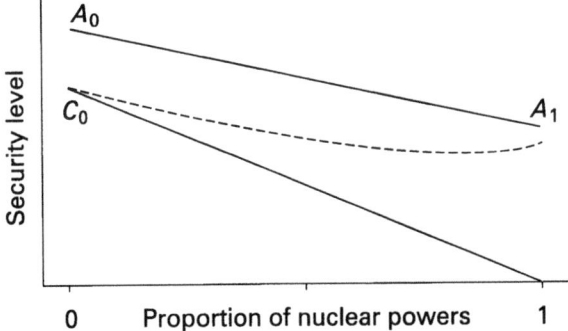

Figure 2.2. International security in a complex as a function of nuclear spread: case 2, C_0 is greater than A_1.

case, as shown in Annex B, the curve of international security always decreases to reach a minimum point when exactly 50 per cent of the complex is nuclear.

When C_0 is greater than A_1 (see Figure 2.2), we have an example of a multilateral prisoner's dilemma. International security now typically reaches a minimum value after more than half the complex has gone nuclear.

Figure 2.3 illustrates the situation described above as 'Waltz-plus', where a completely nuclearised complex enjoys higher security than a completely non-nuclearised one. Even here, however, the process of nuclearisation at first causes international security to dip. But in this case

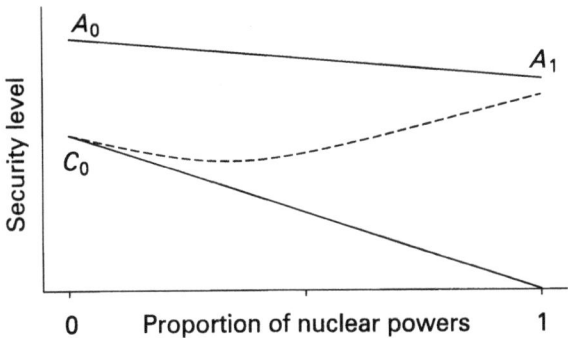

Figure 2.3. International security in a complex as a function of nuclear spread: case 3, C_0 is less than A_1.

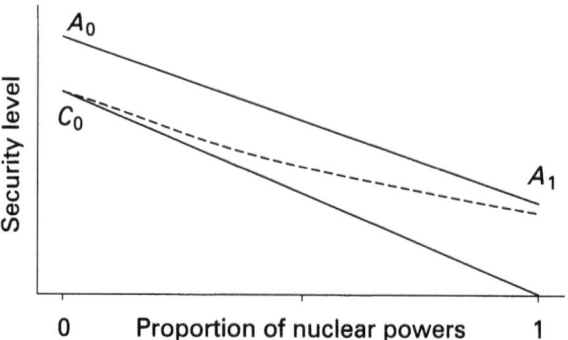

Figure 2.4. International security in a complex as a function of nuclear spread: case 4, C_0 is much greater than A_1.

the minimum point is reached before the point of 50 per cent proliferation.

Finally, the situation shown in Figure 2.4 is typical of what we call above a 'Waltz-minus' situation where – perhaps because of a high risk of accidental nuclear war – average security in a completely nuclearised complex is considerably below that for a non-nuclear complex. In this instance there is no minimum for international security: it simply decreases steadily as nuclear proliferation proceeds through the complex.

As a concluding point concerning Figures 2.1 to 2.4 we can qualitatively at least make an allowance for the possibility that the decline in security for both nuclear and non-nuclear states in the complex as nuclear proliferation proceeds is not linear as shown. In reality it seems much more likely that the decline in average security will initially tend to be steeper than we have so far suggested if we accept the empirical evidence that the first nuclear powers within a complex will be the most capable in terms of the number and range of their nuclear weapons. Historically, the militarily strongest states (in conventional military-industrial terms) in security complexes have always been the first to go nuclear – the USA, the USSR and the UK in that order in the great power complex. The prime candidates for going nuclear in the Latin American complex were Brazil and Argentina. And if the African nuclear-free zone is taken to be a security complex, South Africa took the lead there. As a consequence, the risk of nuclear attack for the non-nuclear members of the complex would rise more steeply at first than with later additions to the nuclear weapons states. This would imply that the minimum point in average security within the complex will be reached somewhat sooner than suggested by the plots shown in the figures.

Summary

The conventional view concerning nuclear proliferation is that it is a bad thing in the sense of the damage it does to international security. On the other hand, the view associated with Kenneth Waltz, primarily, is that nuclear proliferation can be a good thing and helpful to international security. The analysis above firmly suggests that these two positions are not necessarily at odds. In a comparatively small security complex, like the grouping of great powers, after a few such states have gone nuclear it is certainly possible that international security might be improved if further states in the complex were to go nuclear too. In a larger complex, on the other hand, where there is comparatively little nuclear spread already, a small further amount of proliferation will reduce international security and further proliferation, up to a point, will simply worsen the situation even more, but only up to a point. Only in circumstances where the risk of accidental nuclear war is particularly high does it seem likely that proliferation is unreservedly a danger.

In short, laissez-faire will not normally lead to improving international security, as Waltz seems to be suggesting, even if it may do so in certain situations. International security, by contrast, will normally be served by collective cooperative action within a complex to curb nuclear proliferation. If states can so organise themselves to take effective action to curb proliferation they will be jointly rewarded in terms of the deterioration in international security prevented. But such organising is difficult, since each state can always see that whatever other states do it will itself be better off by going nuclear than remaining non-nuclear.

There are two broad approaches to securing the mutually beneficial outcome: the centralised and the decentralised approach. The centralised approach requires a small grouping of the whole to assemble a package of carrots and sticks which they then deploy to restrain the rest of the complex as individual actors from behaving contrary to the interests of the complex as a whole. If this small grouping has the resources to operate in this way, that is not the end of difficulty, since maintaining cooperation within the small grouping may itself, as a form of collective action, prove difficult, since each member of it will have an incentive to seek to minimise its own contribution to the costs of the activity and to 'free ride' on the efforts made by the others. In the case of the NPT, the small grouping was originally, in 1968, made up of some of the great powers (the USA, the USSR, the UK) but with others (France, China) standing outside at first and contributing relatively little to the enterprise. This is presently less of a difficulty, even if complete unanimity within the small grouping is rarely present.

A secondary difficulty with the centralised approach concerns the application of carrots and sticks. For this to be effective, first a system of monitoring the standing of states party to the treaty has to be set up. States verified as abiding by the terms of the treaty qualify for the incentives, while those failing to do so have to face the consequences. The carrots have included a helping hand with peaceful applications of nuclear technology and security guarantees of various kinds. As time has gone on, the helping hand with nuclear technology has become less valued for its own sake as the linkage between commercial nuclear power and economic development has become more tenuous. It has also become less freely offered, as the conversion time between certain nuclear technologies with valid commercial applications (plutonium separation and uranium enrichment) and a military application has become shorter, without a guarantee that there can be an equivalent improvement in the efficiency of the verification apparatus. But one unintended consequence of this has been an increase in black market trading of such technologies, principally involving as suppliers states that are outside the NPT, such as Pakistan.

The decentralised approach works best when the states concerned are relatively few and already enjoying good cooperative relations with each other, as in the ideal nuclear-free zone. No centralisation need be required even to provide timely warning that one of their number was about to go nuclear, since states are usually better informed about their neighbours than they are about states on the other side of the world. 'Recessed deterrence' ('if you go nuclear, so will we') restrains states from defecting from the situation where they have decided to forgo nuclear arms (see the two-state prisoner's dilemma matrices above). States should be reasonably sure that, if they did decide to go nuclear, neighbouring states would not be far behind. Of course, for recessed deterrence to work it is important that commercial nuclear technology is available and that the gap or conversion time between commercial nuclear technology and its military application is not too great.

In practice, the international political arrangements in place to restrict nuclear proliferation are a mixture of the centralised and the decentralised. The forces operating to make the decentralised approach work do not need ideal preconditions. That nuclear proliferation has proceeded much more slowly than was once feared in unpromising areas such as the Indian sub-continent or the Middle East also owes something to recessed deterrence. At the same time, the carrots offered under the centralised approach of the NPT in the form of transfers of commercial nuclear technology have often created the possibility of recessed deterrence where none may have existed before, and the centralised verification system of the NPT eases the setting up of nuclear-free zones in less than ideal circumstances.

Of course there is considerable tension within the arrangements as a whole and recessed deterrence carries the seeds of its own demise, but

Nuclear weapons and international security

arms control arrangements that are worth having always face a risk of failure.

Annex A

Accidental nuclear war

When speaking of the probability of accidental nuclear war it is important to say where. The present analysis concentrates on that security complex of nuclear states united in a mutual recognition of great power status, or close to it. The five states in this category explicitly identified as nuclear powers in the context of the NPT are the USA, Russia, the UK, France and China. India may soon be a candidate for *de facto* membership of the same complex. While the original five possess the capability to launch nuclear strikes against any of the other four, even after absorbing an initial strike designed to prevent retaliation, the same is not yet true of India. India can already launch strikes on China or Pakistan and is working further to extend the range of its launchers.[9]

Calculations of the probability of an accidental war involving the launch of at least one nuclear weapon and it detonating on the territory of another state are based on assigning a probability to this happening for any one nuclear power in any one year (Figure 2.5). This probability must be quite small. The fact that there has been no instance of such a thing in the 50 years since there have been at least two nuclear powers in an adversarial relationship (accidental launches, as we shall see, are more likely in the context of an adversarial relationship), we might think that the value of the probability where two nuclear states are concerned is about 1 per cent. But there is a way of making this estimate somewhat

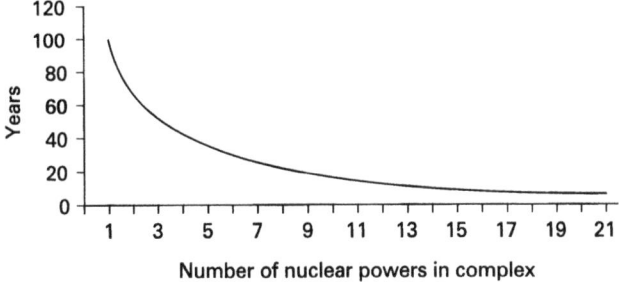

Figure 2.5. Risk of accidental nuclear war as a function of nuclear spread, plotted as the number of years before an accidental nuclear strike may be expected to occur (assuming a 1 per cent per annum risk of accidental launch per state).

more precise and at the same time illuminating the connection between the likelihood of accidental launches and the spread of nuclear weapons already discussed above.

If P is the probability of an accidental launch in a world where there is only one nuclear power, the probability that such an event does not occur in any one year is $(1 - P)$. The probability of no such launch anywhere in a system containing n nuclear powers is $(1 - q)^n$. The new probability, q, is not necessarily the same as P and is now an average figure. And the cumulative probability of no launch after y years is $(1 - q)^{ny}$.

It directly follows that the probability of at least one case of an accidental nuclear strike in y years emanating from within a system of n nuclear states is:

$$(1 - (1 - q)^{ny})$$

The probability of a nuclear state in the system being the target of the accidental attack is about $1/(n - 1)$, to allow for the likelihood that accidental attack will preponderantly be a phenomenon of the relationships between the nuclear powers themselves, but it is of course conceivable that the target of an accidental attack could be anywhere within the range of the launchers at the disposal of the states in question and even directly involve states outside the complex. Indirect involvement of states outside the complex is inevitable to a certain extent, since radioactive fallout will rarely be confined by national boundaries, even if transmission of fallout between, say, the northern and southern hemispheres of the earth will be limited by meteorological considerations (and all nuclear weapons states are in the northern hemisphere).

To make further progress, we can speak in round figures of a global nuclear security complex of five nuclear powers (the USA, the USSR, the UK, France and China) in existence from 1964. In the four decades since then there has been no nuclear detonation on the territory of any state as a result of an accidental launch or any other kind of launch by a nuclear state. This allows us to put a maximum value on q (again, this is an average both over time and over the five states concerned, which will all have different safety procedures). However, what the states in the system will have had in common is a concern for the survival of their nuclear arsenals in the context of the possibility of a deliberate nuclear strike (which would likely be intended to reduce or remove their ability to retaliate with a nuclear strike of their own). This will normally have meant developing a capability for rapidity of response to such an attack – a high degree of readiness for launch in order, first, to stem any losses to their retaliatory forces, which may have begun to happen in a time-scale of minutes and, secondly, on the same time-scale, to strike at that portion of the attacker's forces that may still be awaiting launch or held in close reserve. This same high degree of readiness, because it leaves very little time for checking and double checking the relevant facts of the situation, will translate into a relatively high value for q.

In general, when effective deterrence has a high priority, the danger of accidental launch is also high. When effective deterrence is less energetically sought, the danger of accidental launch diminishes. This should not be interpreted too literally. With the ending of the Cold War, first-tier nuclear states (with the apparent exception of China) have become willing to see the size of their nuclear arsenals fall and their composition to become increasingly weighted towards launchers based on nuclear-powered submarines.[10] And it is true that the deterrent usefulness of these particular weapons does not depend on their being ready for firing as soon as an attack is seen to be under way. But as forces have become smaller – itself reducing the risk of accidental launch, other things being equal – the deterrence efficiency of what remains has become more important, and the general proposition that would equate effectiveness in deterrence with proneness to accident still applies.[11] Commanders of nuclear armed submarines have no way of learning independently whether or not their home country has been attacked. Deterrence is enhanced if the same commanders have authorisation to launch in the event of a total loss of communications, which might after all have been deliberately engineered by the enemy. But two sources of risk of accident are immediately created: insanity on the part of the commander, and an accidental loss of all communication with the home base.

Additionally, accidental war could be the unintended consequence of an innocent change in nuclear operating procedures which is misread by the other side as unmistakable evidence that an attack is being planned and therefore to be headed off by a pre-emptive strike. During the Cold War the USA regularly carried out exercises pushing its whole missile-carrying submarine force out to sea. The Soviets had no such regular programme of exercises and when they did finally order all their submarine forces carrying nuclear missiles out to sea at the same time, this could easily have been read as a first step in a planned nuclear attack on the West instead of the exercise that in fact it was. It is reasonable to think that the multiplicity of communication channels opened up between Washington and Moscow during the Cold War and later, starting with the hot line in 1963, will have largely cancelled out this risk.[12]

To put a reasoned figure on q, we need to make one further calculation, after making a helpful detour. In a situation such as the one described, we can ask about the average time we should need to wait for one of these accidental nuclear strikes to occur. This so-called median time (by definition we are as likely to have to wait longer than the median time as we are to have to wait less long than the median time) is the value of y years satisfying the equation:

$$0.5 = (1 - (1 - q)^{ny})$$

If $n = 5$, and $y = 40$ (from 1964 to 2004 – as an approximation to the median time) are inserted, this produces a value of q equal to 0.0035, or just over a third of 1 per cent, as the average probability per annum of an accidental strike launched by a state in the system. Alternatively, it means that in a system of five nuclear states, in any one year the probability of an accidental nuclear launch anywhere in the system is about 2 per cent. At a minimum only one state in the complex will be affected by this strike, and its destructiveness will be limited accordingly – with a probability of 0.5 per cent. At a maximum or worst case all would be directly affected, putting a reasonable measure of the risk overall for an individual state at about 1 per cent. This may be compared with the figure of 3 per cent for the annual risk of a European state getting involved in war in the period 1850 to 1980,[13] when we are dealing with an equivalent great power, but conventionally armed, complex of about the same size (Austria, Britain, France, Germany and Russia).

Nuclear accident calculations performed elsewhere are broadly in line. Steven Brams and Marc Kilgour take 1 per cent as a probable sort of figure for when there are two states in the system (which leads to essentially the same value of q as obtained above). They also quote Richard Garwin as the source of the idea that a constantly reducing value of q, over time, can compensate for an increase in n.[14] And Paul Bracken, writing earlier,[15] puts the probability of accidental nuclear war occurring in a period of 10 years from the mid-1980s at about 10 per cent. This corresponds to a value of q of 0.002.

We are now in a position to answer questions about accidental launches and nuclear proliferation. If the present five acknowledged members of this nuclear security complex were to increase towards 10, after the sort of expansion projected in the preceding treatment in the main text of the effects of nuclear proliferation on international security within the complex in question, the overall risk of 1 per cent would increase to around 2 per cent. This figure is small enough not seriously to challenge the suggestion also made above that further proliferation within the security complex of great or emerging great powers could actually add to international security within the complex. The risk of accidental nuclear war is not higher than the estimated risk of conventional war involving the complex concerned. And the possibility is left open that a completely nuclearised complex of this size might be only a little less secure (to allow for the more devastating consequences that might eventuate from an accidental nuclear launch) than one that was conventionally armed.

It is true that this assumes that additional members of the security complex will be almost as well equipped as the original members with the technical and political instruments available to contain the risk of accidental war within bounds. Established nuclear powers will increase the safety of their own launch procedures over time (this is not necessarily only a technical matter, as we shall see below). A relatively greater reliance on submarines means a relatively smaller reliance on land-based missiles, such as intercontinental ballistic missiles (ICBMs) and this tends to reduce the average value of q. According to Bruce Blair and Henry Kendall, the minimum accidental launch, for organisational reasons, of US ICBMs is or was likely to be 10 missiles.[16] But the pursuit of effective deterrence with changes in the size and composition of its own and enemy arsenals will tend, as we have seen in the submarine case, to put a limit on how far this might go. Emerging new nuclear powers, whose command-and-control procedures will always be relatively primitive at the start, and for which deterrence will be no less important, will have the effect of further putting a brake on improvements in the average figure in the system as a whole.

On the other hand, there is no reason to think that new nuclear powers will always start off with safety procedures as crude as those adopted by the established nuclear powers when they first acquired nuclear status. Indeed, there is some evidence to show the truth of this. India and Pakistan had a hot line between New Delhi and Islamabad installed before the parallel series of nuclear tests in 1998, even if it was not used during the period of testing.[17] New nuclear powers are at least going to be aware of the existence of, for example, early-warning radar and will often be able to obtain working systems – perhaps not always of the latest design – from overseas suppliers. Technology moves on. On the other hand, safety controls against accidental launch can be so intimately associated with the effectiveness of the nuclear weapons in war or in the deterrence of war that states will be reluctant to advertise their safety arrangements too widely. As an example, an effective safety measure against accidental launch would be a remote means of reliably destroying or disabling in flight any missiles which a state may have launched accidentally. Sharing such a command-and-control safety procedure or even admitting its existence would be an invitation to potential enemies to 'hack into' it. Even when we are speaking of nuclear powers whose relationships are particularly friendly, to the extent of sharing the same launcher technology in the case of the UK and the USA with the Trident D5 submarine-launched ballistic missile, US safety systems have not been wholly incorporated by the British. The British warhead for use in the Trident D5 missile does not incorporate the same safeguards against accidental detonation (not, of course, the same thing as accidental launch, but akin to it) as those used by the USA. Safety procedures are as much a matter of safety 'culture' as technology and, as perhaps illustrated by the case of the failure to use the Indo-Pakistan hot line in 1998, not necessarily very transferable across national boundaries.[18] Geography also comes into it. A state with nuclear weapons deployed on its own densely populated territory will be more safety conscious than one whose territory is thinly populated and where weapons can be based in some remote, more or less empty quarter of the country.

However, the possible emergence of India as a potential 'great power' with a matching nuclear capability is a reminder that calculations of the probability of accidental nuclear war need to be done with care. India's nuclear neighbour, Pakistan, is India's inferior in almost every index of military capability. Its strategic depth is slight and Pakistan has consequently adopted a strategic doctrine of 'first use' of its nuclear weapons. This encourages India to think along pre-emptive lines and promotes accordingly a high degree of strategic readiness on both sides because of the unusual lack of 'strategic warning' at the conventional level inherent in the geography of their relationship. The speed of conversion on the sub-continent from recessed deterrence to explicit deterrence since 1998 will itself create risks of misperception of intentions. For instance, the two countries' busy missile test programmes will force a rapid learning curve on both sides of what is to be ignored as a test flight and what may be an attack disguised as such. Perhaps this is an example – the transition from recessed deterrence to explicit deterrence – of the sort of speedy proliferation that Waltz acknowledged as capable of undermining his general thesis. There were only some days between the formal emergence of India and Pakistan as nuclear powers, as both tested their first acknowledged nuclear weapons within the month of May 1998. India's very first nuclear test explosion, in 1972, was described by New Delhi as a peaceful nuclear explosion and inaugurated the period of recessed deterrence on the sub-continent. The original five nuclear powers had gone nuclear with an average gap between them of almost five years.

It is in the nature of the security complex of the nuclear great powers that an accidental nuclear attack in any part of it may have repercussions for all of it. An accidental attack involving a non-member state will normally have inherently more containable consequences. But India's potential membership of the great power complex carries with it the embarrassment of India's relationship with Pakistan, which threatens to import into the great power complex an exogenous danger of accidental nuclear war. So self-interest as well as the dictates of humanity demand that the five main nuclear powers do what they can to reduce the risks of an accidental nuclear war in the sub-continent while at the same time denying either sub-continental state visible rewards for having breached non-proliferation norms.

Should further nuclear proliferation proceed outside the great power security complex, extreme pessimism about the increased probability of accidental nuclear launches may not be warranted. The various new nuclear powers that have emerged for the most part towards the end of the median time referred to above – Israel, still, India and Pakistan for two decades before 1998, and temporarily South Africa – have not or have not immediately entered into nuclear deterrent relationships in the classical sense of maintaining nuclear retaliatory forces in a high degree of readiness for use. Israel, and India and Pakistan for a time, have practised a recessed form of deterrence, in which a more or less openly advertised potential to develop a nuclear weapons capability quickly is seen as more useful than the capability itself. This potential may deter those neighbouring hostile states that are militarily weaker in terms of conventional forces from setting out to acquire nuclear weapons of their own, while having a number of additional benefits in the form of cheapness and in retaining an ambiguity about the state's position with regard to the NPT and related arrangements to curb the spread of nuclear weapons.

Israel's nuclear capability remains recessed. The South African white minority governments built six or seven nuclear weapons of an enriched uranium 'Little Boy' design (see Chapter 1) but dismantled them before the abandonment of apartheid and the coming of black majority governments to power. These weapons were not developed in order to deter but in an attempt to acquire leverage over Western powers to keep them willing to view apartheid South Africa as an indispensable part of the Western alliance during the Cold War. The weapons were not held ready for use at short notice and will therefore have made a negligible contribution to the risk of accidental launch. But the same is not true of their proneness to theft.

Nuclear theft

Another type of undeterrable event is the acquisition for use, political or otherwise, of nuclear weapons, probably in very small numbers, by non-state groups. This event contributes to the risk of nuclear war unintended by the nuclear states since it puts nuclear weapons in the hands of persons who may be largely beyond the reach of deterrent threats. The likelihood of such groups obtaining nuclear weapons, whether through theft or purchase, or, indeed, transfer from state sources, will increase as the number of possible state sources increases. Any assessment of the scale of this risk would need to take into account the following factors. First, not all terrorist groups will be interested in nuclear weapons or any other weapon of mass destruction while they retain the sort of political objectives that depend on influencing sectors of public opinion within target states favourably. Secondly, the average degree of security with which nuclear weapons are guarded is less significant than the degree of security applying at the weakest point in the system (i.e. where security is most lax). Thirdly, weapons in a deployed state – that is, fitted to or held very close to delivery systems – will enjoy some degree of security from theft or diversion from their intended purpose as a result of the steps taken to secure them from enemy attack. At one extreme, British strategic nuclear warheads at sea fixed to the nose cones of Trident D5 missiles are hardly vulnerable to theft at all, whereas any Indian or Pakistani warheads still held in a semi-recessed state separate from launch vehicles will be more exposed. Fourthly, nuclear warheads stood down from active stockpiles at the end of the Cold War and now in storage pending possible recycling as nuclear reactor fuel are at greater risk of theft than when they were under direct military control. Lastly, theft or unauthorised diversion is least likely when all reserve warheads, and fissile materials involved in the production of warheads, are held in as few well policed distinct sites as possible, but deterrence considerations of vulnerability to attack are likely to argue against concentrating even reserve means of retaliation in a few sites. This is an argument for placing at least some fissile materials from stood-down warheads under international control.

If, for simplicity, it is assumed that nuclear warheads married to or held in very close proximity to their launchers are essentially safe from theft because the same precautions taken in the name of deterrence suffice to deter theft, this leaves the question of exposure to theft confined to warheads held in storage in one form or another. And there are essentially two forms of warhead storage. One form is for warheads surplus to requirements and hence candidates for dismantling and even recycling in the form of nuclear reactor fuel. The other is for warheads that are really in a reserve role or in the process of being manufactured, and in either case earmarked for active nuclear deterrent duties at some point in the future.

Warheads only temporarily surplus to the requirements of deterrence and in reserve, or in the process of actually being manufactured, can hardly be kept in one place because of the risk that this site becomes known and hence an enemy target. Logic would suggest that either they be dispersed, and hence placed relatively in a state of vulnerability to theft, or in the case of reserve stocks be kept physically part of the deterrent force to which they belong – perhaps even in the holds of the submarines from which they would be launched in the event of nuclear war.

Those warheads actually in surplus will still need storage pending disposal of their cores or 'pits' – the term used to describe the key component of all modern nuclear weapons, being the specially shaped kernel of plutonium or highly enriched uranium, the compression of which by a surrounding, shaped, conventional explosive initiates the explosive nuclear chain reaction (see Chapter 1). But it will normally be possible simply to deactivate the pits before storage by crushing them out of shape – an irreversible procedure unless the core is removed, melted down and reshaped, all of which represents a formidable task for an advanced industrial state, especially when the pits are made of plutonium. Here the logic of storage in the one well guarded site does apply, guarding still being necessary because the reconstituting of old cores based on highly enriched uranium into the form of a nuclear bomb of some kind is much less difficult (although this is balanced by the much higher recyclability of highly enriched uranium in the form of nuclear reactor fuel compared with plutonium). Guarding also helps prevent theft of plutonium, not in order to make a nuclear bomb, which will normally be far too difficult for a non-state group, but for use as a radioactive and poisonous contaminant in the context of an ordinary chemical explosion or fire (in a so-called 'dirty bomb'). Only one place would then need to be guarded against theft and this could be unstintingly done, since the resources thieves could bring to bear in pursuit of their efforts would themselves be limited in nature. The place itself should be, as far as possible, bomb proof with regard to conventional explosives or incendiaries and this suggests converted old mine shafts and the like.

Establishing international best practice with regard to disabling, storage and recycling of warhead pits may be relatively easy, since it is something within the reach of the IAEA. The extension of Agency safeguards to monitoring a cut-off or halt in production of plutonium or enriched uranium for weapons purposes currently under consideration at Geneva could logically embrace too the question of safe storage of weapon cores that have been permanently stood down.

Lastly, theft is a matter both of supply and demand. Obstacles erected by the nuclear states against theft will not be as effective against a large number of potential thieves as against a small number. If the risk of nuclear theft is seen as something likely to rise and fall (other things being equal) with rises and falls in terrorist activity, worldwide trends here are difficult to establish. Official US State Department figures going back to 1996 that itemise significant acts of terrorism both within states and internationally (i.e. involving the nationals or territory of more than one state) show a near doubling of incidents worldwide between 1996 and 1999, from 84 to 166. But from 1999 to 2002 the frequency of incidents dropped again, to a plateau of about 130 per annum. In spite of reservations about the comprehensiveness of such a listing, and the failure of simple counting to distinguish the political significance of one incident from another, there does not seem to be much basis for attributing a downward trend to such incidents.

So, to complete the analogy with accidental nuclear war, nuclear theft will become more probable the more nuclear states there are and while the motives for the theft cannot be predicted with certainty, the consequences of the theft would be more serious within the nuclear system than without, thus reducing international security within it.

Outlook

Finally, it has been emphasised that the risk of accidental nuclear war would seem to increase as deterrence policies are more avidly pursued, with even the reverse being true: anti-missile defences offer some hope of containing the consequences of an accidental launch, but at the same time weaken the deterrent balance in adverse relationships. Equally, the risk of nuclear theft would seem to rise as forces are taken off alert or temporarily stood down or kept in a semi-recessed state, with nuclear warheads stored separately from the delivery vehicles, because an efficient deterrent relationship is not being pursued with maximum drive, deliberately or otherwise. A striking illustration comes from the 2002 Strategic Offensive Reductions Treaty aimed at maintaining and building confidence between the USA and Russia. In 2002, the USA kept 6,480 warheads embedded in their deterrent forces (including 1,660 in bombers) and about 2,000 in reserve. By 2012, it plans to have about 2,200 embedded and 5,500 in reserve.[19] The risk of accidental launch will have been reduced. The proportion of warheads to be carried on submarines, as we have seen, is to increase but with the actual total in submarines to be cut to half the 2002 figure. But the number of warheads planned to be held in reserve is almost double the 2002 figure. This may or may not be an invitation to theft in the case of the United States, but the precedent is not encouraging. While there are some special features of the US case, such as a very restricted market for nuclear fuel and therefore little anxiety there to turn nuclear swords into ploughshares, Russia will presumably take advantage of the precedent to argue for similar large reserve stocks and other first-tier nuclear states may feel induced to follow suit and maintain large reserve stocks lest their credentials as modern nuclear states be questioned.

Annex B

Calculating international security

Figure 2.6 illustrates the security levels of nuclear and non-nuclear states within a security complex of size N, according to whether they adopt a nuclear or non-nuclear arms policy. The security trends in each case are assumed to be linear with increasing nuclearisation of the complex, with the number of nuclear powers (n) running from 0 to N. The proportion of nuclear powers in the complex is therefore n/N. For illustrative purposes the model shown corresponds to the N-player prisoner's dilemma, with $A_1 < C_0$. The security level of the non-nuclear state is shown as also reducing with nuclear spread, not necessarily at the same rate, and declines from C_0 to 0.

Nuclear weapons and international security

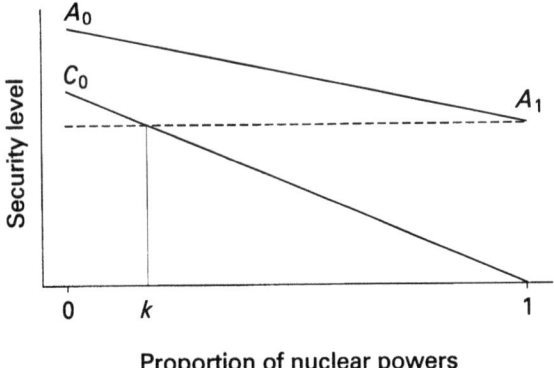

Figure 2.6. International security in a complex as a function of nuclear spread: *k*-value.

In algebraic terms, the security level of a state that has gone nuclear changes with an increase in n, the total number of nuclear powers in the complex, as:

$$-(n-1)(A_0 - A_1)/(N-1) + A_0$$

and for a non-nuclear state:

$$-nC_0/(N-1) + C_0$$

The first thing to notice from the equation for the decline in the security of a non-nuclear state as proliferation (n) increases is that in the circumstance where C_0 is greater than A_1 – in other words when we are dealing with an example of a multilateral prisoner's dilemma – the graph shows that a certain amount of proliferation is tolerable before its security level drops below A_1. This critical value of n is usually called the *k*-value (following Schelling[20]). If the extent of proliferation in a complex is below the *k*-value, no non-nuclear state in the complex is as badly off as it would be in a complex where it and every other state had gone nuclear.

$$k = (N-1)(C_0 - A_1)/C_0$$

Thus when $C_0 = 4$ and $A_1 = 3$ and $N = 10$, k (or the nearest integer below k) = 2.

The force of this simple observation – that it can pay, in security terms, for non-nuclear states to have proliferation restricted even if they cannot have it banned – is amplified when we come to discuss the slightly more demanding and contentious concept of average security in the complex as a function of n.

Since there are n nuclear states and $(N - n)$ non-nuclear states, the total security (S) of the system is:

$$n^2(A_1 - A_0 + C_0)/(N - 1) + n(A_0 - C_0 + [A_0 - A_1 - C_0N]/[N - 1]) + C_0N$$

This is a rather unwieldy expression and its presentation and elucidation are much simplified if we are dealing with a complex where N is comparatively large, such as the 20-strong (or so) security complex typical of a large nuclear-free zone arrangement. The average security of the complex, S/N, in terms of p, the proportion of the complex gone nuclear, is now, approximately:

$$p^2(A_1 - A_0 + C_0) - p(2C_0 - A_0) + C_0$$

The average payoff of a state in the security complex in the presence of nuclear weapons is then expressible as a quadratic equation in p. Inserting $p = 1$, and $p = 0$, respectively, into the equation produces the already known average for when all states are nuclear (A_1) and the average for when none are (C_0).

We can explore the equation further. Average security in the complex reaches a minimum value when p equals:

$$(2C_0 - A_0)/2(A_1 + C_0 - A_0)$$

provided $(A_1 + C_0 - A_0)$ is positive.

We can settle these questions by asking what happens to average security in the complex at either extremity of possibility. When all states in the complex are non-nuclear and one state decides to acquire nuclear weapons, it seems clear that average security in the complex will decrease. Every state but one will be at risk from the new phenomenon of nuclear attack. The one state that is now nuclear will itself be more secure, to the degree to which it has guaranteed itself against large-scale conventional attack. So when p is 0 or nearly 0, dS/dp will be negative. This means that $(2C_0 - A_0)$ is positive. Similarly, if all states but one are already nuclear, the final state to go nuclear will add to its own security while making very little adverse impact on the security of the others (leaving to one side for the present the situation where the risk of accidental nuclear war is high, since in a large complex the final state to go nuclear will not normally add appreciably to this risk). In fact, by going nuclear, the state in question removes itself from the risk of predation from the nuclear powers in the system and removes itself as a possible cause of dispute between them. This means that at $p = 1$ or nearly so, dS/dp will be positive, which means in turn that $(2A_1 - A_0)$ will be positive. We repeat that this argument might not be true of a relatively small complex in which the risk of accidental nuclear war is significant.

If $(2C_0 - A_0)$ is positive and $(2A_1 - A_0)$ is positive (or zero), their sum $(2A_1 + 2C_0 - 2A_0)$ must also be positive, from which $A_1 + C_0 - A_0$ is also positive. This is the requirement for a minimum value in average security to exist as nuclear weapons spread within the complex.

In the main text, particular use was made of the situation where the average security enjoyed in a completely non-nuclear complex was the same as that enjoyed when the complex was all nuclear (i.e. when $A_1 = C_0$). We now return to the main political question, of how far nuclear proliferation must proceed for the minimum average security level to be reached. The answer from the present model is that the minimum level of international security in a nuclearising complex is reached at 50 per cent nuclear, when the average security enjoyed in a completely non-nuclear setting is the same as the average enjoyed when the whole complex has gone nuclear.

When the non-nuclearised level of security is higher than the fully nuclearised value, we have a prisoner's dilemma and the point of minimum international security is reached after the mid-point of nuclear spread. When the reverse applies and we have a Waltz-plus or 'deadlock' situation, the minimum of average security is reached before the 50 per cent point. Therefore, in a complex in which even a substantial amount of nuclear proliferation had already occurred (a half or more states nuclear), in a situation where the states in the complex are in a multilateral prisoner's dilemma, efforts to prevent further proliferation will normally be worthwhile since further proliferation will lead to a deterioration in international security before things begin to improve again.

Finally, to return to the more general case where the security complex is of size N, for any complex, the total security (S) of the system when there are n nuclear states is:

$$n^2(A_1 - A_0 + C_0)/(N - 1) + n(A_0 - C_0 + [A_0 - A_1 - C_0N]/[N - 1]) + C_0N$$

It is easy to show that even in this general case, when average security in a completely non-nuclear complex is the same as average security in a completely nuclearised complex, the minimum in average security in the complex occurs at the 50 per cent nuclear point, as before. This is illustrated for a 10-state complex in Table 2.5 (using the data in Table 2.2).

Table 2.5. Security values for a 10-state complex

n (number of nuclear states)	0	1	2	3	4	5	6	7	8	9	10
Nuclear security		5.2	5.0	4.8	4.6	4.3	4.1	3.9	3.7	3.4	3.2	3.0
Non-nuclear security	4.0	3.6	3.1	2.7	2.2	1.8	1.3	0.9	0.4	0.0	
Mean	4.0	3.7	3.4	3.2	3.1	2.9	2.9	2.8	2.8	2.9	3.0

Values derived from Table 2.2.

Notes

1 Cuba signed the NPT in 2003.
2 Scott D. Sagan and Kenneth N. Waltz, *The Spread of Nuclear Weapons: A Debate Renewed* (New York, W.W. Norton and Co., 2003). The locus classicus of Waltz's thinking is *The Spread of Nuclear Weapons: More May Be Better*, Adelphi Paper No. 171 (London, International Institute for Strategic Studies, 1981). The 1981 date of publication is not entirely an accident. The failure of detente and of bilateral arms control to make progress saw doubts about arms control of a different kind – the NPT and associated arrangements – emerge within US thinking generally. The internal Baruch consensus (see Chapter 5 of the present work) that the spread of nuclear weapons would be harmful to international security and to US security had begun to be questioned, if only transiently, inside the US bureaucracy itself – see Joseph Nye, 'Maintaining a nonproliferation regime', in George H. Quester (ed.), *Nuclear Proliferation: Breaking the Chain* (Madison, WI, University of Wisconsin Press, 1981), p. 32. A brutal summary of these second thoughts about nuclear proliferation would say that international security might be better served by a laissez-faire attitude towards the spread of nuclear weapons than by intervening to stop or reverse it, and that US security might be less hurt by such a development than the security of its chief rival at that time, the Soviet Union.
3 Barry Buzan, Ole Waever and Jaap de Wilde, *Security: A New Framework for Analysis* (Boulder, CO, Lynne Rienner, 1998), p. 198.
4 Bruce Bueno de Mesquita and William H. Riker, 'An assessment of the merits of selective nuclear proliferation', *Journal of Conflict Resolution*, Vol. 26, No. 2, 1982, pp. 283–306.
5 Jon Elster, *Nuts and Bolts for the Social Sciences* (Cambridge, Cambridge University Press, 1989), p. 130.
6 Sagan and Waltz, *The Spread of Nuclear Weapons*, p. 35. Of course, Waltz adds that a nuclear-free world cannot be reinvented.
7 Algeria, Argentina, Australia, Austria, Bangladesh, Belgium, Brazil, Bulgaria, Canada, Chile, China, Colombia, Egypt, Finland, France, Germany, Hungary, India, Indonesia, Iran, Israel, Italy, Japan, Mexico, Netherlands, North Korea, Norway, Pakistan, Peru, Poland, Romania, Russia, Slovakia, South Africa, South Korea, Spain, Sweden, Switzerland, Turkey, Ukraine, United Kingdom, United States of America, Vietnam, Zaire.
8 William Poundstone, *Prisoner's Dilemma* (New York, Anchor Books Doubleday, 1993), p. 218, uses 'deadlock'.
9 Indian government scientists have openly associated that country's space programme with an emerging capability to manufacture intercontinental ballistic missiles (ICBMs). India has already tested a mobile missile with a range of 3,000 km and a one-tonne payload (Agni-3). Its missiles in service in 2004 were below 2,000 km in range. *Military Balance 2003–2004* (London, Oxford University Press for the International Institute for Strategic Studies, 2004), p. 131.
10 The USA and Russia, under the 2002 Strategic Offensive Reductions Treaty, plan to have by 2012 about 75 per cent (USA) and 60 per cent (Russia) of

their missile warheads at sea in submarines, compared with 60 per cent (USA) and 15 per cent (Russia) in 2002. The UK and France already have all their missile forces at sea. See Center for Defense Information at www.cdi.org/issues/nukef&f/database/startab.html (last accessed 8 April 2005).
11 A large nuclear force will almost certainly survive any attack in sufficient strength to threaten unacceptable damage in retaliation, because it is the absolute number of warheads surviving to be used in retaliation that effective deterrence depends upon, not the proportion of the original force. To this extent deterrence and big battalions go together. Smaller forces normally need more careful nursing to ensure their survival in sufficient strength to deter.
12 Long-standing political arrangements are: the 1963 'Hot Line' Agreement concerning the establishment of a direct Moscow–Washington communications link; the 1971 'Accidents Measures' Agreement to reduce the risk of nuclear war; the 1971 and 1984 'Hot Line' Modernisation and Expansion Agreements incorporating technically improved communications links; the 1987 Nuclear Risk Reduction Centres supplementing or backing up the Hot Line arrangements; and the 1988 Ballistic Missile Launch Notification Agreement to give mutual warning of imminent flight tests of ICBMs or submarine-launched ballistic missiles. The end of the Cold War saw in 1991 unilateral measures to put nuclear forces in both countries onto a de-alerted status and in 1994 an agreement not to aim long-range missiles at each other.
13 M. Small and J.D. Singer, *Resort to Arms: International and Civil Wars, 1816–1980* (Beverley Hills, CA, Sage, 1982).
14 Steven J. Brams and D. Marc Kilgour, *Game Theory and National Security* (New York, Basil Blackwell, 1988), pp. 167–72.
15 Paul Bracken, 'Accidental nuclear war', in Graham Allison, Albert Carnesale and Joseph S. Nye, Jr (eds), *Hawks, Doves and Owls: An Agenda for Avoiding Nuclear War* (New York, Norton, 1985), p. 50.
16 Bruce G. Blair and Henry W. Kendall, 'Accidental nuclear war', *Scientific American*, Vol. 263, No. 6, 1990, pp. 19–24.
17 Hilary Synnott, *The Causes and Consequences of South Asia's Nuclear Tests*, Adelphi Paper No. 332 (New York, Oxford University Press, for the International Institute for Strategic Studies, 1999).
18 The UK's nuclear reactors built in the 1940s and 1950s to produce plutonium for the British nuclear weapons programme on the grounds of safety did not seek to copy the US design of such reactors, which employed water as a coolant. This early aversion to water on safety grounds arguably dictated the subsequent shape of the entire British power-generating nuclear reactor programme (for the worse).
19 See Center for Defense Information at www.cdi.org/issues/nukef&f/database/startab.html (last accessed 8 April 2005).
20 Thomas C. Schelling, *Micromotives and Macrobehavior* (New York, W.W. Norton and Co., 1978), pp. 217–22.

3

The International Atomic Energy Agency and safeguards

'Safeguards' is the slightly euphemistic term officially used to describe the measures taken by the Agency (or Vienna Agency) independently to verify the declarations made by states to the IAEA concerning their nuclear material (principally enriched uranium and plutonium) and that the uses it is put to have peaceful ends. The chief method employed for verification is the despatch periodically of inspectors to the territory of the states concerned and with their agreement. The inspectors have the job of identifying and reporting any significant mismatch between what they find 'on the ground' and what written reports and records shared between the state and the Agency had led the latter to believe was the case. The safeguards system pre-dates the 1970 NPT in that they were first applied piecemeal at the request of nuclear exporting and importing states to instances of transfers of nuclear technology or materials, including some done under the 1953 Atoms for Peace initiative (see Appendix B), which had led to the creation of the Agency in 1957. But the chief significance of the safeguards system is its connection with the NPT, under which all non-nuclear states party to the treaty are required to accept Agency safeguards on all their nuclear activities, with relatively minor exceptions. (For a history and the text of the NPT see Chapter 5 and Appendix C, respectively.)

The present chapter looks at safeguards in the context of the treaty. The NPT is interpreted as an example of multilateral arms control, where the collective good of improved international security resulting from a world relatively free of nuclear weapons is maintained in difficult circumstances, where individual states will often see national security benefits in acquiring nuclear weapons. For the treaty to be effective, therefore,

The IAEA and safeguards

centrally organised carrots and sticks are needed. States need, among other things, to be rewarded for adhering to the treaty and to lose these rewards and possibly suffer penalties when they default on their treaty undertakings. Safeguards are a way of giving timely warning that a state is defaulting and therefore part of a deterrent apparatus encouraging states to stay in line.

The deterrent apparatus is in two parts: the first involves the timely detection of an unauthorised diversion of nuclear material from peaceful to military purposes (i.e. detecting diversion rather than preventing it in the first place); the second part is the adverse consequences for the state in question of having been caught (economic sanctions, at a minimum). The present chapter is not directly concerned with the latter and is much more concerned with detection and how this might most reliably be ensured in the triple context of: the limited resources for inspection; the requirement minimally to disrupt the national economic life of states, the majority of which, most of the time, in reality are uninterested in cheating on the undertakings they have given; and the necessity of respecting the principle of sovereign equality between states.

Everything is like something else

Since 'everything is like something else', the present analysis begins by comparing the business of inspection to the procedures used by customs officers to prevent the smuggling of contraband into a country. Essentially what happens is a process of sampling. To stop and search thoroughly every passenger in an airport terminal, say, on every occasion would be regarded as intolerable by the passengers and excessively costly by the customs officers' employers.

Accordingly, deterring smuggling relies on making the sampling process comprehensive enough and the punishment for being caught large enough to make the rational passenger reluctant to run the risk. Of course, some passengers will respond to this state of affairs by accepting that there is a risk of their being searched but looking to avoid the consequences by being especially careful to conceal the contraband in, for example, false-bottomed suitcases. Customs officers are aware of this danger and so react in turn by having particularly intensive search procedures at their disposal. By making every search more intensive to counteract the determined smuggler, a given sampling frequency will see an increase in the number of violators caught. So to maintain the perceived risk of being caught at the original value (we return to this important question below), the customs officers will have the option of sticking to very intensive searches of luggage in every instance but reducing the size of the sample stopped for searching, or keeping the sample at the original size and searching with less than full intensity (or some mixture of the two). Normally there will be very little difference in costs to the customs or average inconvenience to the passengers between the two options. However, 'human' searching is not the only approach. Technology sometimes allows very invasive searching at minimal cost to the customs or to passenger convenience – X-ray machines, sniffer dogs and so forth. Even this is not quite the whole story, since different passengers will be carrying different quantities of luggage and those with a great deal can expected to be 'sampled' more frequently than the norm, even if the customs officers will now have the option of searching the whole of a passenger's luggage or just some sample of the whole.

Lastly, customs officers naturally tend to scrutinise passengers in batches as they arrive from different places of embarkation. Knowledge on the part of the customs that different places of embarkation have different histories when it comes to the law abidingness or otherwise of passengers allows them to tailor the intensity of their searches accordingly. The more prior reason customs have to think that a particular batch of passengers is unlikely to contain smugglers, the more justified they would be in switching their detection resources to another batch.

If the reader were mentally to substitute for customs officers the inspectorate attached to the IAEA and for passengers states party to the NPT, with commercial nuclear installations equivalent to their luggage, the analogy will be found to be reasonably complete. It will also serve as a useful road map through the following game theory model of the inspection process.[1]

The inspection game

Tables 3.1 and 3.2 aim to model the choices faced by a state party to the NPT when deciding whether to violate the treaty by deceiving the inspection teams that pay periodic visits to its nuclear installations to verify that they are being used solely for peaceful purposes. The approach chosen has the merit of plausibility and simplicity, but does not claim to be watertight.[2]

In Table 3.2, n is the intrusiveness costs (per act of inspection) to the state concerned of being inspected, even when completely innocent of any violation. All inspection implies some more or less painful derogation of sovereignty, and there may be specific costs arising from any probability that visits by inspectors may compromise commercial secrets related to the exploitation of nuclear power, and perhaps military secrets too of a non-nuclear kind or even totally defensive in nature. c represents the cost of the specific consequences of being discovered to be in breach. Both are shown as negative (costs are negative and benefits positive). And

The IAEA and safeguards

Table 3.1. Inspection game with qualitative payoffs for the state

State	Inspectorate	
	Inspect	Ignore
Violate	Worst	Best
Comply	Next to worst	Next to best

Table 3.2. Inspection game with quantitative payoffs for the state

State	Inspectorate	
	Inspect	Ignore
Violate	$-c - n$	$+b$
Comply	$-n$	0

b represents the benefit to the violator of getting away with the violation. For some states b will be so small as to be negligible; for others it may be greater.

If we suppose that there is a probability, p, that the inspectorate will make an inspection, then the state in question will always be indifferent between violating and complying when the 'expected cost' of each is the same, or when:

$$-(c + n) \times p + b \times (1 - p) = -n \times p$$

which simplifies to:

$$p = b/(b + c)$$

In other words, whenever p is at all greater than this amount, a potential, rational violator will always choose to comply. When p is much larger than this amount, even a risk-seeking potential violator will choose to comply.

So we have formally established that an effective inspection system can be run on a sampling basis, which has implications as we shall see both for the targets of the inspection arrangements and for the inspecting authorities. A feel for what this may mean can be better obtained by inserting some numerical values, somewhat arbitrary though they may be. If the cost attributable to the consequences of being caught violating the arrangement far outweighed the benefit of escaping detection on any one occasion (not unreasonably we might think, on average, although this might not be true when the violator was very close to the point of having diverted enough material to manufacture a strategically significant quantity of weapons at short notice) – so that c is 100 and b is 10, say, in some arbitrary units – then a would-be violator would choose not to violate provided p was greater than:

$$b/(b + c) = 10/110 = 0.091$$

So in this case, an inspectorate that randomly sampled the targets of inspection (nuclear facilities) in a ratio of 1 in 10 ($p = 0.1$) would be doing enough to deter a rational state from carrying out a violation (for the time being it is assumed that inspection will always uncover a violation).

Implementation

In practical terms sampling would of course have to be weighted according to the type and size of plant involved. Within any given state we might expect to find a variety of nuclear installations, differing both in scale and in function. The ratio b/c will vary from one installation to another because the value of b (for any one state) will vary in part simply with the size of the installation. So, to take nuclear reactors, the rate of plutonium production in reactors of comparable design depends on the power rating of the reactor. A plant of 1,000 MW(e) will produce roughly twice as much plutonium in a year as a 500 MW(e) design (see Chapter 1). Accordingly, inspections for the bigger reactor will normally need to be set at twice the frequency set for the smaller.

The same argument from size will also apply both to plant for the separation of plutonium from spent reactor fuel and to plant for the production of enriched uranium, a normal component of fresh reactor fuel. But the baseline for frequency of inspection will now be set higher than in the case of reactors themselves, since pure plutonium and uranium, especially when highly enriched but even when only moderately enriched in some cases, can be used with little further work as the raw material of bombs – the 'conversion time' is much shorter than would be the case with a batch of spent reactor fuel (for states with the requisite know-how a matter of days in the former case as opposed to months in the latter).

Various important qualifications may sometimes need to be made to the above. For instance, some reactors – usually of a research type or those used for marine propulsion – are actually fuelled with highly enriched uranium and it is their fuel (both in place and in storage) rather than their plutonium production that is then mainly of interest to the inspectors. Among power reactors, most designs are shut down at regular intervals for refuelling, which is a very suitable arrangement as far as Agency inspection is concerned. But certain heavy-water designs, such as the CANDU model, are refuelled on a continuous basis, and this places greater demands on inspectors than would be indicated simply by the power rating of those reactors. And different designs of plant for the enrichment of uranium are differently suited to a quick switch in their output from large quantities of slightly enriched uranium (say 3–4 per cent), such as is suitable for fuel for most reactors, to smaller quantities of highly enriched uranium (80 per cent or more uranium-235) suitable for bombs. But as a guide to the principles involved in a sampling scheme, it is an adequate first step.

In principle, it could be implemented in one of two ways. A state with, say, 60 power reactors each of 500 MW(e) might expect to see 10 of these inspected (at random) every year. Or, alternatively, 30 of them could be visited, and with the inspectors focusing on matching plant records to the actual flows of fuel, as is the norm, but concentrating, again randomly, on the fuel ready to be loaded, or that currently in the reactor, or that discharged in spent form. A plutonium separation plant just large enough to process all the spent fuel from the same 500 MW(e) reactor would obviously merit more attention from the inspectors than the reactor. And one large enough to process all spent fuel from the entire inventory of reactors will receive even more. It is not unusual in practice for large plutonium separation plants to see inspectors permanently in attendance.

While the safeguards procedures adopted by the IAEA feature both the sorts of weighting guidelines outlined above and, as we shall see, a form of sampling too, the Agency has never traditionally sanctioned physical random sampling. A weighting procedure was actually adopted under 'classical safeguards' (the shorthand term to describe the approach of the Agency before the emergence of the Additional Protocol modification to its safeguards arrangements with contracting states in 1997). Where nuclear reactors are concerned, this weighting procedure takes as its benchmark the quantity of plutonium or highly enriched uranium either loaded as fuel in (as in the comparatively unusual latter case) or being produced by a reactor in one year. Where this figure is not more than 5 kg, inspection frequency is not greater than once a year. Where greater quantities are involved, under the stricter and older INFCIRC/66 scheme applicable to states having facilities inspected by the Agency but not party to the NPT, inspection frequency (or rather maximum frequencies) rises pro rata, with continuous right of access by inspectors where amounts exceed 60 kg. A typical, if now obsolescent, Magnox-type reactor of 500 MW(e) will produce about 300 kg of plutonium annually. Under the deliberately laxer INFCIRC/153 inspection regulations, which are the classical basis for safeguards agreements between the Agency and non-nuclear weapons states party to the treaty, the starting point is the same, but the frequency of inspection rises not pro rata arithmetically but at a slower rate, more nearly pro rata logarithmically, it would seem.

So, a state with one reactor of 5 MW(e) might see two inspector-days of inspection a year; 50 MW(e) four inspector-days; and 500 MW(e) eight inspector-days.[3]

In the matter of physical sampling, in reality under classical safeguards a state with 60 reactors of 500 MW(e) (a very extensive nuclear energy programme indeed) will find them all inspected equally. The Agency has considered proposals in the past that, in the interests of saving scarce resources, random sampling should be introduced, but, according to David Fischer,[4] early official Agency estimates of the savings that would ensue amounted to only 4 per cent of its safeguards costs. This figure, if correct, is far too low to compensate for the political difficulties foreseeable when a state with, say, only one reactor has it inspected annually while a state with a large programme has some of its reactors not inspected at all in any particular year. But the question of random physical sampling is now back on the Agency agenda in the context of the new Additional Protocol safeguards arrangements, which emerged in the aftermath of the discovery of Iraq's secret nuclear programme after the 1991 Gulf War (see Chapter 1).

Quasi-sampling

So far so good, but it has been assumed up to now in our formal analysis of inspection that an act of inspection will actually uncover any wrongdoing, whereas in practice there must be a finite probability that the inspection when carried out will be so superficial as to give a determined violator a good chance of remaining undetected. One way of making the model more realistic in this respect, then, is to introduce a new probability, d, that a violator when inspected will not avoid detection, with a corresponding probability $(1 - d)$ that it will, and redo the calculations (see Table 3.3).

The required probability of carrying out an inspection sufficient to deter a would-be violator is now slightly different at:

$$b/d(b + c)$$

Table 3.3. Inspection game with imperfect technique

State	Inspectorate	
	Inspect	Ignore
Violate	$b(1 - d) - dc - n$	$+b$
Comply	$-n$	0

This is the same as before only when $d = 1$, that is, when inspection visits are so thorough that the chance of a violation escaping the attention of an inspector is zero. Otherwise, as d decreases in value, the probability of an inspection being conducted must rise for the deterrent value of the inspections to remain the same. So, to continue with the numerical example already given above, if there was a 50 per cent chance that an inspection would fail to uncover a violation that had in fact occurred, then the original sampling rate of 1 in 10 which was sufficient to deter violations would have to increase to 2 in 10.

But the true practical significance of this illustration comes from working the whole thing backwards. If the inspected state could be persuaded to see d increased in value from our arbitrary 50 per cent by consenting to more thorough or intrusive inspections (see below), it would then be possible to reduce the probability (frequency) of inspections and still obtain the desired level of deterrence. This would normally add somewhat to the efficiency of Agency procedures, from the Agency point of view, since actual acts of inspection (the inspector-days involved) are what costs the Agency money. Increasing the scope of what inspectors are allowed to do on each visit in the name of greater thoroughness would add comparatively little to Agency costs, especially when the inspectors have the assistance of remote-sensing techniques of various kinds and the greater deterrent value of surprise inspections of enrichment or reprocessing plants, as opposed to the classical notified ones, could be achieved at no extra cost to the Agency at all.

If we interpret the Agency's original refusal, under classical safeguards, to countenance random physical inspection as the equivalent of requiring p always to equal unity ($p = 1$), we can rewrite this equation as saying that a potential violator will be deterred when:

$$d > b/(b + c)$$

Thus the term d becomes the equivalent of p in the simpler original model. The Agency does not need to strive to make $d = 1$, even if this were possible: all that is required is for d to be large enough to deter violators. This means that if real random sampling is ruled out, as was the case under classical safeguards, its effect can be reproduced by pseudo-random sampling, where this corresponds to inspections of less than a maximally searching kind. We should note at this point that the larger the term d is, the more thorough and hence more intrusive is the act of inspection normally, and consequently the greater the cost ($-n$) impinging on the inspected state. But equally, instrumentation can allow more searching inspections to be made without a proportionate increase in the intrusiveness cost – hence the encouragement of instrumentation under the minimally intrusive so-called Karlsruhe implementation of INFCIRC/153 (see below). The plots in Figure 3.1 cover both this

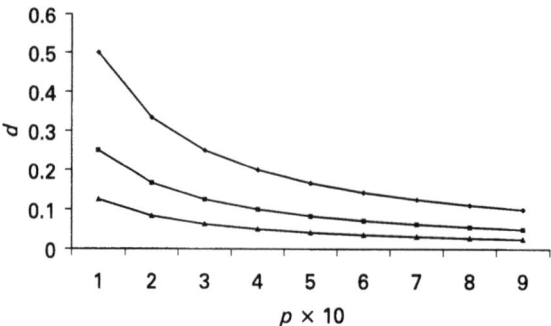

Figure 3.1. Intrusiveness of inspections (d) versus frequency (p).

situation and the post-classical situation, where the possibility of less than 100 per cent physical sampling can be taken seriously in practice.

In Figure 3.1, moving from bottom to top and left to right takes one to situations of increasingly intensive and intrusive inspection overall. Each curve (defined by equating the product of p and d to a range of constant terms) corresponds to a situation of iso-intrusiveness. So, on any given curve, which will correspond to a given level of assurance for the inspectorate that nothing is amiss, any increases in d can be compensated for by reductions in p. A practical example comes from the move by the Agency since the mid-1990s away from classical safeguards with the emergence of the Additional Protocol and integrated safeguards. For instance, the new thinking sees greater scope for unannounced inspections. Plainly these would on average give a better assurance that nothing was amiss at a small uranium enrichment plant, for example, than would a pre-announced visit. This corresponds in our terms to a higher value for d, which would in turn permit a smaller p, which in turn would normally translate into cost savings for the Agency.

Similarly, different states subject to Agency inspection could be dealt with by placing them on higher or lower curves according to how transparently satisfactory (from the Agency perspective) their commercial nuclear programmes already were. There is an obvious analogy with airport customs authorities clamping down on, say, drug smuggling paying closer attention to passengers who have just flown in from some countries than to those from others. If Agency inspectors were able to feel confident that no plutonium separation plant existed within a particular state, perhaps because they had no reason to doubt the comprehensiveness of the accounts presented by that state of the extent and nature of its nuclear industry, then they would be justified in moving to a lower curve of inspection, for example by cutting back on how often or how intensively (or both) they inspected nuclear reactors within that state. Without

The IAEA and safeguards

a separation plant, spent reactor fuel is largely harmless. Reducing the frequency of inspections would again have the most immediate beneficial effect on the Agency's own financial resources.

However, it is important to note that any discrimination between different states should be free of political taint and by putting the onus on the states themselves to provide the Agency with the information upon which it decides how to apportion its inspection resources, this danger may be avoided. This new departure is styled by the Agency 'integrated safeguards'.[5]

In a steady-state or 'neutral funding' situation, which seems to have been the permanent condition of the Agency's inspection budget up until 2003 at least, when an increase in funding in real terms appears to have been agreed,[6] where the greater intensity of inspection inherent in the Additional Protocol and the opportunities provided by integrated safeguards permit a reduction in frequency of inspection, the resources freed can be redirected – possibly towards states that have not signed up to the Additional Protocol or states whose nuclear programmes for whatever reason are not particularly transparent. However, there remains some reason to believe (see the above remarks by Fischer) that the savings in Agency resources obtainable by reducing inspection frequency will not necessarily be very great and that a steady-state or a zero-sum outcome wherein the new departures from classical safeguards effectively paid for themselves may be overly optimistic.[7]

But to return to classical safeguards, with p at a fixed high value, which seems to have been original Agency policy, increasing the sampling rate means travelling vertically from the lowest curve in the direction of the upper curves by increasing the value of d, the pseudo-sampling rate, by making inspections more searching.

The curves in Figure 3.1 also give a good indication, at a given level of instrumentation, of the adverse impact of being inspected on the inspected state itself, since intrusiveness is proportional both to the depth of inspection and to the frequency of the procedure. Moving up and to the right on the graph will normally mean greater intrusiveness unless instrumentation can be used to economise on frequency of inspection (e.g. environmental swipes can be used to derive the operating history of reactors, separation plants or enrichment plants between inspections). Instrumentation can also reduce the intrusive impact of greater depth of inspection, as when atmospheric sampling, perhaps coupled with satellite reconnaissance, can substitute for 'door to door' searches countrywide to establish the presence (or absence) of a plutonium separation facility. In general, instrumentation can allow the Agency to maintain a given degree of confidence concerning the adherence of states to the treaty while at the same time either easing the burden on its inspectors or more usually the burden of intrusiveness on target states, or both.

A simple and long-standing example of where intrusiveness for states may be substantially reduced but at considerable cost to the inspectorate comes from camera surveillance of a critical area, say in a uranium enrichment plant, where physical re-plumbing directly in front of the camera would be necessary to alter the enrichment of the product. The camera obviously sees nothing else, least of all the details of the design of the centrifuges concerned. But the Agency will still need to devote many inspector-hours (if not necessarily on site) to checking the camera footage.

A practical illustration of some of this theorising can be seen at least qualitatively in the development of the Additional Protocol and integrated safeguards. (For more on that Protocol, see the section 'Inspections tighten', below.) The Additional Protocol implies more intrusive inspections, although there is also a promise, in certain circumstances, usually where the Agency already has sufficient information before it on the state in question and its nuclear activities, that actual inspections may be less frequent (it is not yet clear to the present author how far this literally means the emergence of random physical inspection). At a given level of instrumentation, intrusiveness will remain the same, except where the nature of additional information held by the Agency may justify a move to a lower curve on Figure 3.1, for example where it has reliable historical details of all exports and imports of nuclear facilities or their component parts. In some such cases this could avoid altogether the requirement for a countrywide search to establish the correctness of a particular state's inventory of nuclear facilities.

The gains states obtain from participating in a properly functioning arrangement to curb the proliferation of nuclear weapons are not infinite and can only be net of costs involved, which include the costs or the inconvenience of being inspected. In practice, once the principle of inspection has been accepted, the inconvenience cost is normally measured by the extent to which information of commercial or strategic value to the inspected state but of no relevance to the arrangement in question might be compromised by the presence within the country of foreign nationals with a certain licence to roam and ask questions and inquire closely into the function of certain industrial facilities. We have seen how, under classical safeguards, limiting the extent to which this may be necessary by incorporating remote-sensing devices of various kinds into the inspection system will obviously be advantageous. These could include sealed cameras (as above) and other recording devices at key points inside acknowledged plants. Under the Additional Protocol, inspectors can be equipped with devices for analysing air, water and soil to check whether undisclosed activities may be taking place within the state, without requiring them to enter every conceivable industrial building to check that it is not a nuclear installation in disguise.

The IAEA and safeguards

Finally, the model is admittedly rather mechanical. The Agency will want to maintain a degree of mystique concerning its capabilities and will want states on the whole to have an exaggerated view of its surveillance skills. Achieving this when the Agency is, so to say, an employee of the states it keeps under surveillance is easier than it may sound. This is partly because the Agency tends towards secretiveness in general, combined with confidential frankness towards a specific state of concern. But just as important is the normally large gap between the policing facilities available to the Agency, especially when it has the full backing of the major powers, and the deception resources available on average to the states being policed. When subject to inspection a violating state runs a risk of being detected, partly because it cannot always predict how much inspectors may be capable of learning from a given type of access. An example is the environmental swipe technique, which seems to have surprised both the North Koreans and the Iranians, at different times. The Iraqis by contrast took smaller risks and got away with it.

How much is enough?

The above discussion simplifies the problem, quite deliberately, in a number of ways. The numerical attempt to show that a sampling rate of 10 per cent or 20 per cent might be sufficient (or, before the Additional Protocol, a pseudo-sampling rate, where the percentage refers to the degree of thoroughness of the inspection) depended on an estimate of the relative size (or ratio) of the cost to a state of being discovered to be in breach and the benefit to the state of getting away with a programme of violation undetected. In practice this ratio is bound to vary from state to state. A state perceiving its strategic environment to be extremely threatening might attach a great deal of benefit to getting away with a violation of the treaty (e.g. North Korea), or a state particularly vulnerable to external sanctions (e.g. Libya) might have strong reason to fear the international consequences of its being found to be cheating on the arrangement.

In principle, if these payoffs could be known, the inspecting body under classical safeguards could set its (pseudo-)sampling rate at the value needed to ensure compliance from the state for which the temptation to defect was highest (in other words, the state inside the arrangement for which the ratio of the benefit from cheating to the cost of being found out was greatest). But even if this were possible – and it is not clear that it would be, since the cost of being found out ought to include the moral effect (difficult to assess) of being deemed a pariah state as a result – getting the treaty off the ground in the first place is likely to have priority.

The inspecting body in reality would more likely to adopt a 'try it and see' procedure, by pitching the sampling rate of inspection at a rather low level at first. This would have the advantage of helping to establish the immediate attractiveness of subscribing to the arrangement for states that might otherwise have been discouraged by fears of the commercially adverse consequences of very intrusive inspection and/or by the size of the financial contributions they would be called upon to make to the central costs of running a very active inspectorate. Were experience then to show that this sampling rate was too low, as evidence emerged that states were not being deterred from cheating on the arrangement or for some other reason, the logical thing to do would be to increase it until a satisfactory balance had been reached.

Broadly speaking, this is an accurate account of the approach adopted by the IAEA's inspection arm under classical safeguards, from Atoms for Peace in 1953 to the mid-1990s.

Karlsruhe

The political theme for how inspections of non-nuclear signatory states are to be carried out is actually set down in the preamble to the NPT itself (see Appendix C). This so-called Karlsruhe doctrine meant that inspections under classical safeguards were confined to checking the flows of nuclear material (e.g. nuclear reactor fuel),[8] not the installations served by or servicing the fuel flows. Moreover, only certain key flow measurement points in any given nuclear facility are open to the inspectors. Other parts of the plant are normally off limits. The use of instrumentation rather than human observers is also strongly encouraged.

Basically, the procedure starts with states joining the treaty informing the Agency inspectorate of the amounts of all nuclear material in the country and its whereabouts (e.g. which nuclear plant it is associated with).[9] Under classical safeguards this statement is taken on trust, at least initially. Such information is required on: natural and enriched uranium, in the form of reactor fuel and of feed, and the product of uranium enrichment plants; and plutonium and spent reactor fuel as product and feed, respectively, of plutonium separation plants. Agency inspectors then visit the sites indicated to verify that stocks are as reported. Thereafter, the inspectorate is informed of subsequent flows of these stocks, and periodically verifies this information.

In the case of a large nuclear reactor, the plant management will periodically, for its own accounting purposes, find it necessary to make a physical check of the drawdown of stocks of fresh fuel rods (normally containing slightly – 3 or 4 per cent at most – enriched uranium) and the discharge of spent fuel (invariably containing plutonium[10]), by making

The IAEA and safeguards

an actual headcount of the rods (a so-called physical inventory). The spent fuel in question will be on site, since it is too radioactive at first to be easily moved far from the reactor, and is stored under water but in such a way as to be visible to human inspection. There will be a three-way known if approximate correspondence between the amount of electricity produced (for which records also exist), the amount of fuel used and the amount of spent fuel in storage. It will be usual for Agency inspectors (perhaps two) to be present at such inventory checks to ensure that the plant records account entirely (within an acceptable margin of error) for changes in stocks since the last check. If there is a serious discrepancy, the original safeguards agreement theoretically allows for inspectors, with the consent of the state in question, to make a search off site.

Precise balancing of the books will be a rare event. There will sometimes be more spent fuel rods than seems compatible with fresh fuel used up and electricity produced; sometimes the situation will be reversed, with fewer spent fuel rods than expected. The discrepancy is usually called 'material unaccounted for' (MUF), and only when the MUF repeatedly seems to indicate more plutonium being produced than is apparent from a count of spent fuel rods will further action be indicated.

Instrumentation comes into play in the form, for example, of tamper-proof seals placed on fuel stores that are expected to remain untouched between inspections, and film footage, which can be checked to ensure that the reactor has not undergone any undisclosed refuelling cycles between visits. For an average-sized reactor, under classical safeguards the inspectorate probably makes two or three visits a year, with each visit lasting perhaps two days. A small research reactor may have only one inspection a year, but a large plutonium separation plant processing spent fuel from a large number of reactors may require the permanent presence of a small team of inspectors.

All this corresponds to the setting of the impact of inspections at a low level, which would have encouraged states to sign up to the NPT. The contrast for potential signatories was made quite evident. States outside the treaty, importing nuclear equipment from overseas suppliers themselves party to the treaty or in sympathy with its objectives, under classical safeguards were treated more severely under trilateral arrangements between the IAEA, the supplier and the importer. The whole (imported) plant in question was then subject to the attention of the inspectorate, even while it was still under construction; uranium even in its virtually raw material form (yellowcake) within the country came under the inspectors' gaze; and the frequency of inspection was higher than would have been the case had the state in question been party to the treaty. The difference between the two inspection regimes is formally laid out in the two relevant Agency documents. The more intrusive and earlier regime applicable to states not party to the treaty importing nuclear materials or equipment from parties is described in the Agency document INFCIRC/66/Rev.2 (before the NPT, this came into force on a voluntary basis between the importer, the exporter and the IAEA). The less intrusive regime is covered by INFCIRC/153, which is the basis for the negotiation of classical safeguards agreements between the Agency and non-nuclear states joining the NPT.[11]

Inspections tighten

The chief milestones in the learning process whereby the IAEA has reacted to events by a progressive tightening of the intensity of its inspection procedures under classical safeguards since the NPT came into force in 1970 have been five: the original Indian nuclear test explosion of 1974; the Israeli bombing of the Iraqi Osirak reactor in 1981; the discovery after the 1990–91 Gulf War of the extent of the Iraqi secret bomb programmes; the confession soon afterwards of the South African government to a secret bomb programme; and the misgivings publicly raised at the 1990 treaty review conference concerning North Korea's unpublicised building programme involving reactors and plutonium separation plant and the subsequent (rudely terminated) inspections of these plants. (On the review conferences, see Chapter 5.) In fact, only Iraq and North Korea among these were technically in breach (or probable breach in the case of North Korea) of their treaty undertakings. The other states mentioned were not then parties to the treaty, and even North Korea was a rather semi-detached party since it did not actually conclude an inspection arrangement with the Agency until 1992, seven years after it had signed the NPT (states acceding to the treaty are normally meant to conclude an inspection agreement within 18 months and even if North Korea was not the only laggard state in this regard at the time, it was the only one of significance).

The response of the inspectorate to these stimuli was at first confined to a reinforcement of controls on the export of nuclear equipment and materials to states that were not themselves party to the treaty (neither India nor South Africa was). The original Zangger Committee's trigger list, which was drawn up to define the obligations of supplier states as to which exports of nuclear equipment, technology and materials under Article 3 of the treaty were to be connected with safeguards, was tightened and extended by the Nuclear Suppliers' Group (NSG – see Chapter 5) in 1977. This trend reached a high plateau at the start of the 1990s with the attachment of 'full-scope' safeguards to exports (IAEA inspection of not just the exported item but all nuclear material and

The IAEA and safeguards

facilities in the importing state). This was a victory for US policy, which had been pressing for such controls since applying them domestically to its own exports in 1978 under the Nuclear Nonproliferation Act. The same Act aimed to place specific curbs on any state (party to the NPT or not) engaging in the separation of plutonium from spent nuclear fuel (reprocessing) where the fuel or part of it may have originated directly or indirectly from original US supplies. The penalty for ignoring this restriction was to have re-supply of fuel – normally in the form of low enriched uranium – from the USA held up.

The part of the Act relating to fuel reprocessing is an exception to the rule that those states that have not signed the NPT are the main ostensible target of tighter export controls. But the hostile reception accorded to these moves by the supplier states at the 1980 review conference confirms that importing states inside the treaty felt the new pressure too. The cartel-like nature of the NSG suggests a tighter supply situation for all importers of nuclear plant and materials, not solely non-parties to the treaty.

It is not quite true to say that more specific increments to the intrusiveness of inspection faced by treaty signatories had to await the dramatic disclosures concerning Iraq's secret bomb programme and its covert schemes for enriching uranium (see Chapter 1). Experience began to teach the lesson that the Karlsruhe doctrine could not be sustained, with its emphasis on inspection based on instrumentation and the restriction of human access to specific places within a nuclear complex, all in the name of non-intrusiveness. As large-scale plant with plutonium or enriched uranium as product gradually came under the wing of the inspectorate, especially with the voluntary placing of such plant under inspection by the nuclear weapons powers themselves, the inadequacy of the Karlsruhe doctrine became self-evident. The diversion of a quantity of pure plutonium or highly enriched uranium has a much shorter route to travel to the bomb stage than would the diversion of an equivalent amount of either in the form of irradiated fuel rods. And large plant meant that a material balance good to within a fraction of 1 per cent, say, of flow of material could still mean the diversion of a militarily significant amount of material hidden behind MUF. More reliance on human inspectors rather than less, and freedom for inspectors to wander on site, within reason, became standard operating procedure.[12] Instrumentation continued to be developed, in parallel, with Euratom making a substantial contribution here to the common good, and new kinds of instrumentation now allow human inspectors during visits to a plant to deduce something of its operation in the interval since their last visit by using so-called 'environmental swipe sampling'.[13] The intrusiveness of inspections (even those without any specific external trigger) under the treaty began to creep upwards as an unintended consequence of the decision of the nuclear weapons states to invite inspectors into their commercial nuclear plants, as a result of their desire to promote a sense of equal burden sharing among signatory states.

Doubts that the Karlsruhe guidelines were intrusive enough were emerging elsewhere, again in connection with Iraq. Israel officially excused its warlike bombing of Iraq's Osirak reactor in 1981 on three very interesting grounds, as if hoping that some sweet reason would put a rosier hue on its freebooting practical approach to regional security. One was that the IAEA had not been informed about the 'hot cell' facility (laboratory-sized plant for extracting plutonium or enriched uranium from irradiated reactor fuel rods, normally on too small a scale to be of military significance) sold to Iraq by Italy, which could have been used (as a 'one off') to extract unused highly enriched uranium from the Osirak fuel rods. Technically this was correct, in that the rules somewhat vaguely required Iraq and Italy as parties to the treaty to bring the IAEA and its inspectorate into the picture only 'as early as possible' before fissionable materials started to flow into and out of the hot cell.[14] Another Israeli justification for its actions was that it could not fully trust Iraq to be inspected properly when the Iraqi government had arranged for all Agency inspectors of Iraqi activities to be of East European origin. This would have had more force during the Cold War than subsequently, of course, but again it draws attention to a real weakness in the Agency's procedures. In the last phase of the Cold War three-quarters of treaty parties were applying blanket tests to the nationalities of inspectors deemed 'acceptable'. It seems that a simple reason such as the nationality of the inspector mooted being 'wrong' is enough for the hosting state to ask for a replacement to be suggested (although other tests, such as linguistic competence, are also common). In principle, the tendency towards allowing states to select inspectors could, over time, increase suspicions that an element of self-inspection (or at least reciprocity) was creeping in and consequently diminish confidence in the whole system. The third point advanced by the Israelis in mitigation is not wholly within the scope of the present chapter but needs to be mentioned here for completeness. This was a much broader complaint about the NPT – that even member states in good standing could take advantage of their membership, over time, to build up their nuclear know-how to the point when they could, at short notice, break out of the treaty and build themselves nuclear weapons. As we have seen in Chapter 2, in the discussion of recessed deterrence, if states could not do this, the treaty would be much weaker than it in fact is.

But the key incident in forcing a rethink concerning the intrusiveness of Agency inspections was the discovery after the Gulf War in 1991 that Iraq had made substantial progress towards building a uranium enrichment plant, using as a starting point obsolete technology (the calutron), only partly based on imported components, without the IAEA

The IAEA and safeguards 93

nor, it seems, anyone else knowing of its existence.[15] As if to reinforce the lesson, when North Korea finally admitted IAEA inspectors in June 1992 to its Yongbyon complex, where the chief operational declared facility was a 5 MW(e) reactor, the inspectors were unable to reconcile the North Korean claim that only 60 g of plutonium had been extracted from spent fuel from the reactor with the evidence in their possession that larger amounts of fuel had been reprocessed than that necessary to yield such a small amount of plutonium.[16] The inspectors were also shown a plutonium reprocessing plant described as under construction but close to completion.

The foundation for the inspectors' scepticism was in part environmental swipe technology and in part the existence of two undeclared nuclear waste dumps at Yongbyon, which the Agency inspectors in February 1993 said should be the subject of 'special inspections'. The reaction was hostile: North Korea refused the inspection and simultaneously announced its withdrawal from the NPT.

A plausible reconstruction of events (any actual account will have to await declassification, given the secrecy which attends details of all inspections within the context of the NPT) would have inspectors finding evidence at the reactor site of fairly extensive refuelling since the reactor first started operating in 1987 or 1988. Had it been refuelled in such a way as to maximise the amount of plutonium produced, over four years it could have produced about 20 kg of plutonium or enough for three nuclear bombs (and several tonnes of radioactive waste).[17] The reactor seems to have been largely constructed without external assistance and to be of a commercially obsolete design, based on the British Magnox type of plant. Nonetheless, this model of reactor is an efficient plutonium producer and is fuelled using natural uranium, of which North Korea has its own domestic supplies. Admittedly, its existence could be innocently explained by the presence in North Korea of two partly built (one actually on the Yongbyon site), larger reactors of Russian design similar to the Magnox model, for which the 5 MW(e) plant could have been a pilot. But the existence of nuclear waste facilities at Yongbyon (how the inspectors heard of it is unclear) will have suggested the production of waste in industrial quantities, something compatible only with a fairly energetic programme of reprocessing spent reactor fuel. That there were two waste disposal sites is itself mildly odd in that two would seem virtually to double the risks of radioactive leakage into the environment. That one was under military control and the other civilian seems a possible explanation.

The 'special inspection' asked for by the IAEA was technically permitted under the NPT and classical safeguards but was at odds with the non-intrusive Karlsruhe doctrine and had been allowed to become virtually a dead letter. But INFCIRC/153, to which all non-nuclear states party to the treaty are required to sign up, allows the Agency to conduct special inspections anywhere in the state concerned if, in effect, inspectors cannot reconcile the evidence of their own eyes with the state's formal reporting concerning the flows of nuclear materials within the facilities inspected. The demand for a special inspection is then likely to have caught the North Koreans off balance, and there was nothing in their reaction to it to suggest otherwise.

The lesson drawn by the Agency and the principal states behind the NPT from the cases of Iraq and North Korea was not simply to make inspection more intrusive: it was also that it should be made more selective, in fact if not in law. The Iraqi case in particular helped prepare the ordinary states party to the treaty for the idea that inspections might have to be tightened up, while at the same time prepared the leading states without nuclear weapons (which feel the full brunt of any adverse effect of inspections on their commercial competitiveness) for the possibility that the old Karlsruhe formula of non-intrusive interpretation of the Agency's rules had outlived its usefulness. It is also true to say that the fact that almost every state in the world was now party to the NPT meant that it had become much less important to leave an encouraging gap in the intrusiveness of inspections faced by states party to it compared with the others.

Formally, the revisions to inspection procedures were presented by the Agency in two halves: one was a restatement and reminder of what states party to the treaty had already agreed to (as outlined in INFCIRC/153), but which had been partly clouded over by the Karlsruhe interpretation; the other was a new list of additional rights and freedoms to be accorded to inspection teams, laid out in a so-called Additional Protocol in 1997, made public as INFCIRC/540 (corrected). For the Additional Protocol to come into effect, states party to the treaty and bound by IFCIRC/153 individually need to sign up to it as a codicil, so to say, to their original safeguards agreement with the Agency. Other states, including the nuclear weapons states with voluntary safeguards arrangements with the IAEA, and the diminishing number of states outside the treaty but subject to INFCIRC/66 safeguards, were also invited to negotiate new arrangements in the spirit of the Additional Protocol. This will be particularly necessary to maintain the perception of parity of burden sharing between nuclear and non-nuclear states party to the treaty that are active in the exploitation of nuclear energy for commercial purposes, since one clause of the Additional Protocol brings within the reach of inspectors for the first time a state's research and development activities where these are related to the nuclear fuel cycle. It should be added that the depressed state of demand for commercial nuclear energy in domestic and overseas markets has itself created a favourable climate for new initiatives by the Agency on matters of inspection.

The IAEA and safeguards

The sources of the restatement and the Additional Protocol are three: old worries about the inadequacy of the Karlsruhe doctrine and its possibly undue emphasis on material flows; experience with the generally tighter INFCIRC/66 regime; and the lessons of Iraq and North Korea. Under the restatement, against the Karlsruhe interpretation with its emphasis on nuclear material (normally fissile material) and material flows, states are reminded of an obligation to give the Agency information on any new plant before construction or modification, and access to such a plant over the whole of its life. Waiting until fuel begins to flow is no longer good enough. This is meant to meet the Iraqi 'hot cell' case, and a theoretical worry that a decommissioned plant, which logically sees no material flows, under Karlsruhe falls outside the reach of inspectors, but remains in existence and capable of being secretly reactivated. Interestingly, the restatement reminds states that routine inspections are not the only kind they have agreed to and that unannounced inspections will be used to a greater extent in future. This is meant to meet a recurrence of the North Korean case in some other corner of the world. The Agency will now receive information on what might happen between scheduled inspections (it has, until recently, had no information on material flows between inspections) and will be able to supplement scheduled inspections with the use of environmental swipes, to detect evidence of movements of material since the previous inspection.

The Additional Protocol looks to apply to all states party to the treaty what states outside the NPT but importing from suppliers party to it had already come to expect: inspectors' specific right of access to nuclear material, from uranium mines to waste disposal sites, with the Agency receiving notification (in the manner of the NSG) of exports of sensitive nuclear-related technologies (e.g. uranium enrichment plant). In the same vein but in a new departure, importing states are required to give the Agency access to customs-style records of imports. Reminiscent of the old Israeli complaint about Iraq, the Additional Protocol now gives states no choice over the nationality of inspectors and no freedom to withhold visas once issued (in any 12-month period). More clearly linked to the Iraqi and North Korean cases, states are now required to give the Agency information on and access to *all* buildings in any given nuclear complex (this would cover Iraq's undeclared separation of a small amount of plutonium and presumably North Korea's nuclear waste dumps). Plainly arising from Iraq's wholly undeclared uranium enrichment plant, inspectors are given a right to roam off site in order to allow them to take environmental samples. Even so, such sampling of air and water courses will be much more likely to pick up the existence of undeclared plant associated with plutonium – reactors or separation plant – than undeclared uranium enrichment plant.

Conclusion and the way ahead

The success or failure of the Agency's system of inspection and other safeguards, and with it the success of the NPT, can no longer be measured very well by the number of states being brought within its orbit, unless one takes the number of states signed up to the Additional Protocol as a criterion. There are now only three states outside the treaty itself but many more not yet inside the Additional Protocol. Nor can it be measured very well by the number of states it succeeds in keeping away from nuclear temptation. Any arms control arrangement worth having will be constantly in risk of failure. The only test of its success lies in its responsiveness, or rather the responsiveness of its chief sponsors, to experience, and in its ability to adapt its procedures to emerging realities.

A rough and ready critique of the effectiveness of Agency safeguards, that is, safeguards within the NPT and those outside (INFCIRC/66 and nuclear free-zone arrangements) as a whole, would seem to show they have been least effective in deterring weapons programmes where these have been relatively modest, deriving fissile materials either from small nuclear reactors or, more usually, from small-scale but secret installations for enriching uranium. As a matter of record, no large reactor – that is to say a reactor producing electricity on an industrial scale – has ever been implicated in covert military programmes. There are a variety of possible reasons for this. Most such reactors are found in states with no strategic interest in diverting nuclear material to military uses from ostensibly peaceful ones. Also, the dovetailing of such reactors into a country's integrated electricity grid means a very large conspiracy may be needed for a successful clandestine diversion and this may simply be impracticable. It is also true to say that there may be simple technical reasons too. Modern power-producing reactors are nearly all of the light-water type, and are not only relatively inefficient plutonium producers for their size (megawatt for megawatt, Magnox-type reactors, which are now obsolete as power producers, generate twice the plutonium of the more modern, light-water types), but also, when run for maximum efficiency, produce plutonium-239 contaminated with heavier isotopes of the element, which is less suitable for weapons purposes.

Therefore the traditional concentration of safeguards effort on big reactors, while itself playing a part no doubt in creating the situation wherein they have never been used for illegitimate purposes, has probably been excessive. The general direction of the Additional Protocol and integrated safeguards would seem to recognise this lesson. More intrusiveness will help Agency inspectors discover the existence of undeclared small reactors and reconstruction of their operating history becomes relatively simple with environmental swipe technology. And the lighter hand with respect to large reactors implied in the integrated safeguards approach will free up Agency resources for deployment elsewhere.

But the technical trends which have assisted in making the plutonium route to a bomb programme relatively unattractive are at the same time tending to make the uranium route more attractive. The two phenomena are linked at the technical level. The original commercial justification for the recycling of reactor fuel and hence plutonium separation has grown weaker with time. Fuel supplies are no longer perceived to be especially scarce, and extensive new (to the West) uranium deposits in Kazakhstan have come to light since the collapse of the Soviet Union. Light-water reactors, moreover, are efficient users of fuel on a once-through basis. But these reactors nonetheless need fuel in the form of slightly enriched uranium, and this will naturally excite the interest of the proprietors of such reactors in methods of enrichment, since they must be concerned about the security of fuel supplies. Legitimate reasons for this interest include the threat to such supplies that was inherent in the US Nonproliferation Act in the context of that country's original attempt in the 1970s to outlaw entirely the separation of plutonium, except by the acknowledged nuclear weapons states. Keeping this interest within the boundaries laid down by the NPT will not necessarily be easy.

A first important step will be a more general recognition than has as yet apparently been forthcoming that, since its inception, the Agency's safeguards system has tended to concentrate too much on plutonium and too little on uranium. The original reason for this probably lay in the perception, reasonable enough at the time, that the plutonium route to nuclear weapons presented fewer technical obstacles. Of the first five nuclear weapon powers, only China shunned plutonium in favour of uranium, while three – the USSR, the UK and France – focused on plutonium for their first bomb, and the USA pursued plutonium and uranium routes about equally. Of the five most recent (including temporary) members or putative members of the nuclear club (South Africa, North Korea, Pakistan, Iraq and Libya),[18] only North Korea showed interest in the plutonium route and even that seems to have been in harness with a subsidiary interest in uranium.

The swing from plutonium has occurred partly for the negative reason that, in the beginning, the perceived technical difficulties associated with enriching uranium were matched by an equal political determination on the part of the few states (the first five nuclear powers) with the technical know-how to keep it to themselves (with the one exception of Russian help to China). What changed things was the development of the gas centrifuge technique. Unlike the earlier methods of enrichment on an industrial scale, especially the gas diffusion method, the centrifuge technique can be explored quite effectively on a small scale in a concealable installation and can be expanded incrementally without much difficulty, to increase either the capacity of throughput or the degree of enrichment of uranium product. Moreover, the very success of states at keeping gas diffusion technology under wraps stimulated the search for alternative methods, initially and innocently enough in states with an emerging interest in security of supply of fuel for their reactors and especially in Germany, where centrifuge technology had originally been explored during the Second World War. States developing an interest in uranium enrichment with security of supplies of fuel in mind are probably going to be less guarded about dissemination of the technological principles involved than states with national security in mind. It is even possible that the transnational arrangements made in Europe to pool the peaceful exploitation of the centrifuge method under the Urenco umbrella created a particularly leaky structure. Each of the three participating states in Urenco – the UK, Germany and the Netherlands – has its own set of (mainly) nationally based suppliers, as is not uncommon in European collaborative industrial programmes of all kinds. The proliferation of places where leakage of information and components can occur is then self-evident. It is certain that Urenco was implicated, in different ways, both in the start-up of Pakistan's military centrifuge programme and in Iraq's far from half-hearted but brief exploration of the centrifuge method for obtaining enriched uranium for its nascent bomb programme before the 1990–91 Gulf war. In the case of Pakistan, a Pakistani citizen, A.Q. Khan, was the intermediary. Khan, a trained metallurgist, was an employee of a supplier to Urenco in the Netherlands, who had obtained his position through disguising his nationality as someone from the (former) Dutch East Indies. He was secretly an agent of the Pakistani government, and eventually fled to Pakistan with blueprints for centrifuges and a ledger of contact addresses for the supply of key components. Khan seems to have retained his buccaneering ways even after returning to Pakistan and receiving public acclaim as the father of the Pakistan bomb, tested in 1998. While the details remain obscure, including how far he was acting under licence from the Pakistani authorities, it seems as though Khan was instrumental in disseminating centrifuge technology and components also to Iran, North Korea and Libya. Urenco was again involved in the case of Iraq, this time through an approach made to a German supplier (the MAN company) to Urenco by Iraqi scientists (the approach may have been the other way around) in the late 1980s. The German citizen mainly involved, K.H. Schaab, was tried for treason in the German courts in 1999 and found guilty. The fact that he had sold the Iraqis details of the very latest and most cost-effective Urenco centrifuge designs (the 3 m tall supercritical model) counted heavily against him.

Up to a point, the Additional Protocol and integrated safeguards address the problems of small reactors and uranium, but the former more effectively than the latter. The freeing up of resources by cutting back on the excessive inspection of large reactors will mean more resources for other things, like hunting down undeclared facilities. As a general rule, Agency inspectors wondering about the possibility that a secret nuclear site exists within a particular member state and exercising new rights to roam national territory equipped with environmental sampling apparatus would be well advised to apply basic political tests first. Undeclared nuclear sites are unlikely to be close to border areas unless the border is one shared with a friendly power. Moreover, most countries have a heartland and a periphery. In the case of Iraq under Saddam Hussein, it is almost certain that a secret facility of this kind would not have been placed in the Kurdish areas to the north of the country or the Shia areas in the south. In countries with military governments, secret programmes would be most likely to be found in areas tightly controlled by the military (military towns or even the military sectors or cantonments of larger civil conurbations). Countries with a free press would be unlikely to have such programmes at all, but in the very unlikely event of Canada running a secret programme of uranium enrichment it is almost certain that it would not be in Quebec.

Unearthing undeclared small (or large) reactors or plutonium separation plant is considerably assisted by the Additional Protocol's specific provision allowing inspectors to search for undeclared nuclear sites and by the near impossibility of operating such plant without leaving clues in the atmosphere in the form of traces of radioactive gases. Technology also assists in allowing plants once identified to have their entire operating history (if there is one) to be reconstructed using environmental swipe technology. The same can be done for uranium enrichment plants, but the difficulty here lies in finding an undeclared plant in the first place, since the modern types of plant can be physically small enough to be easily disguised as something else and emit few clues, gaseous or otherwise, that an inspector can find. Provisions made by the Additional Protocol to allow Agency inspectors access to state export and import records will help, but only in a limited way. This is partly because of the dual-use nature of traded components that might be secretly intended for a centrifuge plant. For example, the notorious 88 mm diameter aluminium tubes imported by Iraq, from 1999 on, received the following appraisal from the report of the Butler inquiry, set up by the British government to investigate the handling of intelligence on weapons of mass destruction before the 2003 Iraq war:[19]

> The evidence we received on aluminium tubes was overwhelmingly that they were intended for rockets rather than a centrifuge. We found this convincing. Despite this we conclude that the Joint Intelligence Committee was right to consider carefully the possibility that the tubes were evidence of a resumed nuclear programme.

Secondly, import and export records will not help where potential state suppliers of centrifuge technology are themselves outside the NPT, principally India and Pakistan. Nor will they help in cases of black market transactions (Khan- or Schaab-like), which are unlikely by definition to feature, except in heavily disguised form, in any import records.

Of course, integrated safeguards mean openness on the part of the inspectorate to information relevant to its work coming from any quarter. A willingness on the part of the main supporters of the treaty and its safeguards to share intelligence concerning suspicious transactions involving nuclear technology or materials would be an asset. But there are political difficulties. The 'owners' of the intelligence are not always going to be willing to disclose the fact that they possess it because of the risk of compromising the source. Agency inspectors ought too to be nervous about accepting information of this kind when it is offered, since it might seem to compromise their independence should they become seen as agents of the foreign policy of the state sharing the intelligence with them. In an awareness of these and other difficulties, proposals have been advanced that the Agency should possess its own independent reconnaissance satellite. But it is not clear that the cost of obtaining and maintaining such a facility would be the most fruitful way of using the normally limited resources at the Agency's disposal. A more down to earth and pragmatic way around would be for such intelligence to be made public, and then the Agency could act on it or ignore it, according to its judgement of the situation. It is impossible at this stage to be certain, but it seems likely that this procedure was followed in the case of Iran's centrifuge programme.[20] And in line with the more recent thinking within the Agency, foreshadowed in the theoretical section above, whereby the intrusiveness of inspections (as agreed under the Additional Protocol) might be lessened by greater recourse to relevant information already being collected elsewhere, the Agency can make use of commercially available satellite photographs. Pictures with a resolution of 50 cm or less at ground level are now available. These are less revealing than the best obtainable from military satellites (which can make out detail down to the level of 10 cm) but are probably good enough for most Agency needs.[21] Frequent photographic coverage can sometimes disclose not only the construction of a suspect facility but also the subsequent construction of its carapace of disguise.

The state with far and away the widest system of intelligence gathering is the USA. After some original hesitation concerning the Additional Protocol and integrated safeguards and the implied moves away from classical safeguards, President George W. Bush in a 2004 speech defining the position of his (notoriously divided) administration on curbing the spread of nuclear weapons endorsed it, and urged the Senate to consent immediately to ratification of the US signature (as a nuclear weapons state) to the Protocol.[22] Indeed, the speech went much further, proposing that only states party to the Additional Protocol (as of 2005) should be permitted to import any civil nuclear equipment at all, which will seem to many a reasonable extension of the 'full-scope safeguards' norm already applying. In addition and much more contentiously, and very reminiscent of the earlier attempts by the USA to outlaw the reprocessing of plutonium everywhere, Bush proposed that the NSG should trade plant and technology for plutonium separation and uranium enrichment only with states already possessing full-scale plant for such purposes. This is an attack on the uranium problem, but creates problems of its own. Like Carter's initiative on plutonium separation 25 years before (see Chapters 1 and 5), it raises questions of principle with the respect to the bargain contained in the treaty that assures signatories in good standing complete access to nuclear technologies for peaceful purposes. And of course, as before, it raises practical questions about the security of fuel supply.

In spite of repeated institutional urging, states have been slow to sign up to the Additional Protocol – it was in force for 14 states only by 2000, and for 56 by 2004; a perceived lack of US enthusiasm, now at least partly put right, may have had something to do with it (delay on the part of EU states in order to be able to coordinate their positive response also needs to be factored in). But it is not the only explanation. Part of the original incentive for states to sign up to the inspection provisions of the NPT was a pitching of the intrusiveness of inspection procedures at an initial low level, after the Karlsruhe formula. Moreover, the promised impact of safeguards on state sovereignty under INFCIRC/153 was less than that under INFCIRC/66, which already governed safeguards operations with some states. Subsequent tightening was by and large incremental. The Additional Protocol, which as we have seen has to be signed up to separately from the original safeguards agreements, by itself represents or can be easily seen as representing a reverse procedure. It is presented inevitably as a tightening of INFCIRC/153, as a corrective to the apparent failures of the latter in Iraq and perhaps North Korea. It is only after states have signed up to it that they can qualify for easier treatment under integrated safeguards – jam tomorrow rather than jam today.

Notes

1 Henry Hamburger, *Games as Models of Social Phenomena* (San Francisco, W.H. Freeman and Co., 1979), pp. 71–4.
2 A more rigorous approach might consider situations where the players were other than risk neutral (e.g. valuing a 50 per cent chance of getting £1,000 as worth exactly the same as a definite £500) as they are assumed to be here. For how this might matter, and how it should be dealt with, see Avinash Dixit and Susan Skeath, *Games of Strategy* (New York, W.W. Norton and

Co., 1999), pp. 173–7. And a more comprehensive approach would not necessarily assume the sort of asymmetry between players that is assumed here, where the privilege is granted, quite reasonably, to the inspectorate of announcing, or, more accurately, committing itself to, an inspection strategy. The analysis of more symmetrical situations is normally more complex. A more symmetrical situation might arise in the present context where an inspectorate is faced with a single state somehow already identified as a likely violator and judging how best to carry out an inspection that will confirm the matter. See for example Ken Binmore, *Fun and Games: A Text on Game Theory* (Lexington, MA, D.C. Heath and Co., 1992), pp. 257–61. Finally, the simple arithmetical combination of costs and benefits in the payoffs ought in a more rigorous study to be replaced by an indifference curve approach. For a generally comprehensive, but rather technical, chapter-length game theory treatment of inspection, with a good survey of earlier literature, see Steven J. Brams and D. Marc Kilgour, *Game Theory and National Security* (New York, Basil Blackwell, 1988), pp. 143–68.

3 This approximates to practice. The text of IFCIRC/153 is vaguer, in that it promises only that no reactor will attract more than 50 inspector-days of inspection in a year.

4 David Fischer, *Towards 1995: The Prospects for Ending the Proliferation of Nuclear Weapons* (Aldershot, Dartmouth Publishing Co. for the United Nations Institute for Disarmament Research, 1993), p. 67.

5 Jill N. Cooley, 'Integrated nuclear safeguards: genesis and evolution', in *Verification Yearbook 2003* (London, Vertic, 2003), pp. 29–44. See, too, Pierre Goldschmidt, 'IAEA safeguards: evolution or revolution?', in 41st Annual Meeting of the Institute of Nuclear Materials Management, New Orleans, 2000.

6 Cooley, 'Integrated nuclear safeguards', p. 30.

7 C. Xerri and H. Nackaerts, 'Integrated safeguards: a case to go beyond the limits', in 44th Annual Meeting of the Institute of Nuclear Materials Management, Pideni, 2003.

8 Fischer uses this term to describe concessions in the original wording of the treaty designed to meet German (then West German) fears for their commercial nuclear industry that inspections would be too intrusive. Advice from the Karlsruhe Nuclear Research Institute seems to have been influential in formulating the German position. Of course, a treaty with German support was much more valuable than one with the Germans outside. See Fischer, *Towards 1995*, pp. 55–6.

9 This account of inspection procedure borrows heavily from Fischer, *Towards 1995*, pp. 237–9, but is also based on the author's own experiences.

10 Reactors fuelled with thorium and uranium-233 produce no plutonium at all, but there are very few of these in existence.

11 INFCIRC stands for information circular. These are public documents containing the gist of classified (normally) versions of the same (in this case, agreed) documents issued by the Agency to member states. For INFCIRC/66/Rev.2 and INFCIRC/153 see David Fischer, Paul Szasz and Jozef Goldblat (eds), *Safeguarding the Atom: A Critical Appraisal* (London, Taylor and Francis for the Stockholm International Peace Research Institute, 1985), pp. 75–86.

12 Fischer, *Towards 1995*, p. 57.
13 International Atomic Energy Agency, 'The IAEA's safeguards system', para. 6. Available at www.iaea.org/Publications/Booklets/Safeguards2/part7.html (last accessed 29 April 2005).
14 Fischer et al., *Safeguarding the Atom*, p. 80.
15 The assessment of the British government's Joint Intelligence Committee (JIC) of September 1990, on the eve of the first Gulf War, stated Iraq to be three years away from being able to produce fissile material (enriched uranium). But it based this assessment on the assumption that the Iraqis were working on centrifuges only. The JIC knew nothing about the calutron. See *Review of Intelligence on Weapons of Mass Destruction*, Report of a Committee of Privy Councillors, Chairman Lord Butler, HC 898 (London, The Stationery Office, 2004) (henceforth the Butler report), p. 42.
16 Published accounts differ. The present account leans on Larry A. Niksch, *North Korea's Nuclear Weapons Program*, Issue Brief for Congress (Washington, DC, Congressional Research Service, Library of Congress, 2002).
17 See data for a typical Magnox reactor in A.A. Farmer, 'Recycling of fuel', in Walter Marshall (ed.), *Nuclear Power Technology, Volume 2* (Oxford, Clarendon Press, 1983), p. 16. The isotopic composition of plutonium from such a reactor is, moreover, 80 per cent plutonium-239, the isotope most suitable for bomb manufacture.
18 It cannot be denied that there is an unavoidable subjective element present here. But if one were to list alphabetically all states credibly claimed to have taken either firm or provisional decisions to acquire nuclear weapons since the signing of the NPT (in 1968), whether or not these decisions have been subsequently been confirmed or rescinded, the same broad impression emerges. Of Algeria, Argentina, Brazil, Iran, Iraq, Libya, North Korea, Pakistan, South Africa, South Korea and Taiwan, three (Algeria, South Korea and Taiwan) took no interest in uranium. North Korea seems to have been mainly interested in plutonium, but kept uranium in the picture. As for the rest, uranium seems to have been the chief or only interest. See David Albright, Frans Berkhout and William Walker, *Plutonium and Highly Enriched Uranium 1996: World Inventories, Capabilities and Policies* (Oxford, Oxford University Press for the Stockholm International Peace Research Institute, 1997).
19 Butler report, p. 133.
20 This is in contrast to Iraq in the previous decade. As we have seen, the British intelligence organisation, MI6, knew of the existence of the Iraqi centrifuge programme before the 1991 war (Butler report, p. 42), even if it did not know of the calutrons, but it did not share this information (as far as can be seen) with the IAEA.
21 See Hui Zhang and Frank N. von Hippel, 'Eyes in the sky', *Bulletin of the Atomic Scientists*, Vol. 57, No. 4, July/August 2001, pp. 61–6.
22 'President announces new measures to counter the threat of WMD: remarks by the President on weapons of mass destruction proliferation', White House press release, 11 February 2004, available at www.whitehouse.gov/news/releases/2004/02/print/20040211-4.html (last accessed 11 April 2005).

4
Understanding nuclear-free zones

The purpose of this chapter is to identify the properties of an ideal nuclear-weapon-free zone (nuclear-free zone for short) and then to compare it with actual nuclear-free zones in being or seriously proposed.

An ideal nuclear-free zone should first of all be worth having; that means it should do a job of work in solving a multilateral security dilemma, by maintaining a desirable level of international security for the participating states in the face of temptations on the part of individual states within the zone to improve their national security by going nuclear. The job of work is never done and there is always a risk that the arrangement will fail to hold, as there must be in any arms control arrangement that is worth having. This puts it on a par with the NPT, but its narrower geographical scope than the NPT is both beneficial to the nuclear-free zone and a problem for it.

It is beneficial in as much as resolving the multilateral security dilemma is on average easier the smaller the number of participants involved, but more difficult in that no grouping of states is an island, and the introduction of nuclear weapons into the zone from outside may be difficult to insure against. Of course, written guarantees from outside powers that they would not do such a thing may be obtained, but covenants without the sword are but words. The best that may be hoped for is an explicit or tacit undertaking by external nuclear powers to desist from introducing nuclear weapons into the zone, coupled with pledges from the same that they would assist any state within a zone subject to a nuclear threat from the outside; this would comprise a so-called 'positive' security assurance. But the most that has been achieved in practice are specific guarantees of the 'negative' sort – a conditional undertaking not

Understanding nuclear-free zones

to issue nuclear threats against a party to the zone arrangement – and these are much less desirable in this sort of application (where a promise of action is inherently more supportive of the goals of a zone than a promise of inaction).

Of course, any mutual restraint on the part of external powers is more easily achieved in circumstances where the strategic motivation on the part of any external power to introduce nuclear weapons into the security affairs of the zone is slight to begin with. This implies that the ideal nuclear-free zone should itself constitute among its member states a 'security complex' (see Chapter 2). By security complex is meant a grouping of states out of whose interrelationships with each other arise 100 per cent or nearly so of all their external security concerns. It then follows that the motivation for external states, nuclear or not, to concern themselves strategically with states within the zone will be weak.

Additionally, the ideal zone should contain states that have shown themselves to be capable of solving their security dilemma in a historical conventional setting. That is to say, their record for settling international disputes among them peaceably ought to be good, and this will normally be reflected in a long record of low defence expenditures within the zone. Further, in order to deter a state within the group nonetheless deciding to go nuclear, there should be resources within the group to allow a counter-move to be made to deny the first mover its nuclear monopoly, and one requirement for this is a system, probably based on inspections, designed to produce timely warning. Basically, when the zone arrangements are doing a job of work, this means that nuclear technology for peaceful purposes should have a foothold in at least two states within the zone. A more general 'punishment' held in reserve for those that fail to observe the provisions of the treaty is also useful, in the sense that the NPT threatens delinquent states with the withholding of commercial nuclear technology (and security guarantees).

Lastly, nuclear-free zone arrangements should reflect underlying power realities within the zone itself. Larger and more capable (i.e. normally more nearly nuclear capable) states within the zone will find it easier to survive a collapse of the zone arrangements (or a failure for one to be agreed in the first place) and will accordingly expect privileges for themselves in the details of the arrangement; without such privileges the arrangement will be weaker.

Lest this long definition may be found unduly subjective, it will be seen that a relatively high level of defence expenditures within a zone is hardly consistent with the ideal, since it will reflect either arms racing behaviour between members of the zone, which challenges the idea of the zone states being capable of solving their security dilemma, or some powerful external threat, which immediately challenges the idea of the zone comprising a security complex.

While the ideal nuclear-free zone is perhaps to be found only laid up in some Platonic heaven, there are at least seven different international arrangements either in place or which have come close to being put in place that have actually attracted the title of nuclear-free zone. Every one of these represents a departure from the ideal just described, but the one that comes closest was among the first to be put into place, the nuclear-free zone for Latin America under the Treaty of Tlatelolco, opened for signature in 1967.[1]

However, we begin with a chronological approach, since there is no doubt that newer zones have to an extent modelled themselves on earlier ones and on earlier 'non-armament treaties'.

Non-armament treaties

Antarctic

The very first arrangement to be put in place was the Antarctic Treaty, with the Antarctic continent the zone in question, and which entered into force in 1961.[2] It is not specifically about nuclear weapons, except that its Article 5 seeks to prohibit nuclear explosions there and to prevent the continent being used for the disposal of radioactive waste. In fact it prohibits any measures of a military nature being taken on the continent by any of the signatory states, who are the so-called Contracting Parties (circa 25, including the five original nuclear powers), which comprise all those states with mutually acknowledged but indefinitely suspended territorial claims on the continent. Of course the continent is uninhabited (except by small scientific outstations belonging to the Contracting Parties). The arrangement satisfies some of the criteria of the ideal type, in that the Antarctic is militarily/strategically uninteresting to external states, compared with the Arctic, for instance. And the arrangement specifies a right on the part of signatories to carry out inspections anywhere in the zone, including over-flights, in order to verify that signatories are sticking to the agreements. It is not so clear that it is doing a job of work of any kind and is therefore anything more than symbolic, except that the example of the Arctic shows that polar regions need not be strategically uninteresting; also, the treaty could be deemed pre-emptive, in that it will create obstacles to military use should circumstances change, for example if polar bases (and polar orbits of the earth) acquired a new significance in the context of the militarisation of outer space.

The Antarctic Treaty was to prove a model for the non-nuclearisation of two further uninhabited regions: outer space and the seabed.

Outer space

The Outer Space Treaty came into force in 1967, sponsored by the USA and the USSR but open for universal signature.[3] Parties undertake not to place weapons of mass destruction, and specifically nuclear weapons, in space or onto objects in space, from earth orbit 'upwards'. In addition, and more specifically reminiscent of the Antarctic Treaty, it forbids militarisation of any kind where natural bodies in space are concerned (the moon and other 'celestial bodies'). The Outer Space Treaty does more of a job of work than does the Antarctic Treaty, in that it was far from clear at the time that there were no military advantages to be had in placing nuclear weapons in earth orbit, and it remains today pre-emptively in the background as a moral if not legal obstacle facing US plans to construct defences against ballistic missile attack. The abandoning (in June 2002) by the George W. Bush US administration of the Anti-Ballistic Missile (ABM) Treaty of 1972, with its specific restrictions on the use of space-based defensive weapons, increases the possibility that the new plans for anti-ballistic missile defences envisage the use of earth orbit for actual weapons, if not of a nuclear variety. This is almost certainly the reasoning behind the position taken by Russia and China with their joint 2002 proposal to the Conference on Disarmament for a new Outer Space Treaty, even more like that on the Antarctic, banning all space weapons – specifically 'not to place in orbit ... any object carrying any kinds of weapons'.[4] These same states are making further movement on a well advanced proposal within the Conference on Disarmament, namely to supplement the NPT with a monitored cut-off in the production of fissile materials for nuclear weapons by the nuclear states, conditional on progress on a new Space Treaty proposal.

But unlike the Antarctic Treaty, the Outer Space Treaty fails to include specific machinery for mutual inspection procedures as part of the apparatus to deter defection. This is an important defect, given the level of interest in military uses of outer space then and now.

Seabed

The same level of military interest has never applied in the case of the third of these multilateral non-armament treaties – the Seabed Treaty, which entered into force in 1972.[5] Its chief clause is a prohibition on parties placing nuclear weapons or other weapons of mass destruction on the seabed and ocean floor beyond coastal waters (this zone then defined as extending 12 miles, or some 20 km, from the coast). This scarcely appears to do any job of work at all, although during the decade before the treaty came into force there was an upsurge of interest in the economic exploitation of the seabed and how this might be internationalised. But this international interest in orderly exploitation of the riches of the seabed did not long outlive the rekindling of faith in liberal (that is to say competitive) economic policies that coincided with the Reagan years at the White House.

Nuclear-free zones

Tlatelolco

The first zone to come into being for a populated area of the world, if not the first such zone to be seriously considered, was the Latin American nuclear-free zone, the treaty establishing which was signed in 1967 by the regional states chiefly involved at Tlatelolco, a place of significance in Aztec times and now a suburb of Mexico City.[6] The original suggestion for such a treaty seems to have come from Costa Rica, at a meeting of the Organization of American States in 1958, but it was the Brazilian delegate to the UN shortly before the Cuban missile crisis of 1962 who gave the idea a decisive push. And he repeated the call for a zone in the form of a draft UN resolution calling for such a thing during the crisis itself. The Mexican government then took over the baton and under the tutelage of Garcia Robles, the ambassador of Mexico to Brazil, the Mexican President the following year announced that five Latin American countries – Bolivia, Brazil, Chile, Ecuador and Mexico – were prepared to go ahead with the suggestion.

The principles of the zone are laid out in its Article 1. Treaty parties undertake to use their nuclear facilities and materials exclusively for peaceful purposes and not to receive on to their territories nuclear weapons from whatever source for any purpose, including testing.

The fact that the treaty did not substantively come into force until 1994 illustrates that it sought to perform a job of work in as much as it met with resistance among potential signatories that was only gradually worn down. The treaty was opened for signature in 1967 but even by 1990 Argentina had signed but not ratified; and Brazil and Chile had ratified but chosen not to bring it into force for themselves. The treaty automatically comes into force for all once every eligible state has ratified, but it can come into force sooner, on a state-by-state, piecemeal basis. This requires a ratifying state explicitly to waive its right to wait for universal ratification before having the treaty come into force for itself. This provision, in Article 28 of the treaty, was a piece of drafting skill that anticipated the sorts of difficulties Argentina, Brazil and Chile would have in accepting the effects of the treaty on their freedom of action and at the same time avoiding having this prevent any sort of progress at all. The subtlety of the arrangement is that it allows the treaty to come into force gradually not only in a geographical sense but in another sense also. States planning nuclear programmes of any kind and having doubts about the prudence of being fully bound by the treaty were able, as Argentina, Brazil and Chile were, to take partial, less than fully binding steps in the direction of the treaty, with further steps no doubt to be conditional on the wisdom of taking the partial steps in the first place being borne out by events. Subtlety was also shown in the definition adopted concerning the seaward extent of the zone. States party to the arrangement had as side-payments the backing of the arrangement for claims to jurisdiction over territorial waters extending 200 miles (320 km) off their coastline.

The first milestone came in 1969, when the stipulated number of states (11) had exercised the Article 28 waiver for themselves, at which point according to that Article the same 11 would set about creating a regional agency for safeguards – the Agency for the Prohibition of Nuclear Weapons in Latin America (OPANAL). OPANAL was designed to be supplementary to the IAEA, with which body treaty parties (under Article 13) were required singly or jointly to enter into safeguards agreements. The significance of the regional body, at least on paper, was in three parts. Most interestingly, it took powers to carry out what in today's usage would be described as challenge inspections. Any treaty party suspecting another party of contravening the treaty can complain to the OPANAL Council, which will then immediately arrange inspections to clear the matter up. The Vienna Agency under the NPT did not then and does not today possess such powers. The second aspect of OPANAL was its wider remit than the Vienna Agency in another sense, in that the IAEA had no standing with respect, for example, to the emplacement of allied nuclear weapons on West German territory during the Cold War, whereas the banning of such weapons is very much OPANAL's business. And thirdly, much more explicitly than the Vienna Agency within the NPT, OPANAL envisages a role for itself in ensuring that peaceful nuclear explosions carried out by treaty parties are that and only that (on peaceful nuclear explosions, see below).

The question of states external to the zone arose in two distinct forms. One was the subject matter of Protocol I to the treaty, which asks states geographically outside the defined zone of the treaty but which have international responsibility for territories within the zone to respect the terms of the treaty. All four external powers concerned had ratified Protocol I by 1992: France in 1992, the USA on behalf, inter alia, of Guantanamo Bay in Cuba in 1981, the Netherlands in 1971 and the UK in 1969. Under Protocol II of the treaty all nuclear weapons states at the time were asked to respect the status of denuclearisation of the designated geographical zone covered by the treaty and were asked for a commitment not to use or threaten to use nuclear weapons against parties to the treaty. All five nuclear powers had ratified their accession to Protocol II by 1979: the USSR did so in 1979, and France and China in 1974; the USA did so in 1971 but with the proviso consistent with 'negative security' guarantees given elsewhere that should it be attacked by a treaty party allied to a nuclear weapons state, it would view the former to be in breach; and a similar proviso was made by the other nuclear weapons states, including the UK, which ratified in 1969.

In its ratification of Protocol II the USA added its own understanding of another role to be played by external nuclear powers. This concerned Article 18 of the main part of the treaty, which deals with peaceful nuclear explosions in a very accommodating manner, saying that parties may carry them out, even 'including explosions which involve devices similar to those used in nuclear weapons'. Article 18 also stipulates on-site inspection to ensure that the type of explosion carried out is in line with the compulsory notification of impending explosions the Article also asks for. This generously dimensioned room permitted for treaty parties to carry out peaceful nuclear explosions, inserted as a sop to Brazil and a reflection of its bargaining power, was too much for the USA (and not enough for Brazil). In the interpretation the USA attached to its ratification of Protocol II, it unilaterally defined a peaceful nuclear explosion allowable under the treaty as one carried out by the USA on behalf of a treaty party. In fact, the restrictive US position on the question of peaceful nuclear explosions – a 180-degree turn from the permissive attitude US weapons laboratories incidentally did much to promote in the 1950s and 1960s – is not far out of line with most other states' understanding that a nuclear device capable of producing peaceful nuclear explosions is indistinguishable from a bomb. Indeed, Article 5 of the NPT is almost as restrictive on the matter of peaceful nuclear explosions, in that it suggests similarly that these are to be made available to non-nuclear states desiring them, but only from the outside, either bilaterally or through a multilateral body.

Argentina and Brazil were not parties to the NPT and were especially opposed to any restrictive interpretation being given to Article 18 of the Tlatelolco treaty, since as it stood it gave them an extra cover of respectability, if required, for any domestic projects involving the actual production in separated form of fissile material, plutonium or highly enriched uranium, neither of which activity is normally economically compatible with a commercial application of nuclear energy unless that programme is unusually ambitious in scale. But it was to be movement on the specific matter of Article 18 on the part of Argentina and Brazil in 1991 that signalled the start of a greater detente between the two on nuclear matters, and paved the way for their full accession to the

Tlatelolco treaty. In a joint declaration each undertook to ban in its territory 'the testing, use, manufacture, production or acquisition by other means of any nuclear explosive device, as long as no technical distinction can be made between nuclear explosive devices for peaceful purposes and those for military purposes'.[7] Since very few modern nuclear weapons are unsuitable for peaceful uses (such as digging canals), and since what makes for a good nuclear weapon (compactness, portability, safety in handling) also makes for a good peaceful nuclear device, the final clause of the preceding sentence is simply face saving. These developments with regard to Article 18 were only the latest in a series of steps taken by Argentina and Brazil to bring themselves closer to the spirit and letter of the treaty. Along the lines of 'truth and reconciliation', in 1983 Argentina had admitted to the existence of a small gas diffusion plant for enriching uranium, while excusing itself on the basis that the objective of the plant had been commercial. In 1990, with greater candour, Brazil announced the decommissioning of a nuclear weapons testing site in the Amazon basin and the cancellation of an equally secret bomb project, called Solimoes, which had been in existence since 1975, based on enriched uranium from centrifuges run by the Brazilian navy (see Chapter 1).

In 1992, in a more ambiguous move as far as their detente was concerned, Argentina and Brazil were joined by Chile in seeking to amend – in fact diminish – the powers of the OPANAL in the area of safeguards. In keeping with a wider tendency for challenge inspections to be admired on paper but to be found difficult to live with in practice, the three states successfully argued that Article 16 of the Tlatelolco treaty should be amended to allow 'special inspections' (i.e. challenge inspections) still, but to limit them to the hands of the IAEA, which, as we have seen (Chapter 3), has no experience with such intrusive techniques, even if it has vastly more experience than the OPANAL of the art of safeguarding as a whole.

More interestingly, Argentina and Brazil had come to a further exclusive bilateral arrangement between themselves – the Treaty of Guadalajara in 1991 – the effect of which was officially to anticipate their both coming fully into line with the Tlatelolco treaty and the NPT, which neither still had done, but with a caveat. The caveat was to be in the form of a privilege for the two states to be less nakedly exposed to the safeguards inspection arrangements of the IAEA than the rest of the Tlatelolco parties. This was to be achieved by the creation of a new safeguards body, known as the Brazilian–Argentine Agency for Accounting and Control of Nuclear Materials (ABACC).[8] This body would act as an intermediary between the civil nuclear programmes of the two and the IAEA inspectorate and seems to have been partly inspired by the Euratom arrangements in Europe, which gave Germany in particular additional confidence that commercial confidentiality in the area of nuclear technology would not be compromised by IAEA inspectors (see the Annex to the present chapter). The freedom of states party to the NPT to negotiate safeguards agreements multilaterally with the IAEA rather than on a national basis is written into the NPT itself (Article 3).

On the one hand it could be argued that diminishing the powers of the OPANAL relative to those of the IAEA as a safeguarding body adds externally to the perception of the Tlatelolco treaty as a serious regional institution, confident enough to put its safeguards procedures in neutral hands, and moreover willing to see state parties accept, via the IAEA in the form of challenge inspections, an additional layer of safeguarding that other states party to IAEA safeguards agreements do not have to tolerate. On the other, a regional safeguards arrangement has certain advantages over a global one like that run by the IAEA, not least in the quality and quantity of information neighbours naturally have about each other compared with strangers. As a very minor instance, nearly all Tlatelolco parties are Spanish-speaking.

If the health of a multilateral arms control treaty correlates at all with the size of membership, then by the early 1990s the signs for the Tlatelolco treaty were good. In 1990 the treaty became one of denuclearising Latin America *and* the Caribbean, as some English-speaking states there became parties to the treaty for the first time. Belize, having attained independence from the UK, now became eligible. The obstacle to Guyana – involved with the UK in a territorial dispute with other Latin American states, pre-dating the Tlatelolco treaty – was removed by a redrafting of Article 25.

In 1994 Argentina, Brazil and Chile all became fully party to the Tlatelolco treaty and even Cuba, the last camel in the train, signed in 1995 and ratified in 2002. It is (as of 2004) ratified and in force for all 33 possible states within the zone. In 2003, to celebrate this, the parties issued the Havana declaration, which confidently called on the nuclear weapons states to be more mindful of their obligations both with respect to nuclear-free zones and under Article 6 of the NPT.

So to summarise, in comparison with the ideal nuclear-free zone described above, the Latin American zone scores well along most dimensions. First of all, it does a job of work. Argentina and Brazil had both been exploring a nuclear weapons option, which we must assume the treaty helped to keep within bounds. In a treaty doing a job of work we would not expect that job quite ever to be over, and we must expect it to play a part in assisting Argentina and Brazil to remain in the relationship of recessed deterrence with respect to each other. Secondly, the Latin American zone is a reasonable approximation to a security complex, if a slightly odd one. The security attitude of the USA is one of benign neglect, tempered by a fierce interventionist streak whenever it believes other outside powers are acquiring an active security interest in the zone for themselves either directly (as in Cuba) or indirectly (as in Salvador

Table 4.1. Defence expenditure as percentage of gross domestic product within nuclear-free zones[9]

	1985	2002
Tlatelolco	2.7	1.7
Rarotonga	2.6	1.9
Pelindaba	3.5	3.2
North Africa	4.9	4.1
Sub-Saharan Africa	2.7	2.6
Bangkok	4.0	3.6
World	6.2	2.6

Allende's Chile of the early 1970s). This has a deterrent value in that external security involvement in the zone is apt to be limited by this fact of US policy. Thirdly, in the matter of self-policing, the zone has been both ambitious and less than sure-footed in the matter of inspection and safeguards. But the mutual recessed deterrent value of the Argentine and Brazilian pre-nuclear weapons programmes is clear, and the ABACC bilateral safeguards arrangement between Argentina and Brazil is probably a small price to pay to satisfy the natural wish on the part of these big powers in the zone for privileges not granted to the common herd. That there is nonetheless a price to be paid is illustrated by the difficulties the IAEA discovered in 2004 in establishing a satisfactory inspection regime with regard to Brazil's centrifuge enrichment plant. And finally, the historically very low incidence of war in the zone and the long record of low defence expenditures by Latin American states (see Table 4.1) both indicate a capacity for discovering cooperative solutions to the security dilemma, and tend to ratify the idea that the zone is a reasonable approximation to a security complex.

Rarotonga

Chronologically, the next nuclear-free zone to be established was for the South Pacific, in the form of the Treaty of Rarotonga, which has been in force since 1986.[10] As with Tlatelolco, the chief original motivating state was the largest in the region, Australia. The other original parties were the Cook Islands, Fiji, Kiribati, Nauru, New Zealand, Niue, Papua New Guinea, the Solomon Islands, Tonga, Tuvalu, Vanuatu and Western Samoa. Further similarities to Tlatelolco are found in its substantive content, which seeks to denuclearise the zone, and by means of

Protocols have external powers respect the zone's denuclearised status. Innovatively, the treaty aims to exclude the dumping of radioactive waste from the territory of the zone. Otherwise, Rarotonga falls rather short of the ideal zone. For one thing, it is very unclear that it is doing a job of work of any kind, in the sense that it is hard to see what aspect of nuclear proliferation it is actively seeking to prevent. That it was asking very little of its potential parties is shown by the fact that it took only three years from its inception to come into force – Tlatelolco took nearer 30. While it cannot be said to fail the quantitative defence expenditures test of its status as a security complex, there is the awkward fact that its largest member, Australia, is the chief ally of the USA in the southern hemisphere and is a key site for ground stations serving active and passive US military uses of space. On the other hand, while it is perhaps far-fetched to suppose that future New Zealand and Australian governments could find in Rarotonga machinery which would better allow them to reach a state of recessed nuclear deterrence with each other, that does not mean that Rarotonga is useless. Its safeguards arrangements are those of the IAEA, but there is provision (as with the OPANAL) for challenge inspections and this might deter some future Australian government, anxious for foreign exchange, from cutting corners when selling enriched uranium (from some future enrichment plant) on some future sellers' market to a less than respectable buyer. And it is not impossible that the USA might in the future lose interest in overseas bases for space-related communications, even if the current trend, towards defences against ballistic missile attack, is in the opposite direction. So, there is a pre-emptive aspect to Rarotonga, if not a very marked one, and in 10 years' time it may look more worthwhile than it does at present.

Pelindaba

The African nuclear-free zone under the Treaty of Pelindaba,[11] which was opened for signature in 1996, is nearer to the ideal than the Rarotonga treaty, chiefly in respect of the fact that, at least theoretically, it has a job of work to do. Within the zone, which is the whole continent of Africa, three countries – South Africa, Algeria and Libya – have shown apparent interest in acquiring nuclear weapons in the past. There is no doubt about this in the case of South Africa, with its secret uranium-based bomb programme admitted to and dismantled very shortly before the collapse of apartheid. In the cases of Libya and Algeria, in 2003 the former disclosed details of a practical interest in centrifuge methods of uranium enrichment, about which it had failed to inform the IAEA as its membership of the NPT almost certainly obliged it to do (legally, new facilities are to be reported to the IAEA not at the point when construction is begun but only shortly before they begin actual throughput of fissile materials). In December 2003 Libya informed the IAEA that it had imported natural uranium and centrifuge parts and that it had built a small-scale centrifuge plant during the 1980s and 1990s.[12] Algeria did not become a party to the NPT until 1995, four years after it became known that it was building a secret nuclear reactor (15 MW(th)) in the Atlas mountains. The reactor was supplied by China under a 1983 agreement, together with a small plutonium separation facility.[13] The whole assembly could produce sufficient plutonium for at least one bomb every two years or so.

While the Pelindaba treaty has in the African Commission on Nuclear Energy (AFCONE) an equivalent to the OPANAL within the Tlatelolco framework, which, like the latter, has powers to authorise challenge inspections, and like the Rarotonga treaty has as a sort of side-payment a prohibition against radioactive dumping in the waters of participating states, it is seriously compromised by its failure to represent a security complex. Like the Rarotonga treaty, it excludes from its remit 'facilities [on African territory] serving nuclear strategic systems of the nuclear powers',[14] but this is not the worst of it. Africa south of the Sahara might have some claim to status as a security complex but the whole continent is the wrong unit, being simultaneously too large (by taking in North Africa – defined as comprising Algeria, Egypt, Libya, Mauritania, Morocco and Tunisia) and too small (by not extending to the Middle East). Algeria and Libya are two countries whose principal external security linkages are to the Arab–Israeli conflict and to conflicts involving traditional and modernising Arab and Islamic societies. Israel might be deterred from openly joining the nuclear club by considerations of how, among others, Algeria or Libya might respond, and even vice versa, but it of course plays no part in the Pelindaba arrangements.

It is unclear, however, whether the founding fathers of the Pelindaba treaty (post-apartheid South Africa and Nigeria) would necessarily have had much time for this argument, since it quite remarkably not only bans nuclear weapons in the zone but also research and development towards the production of these weapons. How this may be verified is in question, although the IAEA with its Additional Protocol now envisages peaceful nuclear research and development facilities as being open to inspection and there is an implied capability somehow to detect those not declared. But the more serious point is how to deter a neighbour from going nuclear if a state does not have a capability to follow that neighbour down that route before too long.

Africa as a continent of independent states, even if relatively recent in formation, is not particularly warlike in the inter-state sense and may be thought to have the capacity to solve the multilateral security dilemma in a cooperative direction. But it is markedly weaker along this dimension than Latin America. Comparison of military expenditures – even if some such expenditure is for internal security purposes – provides a clue. The average military expenditure over the North African states as a whole in 2002 as a proportion of gross domestic product was 4.1 per cent (a reasonably typical figure for any time in the previous decade and a half). Average military expenditures as a percentage of gross domestic product for sub-Saharan Africa (more of a security complex than the continent as a whole) in 2002 was 2.6 per cent (also a typical figure for any time in the previous 15 years). The equivalent figure for the whole of the North Atlantic Treaty Organisation (NATO) for 2002 was also 2.6 per cent. The corresponding figure for Latin America was 1.7 per cent for 2002, after registering a downward trend from 2.7 per cent in 1985 (see Table 4.1).

What sense of cooperative cohesion there is in Africa is closely bound up with a common antipathy towards colonialism. The original stimulus for the creation of a nuclear-free zone in Africa was the testing of nuclear weapons in the Sahara by France in 1960 (and 20 years later the French testing programme in the South Pacific helped produce Rarotonga). But memories of colonialism and the common cause it created are now fast receding.

Bangkok

The last of the Tlatelolco-model treaties to be discussed is the 1995 Treaty of Bangkok, which created the South East Asia Nuclear Weapon-Free Zone (SEANWFZ).[15] The original proposal came from Indonesia in 1984, in an attempt to put substance into quite plausible earlier assertions of, and claims to, an evolving regional identity and uninterest in the use of force in their mutual relations made by the member states of the Association of Southeast Asian Nations (ASEAN) (then only six – Brunei, Indonesia, Malaysia, Philippines, Singapore and Thailand[16]). In 1971 these states had already declared themselves to be a Zone Of Peace, Freedom And Neutrality (ZOPFAN). ASEAN was founded in 1967 and a history of unusual cooperativeness between its members certainly exists. The record of cooperation within ASEAN since its creation more than offsets the earlier instances of the contrary – especially the hostile relations between Indonesia and Malaysia – even if, as within the EU, regional cooperativeness has been expressed most markedly along the economic dimension. The more recent expansion of ASEAN membership has brought inside it, and inside the Bangkok treaty, new member states like Vietnam and Cambodia, whose history of neighbourly cooperativeness is short. And while the simple fact of enlarged membership raises the usual sorts of questions about whether an expansion of a successful regional organisation is always compatible with cohesion, expansion is also a sign of success.

The trigger for the original Indonesian proposal for a nuclear-free zone to be taken up was again an external event, but this time a positive one, when US armed forces began their post-Cold War withdrawal from their bases in the Philippines, taking their tactical nuclear weapons along with them. Interestingly, while the updating of Tlatelolco and the drafting of Pelindaba involved the IAEA very closely in an advisory role, the Bangkok treaty was a more wholly home-spun and truly bottom-up affair, even if it envisages (like the other nuclear-free zones) a major role for the Vienna Agency in the inspection of commercial nuclear activities within the member states.[17] And it is equally clear that the drafters of the Bangkok treaty had studied the 'constitutions' of other nuclear-free zones closely. Like Tlatelolco and Pelindaba, Bangkok supplements IAEA safeguards through the regional provision of a scheme of challenge inspections, although one that is less uncompromising than the original OPANAL scheme. Like Tlatelolco, it also has side-payments in the shape of ambitious seaward cover, comprising the exclusive economic zones of the parties, and like Rarotonga seeks to ban radioactive dumping in its waters.

Where Bangkok suffers in comparison with Tlatelolco (or for that matter Rarotonga), at least as badly as Pelindaba does, is in the matter of isolating itself and its member states from the strategic concerns of external nuclear powers and the credibility of its claims, like all nuclear-free zones, to be able to do so. The United States and the former Soviet Union lost strategic interest in the area only very recently, and one Bangkok treaty member (Vietnam) has fought wars against two external nuclear weapons powers (the USA and China) and been allied with a third (the USSR). Another member state – Myanmar (Burma) – shares a border with two nuclear weapons states, China and India. On top of this, the creation of nuclear-free zones always involves much work for cartographers when it comes to delimiting their precise extent, especially where the outer limits of the territorial seas to be brought within its reach are concerned. The Bangkok treaty, as we have seen, extends its zone seawards to encompass the continental shelves of member states and their exclusive economic zones. Unfortunately, in the South China Sea there are unresolved national claims to territorial waters and island territories, some of which are believed to be of economic significance, involving not only ASEAN members but also China and other external powers besides.

Again, statistics of defence expenditures provide a clue (see Table 4.1). In 2002 defence expenditures across the Bangkok treaty states as a proportion of gross domestic product averaged 3.6 per cent, and they are not markedly on a declining trend. This is high by international standards, and while, as always, allowance has to be made for the fraction of this expenditure that is directed at internal security, it is not easy to reconcile with the status of an ideal nuclear-free zone.

Low defence expenditures within a zone like Latin America normally reflect the simultaneous, relative absence of two things: arms racing among the constituent states and fear of attack on states within the zone from outside. Relatively high defence expenditures, on the other hand, suggest the presence of at least one of these two features. In the case of Bangkok, the probability is that the latter is more significant.

Nonetheless, the Bangkok treaty carries the usual protocol under which the external nuclear powers promise to respect the zone and, unusually, it sets out procedures which allow it to investigate alleged breaches of the protocol. The difficulty is that outside nuclear powers have strategic interests within the zone – hence the high defence expenditure of Bangkok parties – and the mutual deterrence effect of 'negative' security assurances is slight.

Rapacki and Korea

The four nuclear-free zones discussed above all to a greater or lesser degree deal with countries within the southern hemisphere (to the greatest degree the Tlatelolco countries; to the least degree the Bangkok countries). Nuclear-free zones within the southern hemisphere are to nuclear-free zones in the northern hemisphere as the Antarctic is to the Arctic. That is to say, the relative concentration of the security interests of the nuclear weapons states within the northern hemisphere makes it intrinsically much less propitious territory for nuclear-free zones. Two important but failed attempts at these have nonetheless been made, 30 years apart – the Rapacki Plan and the Korean Declaration, one very much a mirror image of the other.

The Rapacki Plan was devised or at least put forward by the Polish foreign minister Adam Rapacki between 1957 and 1958 and was aimed at central Europe. The plan was that Czechoslovakia, Poland and both parts of the divided Germany should be made free of nuclear weapons. The attractive aspect of this proposal to both East and West was the creation of a nuclear-free buffer zone on the front line of the Cold War. Even if the perceived disparities in the conventional balance of forces in Europe favouring Warsaw Pact countries eventually ensured that, in the end, the proposal was too much for the West to swallow, it originally had some support on both sides of the Iron Curtain. For the UK it contained echoes of the earlier plan by British Prime Minister Anthony Eden for a demilitarised zone in central Europe, and for the Scandinavian NATO member states at least it portended a welcome de-emphasis on nuclear weapons within NATO strategy. But that the Rapacki Plan foundered on the nature of security balances outwith the actual zone of the proposed plan is simply evidence that the zone itself did not meet the security complex test.

The Korean Joint Declaration of 1992 on the denuclearisation of the peninsula is from the Rapacki mould and, indeed, is a curious Asian mirror image, with updated features, of the earlier proposal for central Europe. The suggestion that the two halves of Korea should become a nuclear-free zone came from the South Korean government in 1990. With the ending of the Cold War, even if this event was more clearly to be discerned in Europe than in Asia, the revision of US thinking on the forward basing of its tactical nuclear weapons had enabled the South Koreans to state that their end of the peninsula was free of nuclear weapons, and to propose the denuclearisation of the whole peninsula. Talks began between the two Koreas in 1990 and resulted in the Joint Declaration on the Denuclearisation of the Korean Peninsula, which officially entered into force in 1992. This short document (its English version amounts to only one side of A4)[18] speaks of the establishment of a control commission to carry out inspections in North and South Korea of unspecified (but presumably nuclear-related) facilities, and quite remarkably completely bans either party from enriching uranium or reprocessing plutonium even for commercial purposes and under safeguards.

In the same year (1992), seven years after it had originally signed the NPT,[19] North Korea finally entered into a safeguards agreement with the IAEA, declaring the nature and whereabouts of its (by definition peaceful) nuclear sites and arranging for their initial and subsequent inspections.

Like the Rapacki Plan, the Korean Declaration had some appeal for both sides in which we must include the USA and Japan on the South Korean side and China on the North side, but now the 1950s Cold War roles were reversed. A nuclear-free Korea would again mean highlighting the balance of conventional forces in a strategically significant area. At this stage in the north-east Asian theatre of the Cold War, it was now the West that stood to benefit strategically.

At any rate, North Korea almost immediately began to signal a change of heart. The first IAEA inspection under the NPT found anomalies in the material accounts which suggested, at a minimum, that North Korea had not declared to the Vienna Agency the whereabouts of all its nuclear plant. Pyongyang protested (too much, it was widely thought) in 1993 by threatening to withdraw from the NPT. The situation was brought partially back under control in 1994 by the creation of the US-sponsored KEDO (see Chapter 1), which undertook to make aid available to ease the chronic energy shortage in the North, in exchange for the North agreeing: to abandon a nominally peaceful commercial nuclear energy programme that threatened to produce large quantities of weapons-grade plutonium as a by-product, to accept IAEA safeguards within the NPT and to take steps to implement the 1992 Joint Declaration on the Korean nuclear-free zone.[20] Funding for KEDO comes from Seoul, Japan and the EU. But for every two steps forward, the North continues to take at least one step back (see Chapter 1) and the Joint Declaration is yet to be implemented.

In the context of the present chapter the trouble with the Korean Joint Declaration was not that it did not attempt a job of work. Nor was the problem even a lack of recessed deterrence possibilities – a South Korean bomb programme in retaliation for a North Korean one is certainly not something the North Koreans themselves would necessarily bet against. The South had openly explored the bomb option in the 1970s, and the question of missiles as delivery systems, before Seoul was eventually corralled within the NPT as a result of US pressure. Nor evidently was verification a difficulty. The trouble was simply that the Declaration did not deal with a security complex; nor did it deal with states that had established some historical ability to solve the security dilemma between themselves. Evidence of the absence of arms race behaviour was not apparent. As we have seen, we should expect such an unfavourable situation for a nuclear-free zone to be reflected in unusually high defence expenditures, by international standards, relative to the wealth of the countries concerned. Reliable data on defence expenditure show that in 2002 North Korea was spending 25 per cent of its gross domestic product on defence and South Korea 2.8 per cent (the global average for the year, or the NATO average, which is much the same thing, was 2.6 per cent).[21] In 1992 the North Korean effort was slightly less and that of the South somewhat greater.

End-point

A successful nuclear non-proliferation treaty ought to resemble a successful nuclear-free zone, writ large. Certainly there is no problem concerning the identity of the reach of the NPT and the security complex incorporating the states concerned (but see Chapter 2). And it is reasonable to expect that even the NPT would benefit from a comparatively low level of global defence expenditures. That the slide in the global average of defence expenditure as a proportion of gross domestic product from 6.2 per cent in 1985 to 2.6 per cent in 2002 was accompanied by the successful negotiation in 1995 of the indefinite extension of the NPT on the expiry of its first 25 years, and the 50 per cent increase in treaty membership over the same period (to near saturation point), may not be a complete coincidence. However, the inclusion of the world's largest powers, whether along the military or economic dimension, within the NPT produces a feature largely absent from nuclear-free zones – the possibility of hegemony or leadership on the part of the bigger member states and the employment by these states of various carrots and sticks to herd smaller states within the confines of the treaty.

The future of nuclear-free zones is uncertain, even problematic. The southern hemisphere, where zone creation was easiest, at least during the Cold War years and for a time afterwards, is now saturated. The northern hemisphere now houses seven declared nuclear powers, itself an obstacle to the emergence of new nuclear-free zones. At the same time, there is a reorientation of strategic concerns on the part of some nuclear powers towards the consequences for their security of weak or failing states, which lie predominantly in the southern hemisphere. Projecting their military power into such areas may not overtly involve nuclear weapons, particularly where peace-making or nation-building enterprises are being carried out, but it would be unusual for major military deployments anywhere to be unaccompanied by a reserve stock of nuclear weapons in case of an unexpected escalation of the conflict in question.

Annex. Euratom

One curious hybrid arrangement superficially reminiscent of a nuclear-free zone and the NPT but different from both is the European Atomic Energy Community or Euratom, set up under the Treaty of Rome. Every member state of what is now the EU, nuclear or non-nuclear, has been required since Euratom's inception in 1957 to open its non-military nuclear activities to international inspection conducted by Euratom's own inspectors. From the beginning, Euratom had both international and transnational elements. The former were as might be found in any miniature version of the IAEA safeguards apparatus under the NPT, except that even from the start there was no freedom from inspection for the civil nuclear installations on the territory of nuclear weapons states. Thus France was a Euratom member from the beginning but tested its first nuclear weapon in 1960. At the same time Euratom had transnational elements too, in the sense that its dealings were directly with the operators and management of nuclear plants, not with governments, and it was blind to the nationality of inspectors, so that German inspectors (or rather Euratom inspectors of German nationality) could in practice inspect German plants. As a transnational operation it does for EU states what the French government, say, does for France, with regular inspections directed from Paris of French civil nuclear plants to ensure that the whereabouts and movement of fissile and related materials within the large French commercial nuclear programme are fully accounted for.

Euratom's actual on-site inspection procedures tend to be at least as robust as those of the IAEA. Euratom interests itself in more of the fuel cycle than does the IAEA and concerns itself even with movements of uranium ore. Interestingly, Euratom operates tighter standards concerning how much 'missing' fissile material can be tolerated as MUF (see Chapter 3), and has powers to impound material apparently in excess of what may be accounted for by the host facility. The dual nature of Euratom reflected the unusual nature of relations between the member states – still sovereign but at the same time embarked on a long and still unique experiment for the dilution and merging of their sovereignty. For this reason it was never possible properly to see in Euratom a model for the regional nuclear-free zones discussed above. And at the same time it was equally difficult for non-Euratom states within the NPT to feel comfortable with the notion that Euratom inspections could substitute for those conducted by the IAEA. We have only to ask ourselves how much confidence the outside world would repose in the inspection procedures of, say, a Middle East version of Euratom for Arab states? Original Soviet suspicions of Euratom as a self-inspection scheme and an inadequate restraint on what it saw as West German nuclear ambitions helped to ensure that Euratom states party to the NPT were inspected twice: once by the IAEA and once by their own inspectorate. A minor quarrel over the status of Euratom, which the USA was initially willing to see as fully capable of acting as a proxy for the IAEA for its members,[22] was about the only NPT-related issue the Soviets and the Americans were unable to agree on.

The progressive expansion of the EU, the anomaly that Euratom member states unlike any other NPT parties were actually inspected twice, and the fact that they were of course paying for this privilege, produced an early attempt to rationalise relations between Euratom and the Vienna Agency. In 1977, under INFCIRC/193, an agreement was reached on paper that seemed to indicate that Euratom could become for its member states a sort of subcontractor to the IAEA, with Euratom doing the verification work on the ground and the IAEA verifying that Euratom had done its work properly. In practice this did not happen and duplication of effort continued. Part of the explanation may have lain in the Cold War and a west European wish not to seem to surrender to Soviet preferences in this matter any more than they could help, since a subcontractor does not normally have the prestige of a main contractor. But persistent uneasiness at the blatant waste of resources involved and a change in the general political climate meant a new attack on the problem in 1992. In that year Euratom and the IAEA agreed the 'New Partnership Approach' in a fresh attempt to make INFCIRC/193 work better.[23] But, again, rather less progress seems to have been achieved than was hoped for. The 'one job, one person' theme of the New Partnership Approach, which simply means that actual inspections should not be duplicated by the two bodies, seems to have been only partially implemented. Thus an inspection requiring two inspector-days might see one inspector from each body sharing the work evenly, but an inspection requiring one inspector-day posed the apparently awkward question as to which body should provide the inspector. Even less seems to have been achieved in areas outside the rather uninteresting inspection of (relatively proliferation-proof) reactors. Moreover, it seems to have been implemented on a one-way basis. The IAEA seems to have had no problem 'trusting' Euratom to sponsor inspection of a given nuclear facility falling under the rubric, but Euratom seems to have faced constitutional difficulties at the level of Brussels in always 'trusting' the IAEA to provide the 'one person' for the job in question. These problems at least had the silver lining that innovative ways of substituting instrumentation for human inspectors were encouraged as a possible way out of these political difficulties. Even so, and not surprisingly, by 2003 there were complaints that the New Partnership Approach seemed to have saved the IAEA money but Euratom less so.[24]

By the late 1990s, two developments suggested that a further rethink of relations between Euratom and the IAEA would be necessary. One was the impending sharp increase in the size of the EU to 25 member states, portending a steep rise in the costs of running Euratom without much in the way of additional resources to meet these costs, given the relative weakness of the economies of the new members. The other was the revision of thinking at the IAEA subsequent to the alarms created by the discovery, in the aftermath of the first Gulf War, of Iraq's secret bomb programme. This led to the emergence of the Additional Protocol and integrated safeguards, to which NPT parties individually and collectively under INFCIRC/193 are expected to sign up (see Chapter 3). The gist of the Additional Protocol is that more intrusive inspection (such as unannounced or 'surprise' inspections) may be traded for less frequent inspections of at least some types of facility, provided the Agency receives compensation in the form of good general levels of information concerning a state's commercial nuclear programme as a whole. In practice this will tend to mean a lower level of actual inspection activity than at present obtains in those parts of the world with mature commercial nuclear programmes, such as the Euratom membership.

The net result of the coming into force for EU states of the Additional Protocol and integrated safeguards, and the looming costs of extending Euratom procedures undiminished to cover the whole 25-state membership of the EU in May 2004, was for Euratom to decide to accept a smaller role for itself in the future compared with the Agency. Euratom will take no part in the positive implementation of the Additional Protocol and, in particular, unannounced inspections will be left entirely to the IAEA.

But Euratom will at the same time go along with the reduced frequency of traditional inspections likely to accompany the implementation of the Additional Protocol for the countries of the EU. This is not only expediency. The report to the European Commission in 2003 on the future of Euratom (from the High Level Experts Group) advised that Euratom in future should comport itself less like the IAEA and move away from considering European operators of nuclear plants as potential 'diverters' of nuclear materials from peaceful to military uses.[25] Whereas the operating model for Euratom had always been, as we have already indicated, somewhere between the IAEA safeguards division and the French national system for ensuring French nuclear facilities are run on a basis of proper accounting for nuclear materials, the pendulum has now swung towards the latter. This indicates a belief that the widening of the membership of the EU is not seen, in nuclear matters at any rate, to be inconsistent with a 'deepening' of the nature of the Union.

Notes

1. Treaty for the Prohibition of Nuclear Weapons in Latin America, opened for signature in 1967.
2. For the text see *Arms Control and Disarmament Agreements: Texts and Histories of the Negotiations* (Washington, DC, US Arms Control and Disarmament Agency, 1990).
3. Treaty on the Principles Governing the Activities of States in the Exploration and Use of Outer Space, including the Moon and Other Celestial Bodies. For text see *Arms Control and Disarmament Agreements*.
4. See Michael Krepon and Christopher Clary, *Space Assurance or Space Dominance? The Case Against Weaponizing Space* (Washington, DC, Henry L. Stimson Center, 2003), p. 108.
5. Treaty on the Prohibition of the Emplacement of Nuclear Weapons and Other Weapons of Mass Destruction on the Seabed and the Ocean Floor and in the Subsoil Thereof. For text see *Arms Control and Disarmament Agreements*.
6. For the text see Appendix D.
7. Jozef Goldblat, 'Nuclear weapon free zones', *Nonproliferation Review*, Vol. 4, No. 3, spring/summer 1997, p. 20.
8. Julio C. Carasales, 'The Argentine–Brazil nuclear rapprochement', *Nonproliferation Review*, Vol. 2, No. 3, spring/summer 1995, p. 42.
9. *The Military Balance 2003–2004* (Oxford, Oxford University Press for the International Institute for Strategic Studies, 2003).
10. For the text see David Fischer, *Towards 1995: The Prospects for Ending the Proliferation of Nuclear Weapons* (Aldershot, Dartmouth Publishing Co. for the United Nations Institute for Disarmament Research, 1993), pp. 271–82.
11. For the text see www.armscontrol.org/documents/pelindaba.asp (last accessed 10 July 2005).

12 *Trust and Verify*, No. 112 (London, Verification Research, Training and Information Centre, January/February 2004). Libya had already been confronted with Western intelligence, some of it made available to the IAEA, accurately detailing its secret nuclear programme. See *Review of Intelligence on Weapons of Mass Destruction*, Report of a Committee of Privy Councillors, Chairman Lord Butler, HC 898 (London, The Stationery Office, 2004) (henceforth the Butler report), p. 21.
13 David Albright, Frans Berkhout and William Walker, *Plutonium and Highly Enriched Uranium 1996: World Inventories, Capabilities and Policies* (Oxford, Oxford University Press for the Stockholm Peace Research Institute, 1997), p. 363.
14 Goldblat, 'Nuclear weapon free zones', p. 25.
15 For the text see www.aseansec.org/2082.htm (last accessed 10 July 2005).
16 Joined in 1995 by Vietnam, in 1997 by Laos and Myanmar (Burma) and in 1999 by Cambodia.
17 Jan Priest of the IAEA describes Bangkok as having taken the Vienna Agency by surprise. See the Carnegie Endowment Non-Proliferation Project website text of her paper on nuclear-free zones read to the Carnegie-sponsored 1996 conference Non-proliferation and the Millennium, at www.ceip.org/files/events/Conf96IAEA.asp?p=8 (last accessed 11 April 2005).
18 The English version of the text is reproduced in Appendix E.
19 Perhaps surprisingly, seven years is not an unusually long time for NPT states to complete their negotiations with the IAEA, but it is unusually long for a state, like North Korea, with facilities requiring inspection on its territory.
20 If North Korea accepted the Joint Declaration with its suggested verified ban on all reprocessing of nuclear fuel, it is hard to see why it also has to tear up its plans for nuclear power and replace them with the KEDO version.
21 *The Military Balance 2003–2004*, pp. 335, 340.
22 Fischer, *Towards 1995*, p. 241.
23 K. Murakami, G. Zuccaro-Labellarte, L. Bevaart and A. Tolba, *Beyond NPA and Toward Integrated Safeguards in Countries of the European Union*, IAEA-SM-367/11/07 (Vienna, IAEA, 2001).
24 S. Tsalas, U. Blohm-Hieber, K. Martin, S. Synetos, R. Clarke and F. MacLean, *The New Orientation of Euratom Safeguards* (Phoenix, AZ, Institute of Nuclear Materials Management, 2003).
25 Tsalas *et al.*, *The New Orientation of Euratom Safeguards*.

5

United States policy on non-proliferation and the Nuclear Non-proliferation Treaty

The history of the attitude of the United States towards the spread of nuclear weapons has been one of continuous opposition, tempered now and then by the judgement of the government of the day as to whether in particular instances the exigencies of the moment outweighed the force of the general principle.

From Baruch to Eisenhower

The starting point or the rough first draft for the US policy of hostility towards the spread of nuclear weapons is the Baruch Plan, presented in 1946 to the newly created UN Atomic Energy Commission by the US representative on the Commission, Bernard M. Baruch. At least it is taken to be so in the present chapter for heuristic purposes (and is reproduced in Appendix A). It is not suggested that US policy makers in practice have ever since turned to the Baruch Plan for guidance, any more than the US foreign policy establishment has kept the Kennan 'long telegram' of the same year constantly at their elbows (see below). But the heuristic value of interpreting US Cold War policies through the lens of the Kennan document is well established, and there is reason to think that the Baruch Plan can do similar service for the understanding of US non-proliferation policy.

The Baruch Plan aimed to harmonise an anticipated widespread international interest in the use of nuclear energy for peaceful purposes – the production of electrical power and the production of radioactive substances in relatively small quantities as therapeutic or tracer elements for medical or industrial applications – with a US-inspired closing of the door everywhere to the production of nuclear weapons. The Plan envisaged the creation of an international atomic development authority that would itself largely monopolise 'dangerous' activities in the area of nuclear energy and act as a licensing and inspecting body for activities, of a less dangerous kind by and large, which would be carried out essentially by, and on the territory of, UN member states. 'Dangerous' activities referred to those stages in even the most innocent programmes for the commercial exploitation of nuclear energy involving the production or separation of either highly enriched uranium or plutonium-239, each directly usable as material for a nuclear bomb. Either of these fissionable materials was seen as a by-product of nuclear power generation, but any produced in pure form could just as easily be used and in comparatively small (kilogram) amounts to form the cores (or pits) of nuclear weapons (as we have seen in Chapter 1). The Plan also envisaged a halt to the manufacture of nuclear weapons, and the disposing of existing bombs, once the international convention envisaged by (and incorporating) the Plan was in force. At the time, of course, the only acknowledged bomb programme or bomb stockpile belonged to the USA itself.

There were two key differences between the Plan as presented to the UN and the earlier attempts by the US government to elaborate schemes for the international control of nuclear energy. The Acheson–Lilienthal report,[1] commissioned by the State Department and made public ahead of the Baruch Plan, had taken a stronger view of the necessity of keeping all 'dangerous' processes and materials centrally under the wing of the international atomic development authority, with less willingness to rely on licensing and inspecting by the authority to ensure that no warlike diversions of fissionable material were occurring at the national level. And at the same time, the Baruch Plan ensured its unacceptability to international opinion, in the view of Dean Acheson, then US Undersecretary of State[2] and co-chairman of the committee that produced of the Acheson–Lilienthal report, by its insistence on specifying that states caught breaking the rules envisaged by the Plan concerning the manufacture and use of dangerous materials would be subject to 'immediate and certain' punishment (up to and including armed attack, it was presumed), concerning the application of which the operation of the veto within the UN Security Council would not apply.

There were a number of reasons why the Baruch Plan failed. There was plainly disagreement within the US administration over details of the Plan itself. We have noted Acheson's scepticism. And it is hard to see the Baruch Plan fitting in with Kennan's long telegram advice that there was no point seeking a *modus vivendi* with the Soviets. Even without Baruch's insistence on the punishment clauses, Stalin's Moscow 'election' speech of February 1946 seemed to show that the USSR, now known at the time already to be working on a bomb of its own, had no faith in the prospect of a peaceful international order. Stalin's claim that the same forces which had caused the recent war were still in control abroad and the hostile tone of the speech overall prompted Washington to ask its chargé d'affaires in Moscow, George Kennan, for a clarification of the likely direction of Soviet foreign policy. And this took the form of the 'long telegram'. Elsewhere, the British Attlee government was swiftly being made aware that the close wartime cooperation with the USA in nuclear energy matters, military and civilian, was being swept away. The McMahon Bill had already passed through all its stages at the time of Baruch's speech to the UN (it became an Act in August 1946), and it provided for an energetically patrolled fence of secrecy to be erected around all US work in the nuclear field, with the British along with everyone else placed on the other side of the fence. With two of the 'Big Three' of the time thus put on their guard, the USSR by the wording of the Plan itself and the British as much by the signs of extremism in US non-proliferation policy, it is not surprising that it foundered.

This is not to say that the whole episode was doomed. A contemporary disinterested observer, Bertrand Russell, who understood the technicalities of nuclear energy, praised the Plan as wise and generous,[3] and found Stalin too suspicious for the good of the USSR, which Russell felt had nothing to lose from the Baruch Plan (in view of the regional superiority in conventional arms enjoyed by the Soviets in Cold War Europe, this is not an unreasonable suggestion). Indeed, Russell's enthusiasm for the scheme led him to advocate that nuclear threats be used to force Moscow to accept the Plan. Certainly the USA had nothing to lose from the Baruch Plan. Were the whole to be carried through, while the USA would be required to disband its nuclear force (small at the time, perhaps a dozen actual bombs) and place its nuclear reactors and uranium enrichment plants and plutonium separation plants at least in part under international control, it would still be in a recessed deterrent position. In the event of the Baruch arrangements failing, the USA would be able rapidly to reacquire nuclear weapons, as it would retain something like a monopoly of understanding and know-how concerning their manufacture. This fact by itself would have had a deterrent effect on other states contemplating violating the principles of the Plan, at least in its earlier stages. This *realpolitik* aspect of the Plan is an important aspect but not the only one. The utopian theme of the Plan, with the envisaged abolition of nuclear weapons, has also resonated over the years, if more infrequently, in US thinking. Perhaps it peaked with the nuclear abolition proposals of the Reagan presidency when, in 1986, at the Reykjavik summit, the United States proposed the complete elimination of all ballistic missiles by 1996, provided the Soviets agreed that US work on defensive missiles could proceed unhampered (this the Soviets were unprepared, in the end, to agree to).

US policy on non-proliferation and the NPT 129

The Baruch Plan helped set the agenda for US anti-nuclear proliferation policy for the rest of the century and beyond. The tug of war between Baruch and Acheson over central control of dangerous activities and devolved control accompanied by inspection to ensure there was no diversion of fissile materials to military purposes persists to the present day, albeit in a modified form.[4] Devolved control over nuclear energy is the core philosophy of the 1970 NPT, with national programmes submitting to international inspection. But almost from the start, the freedom of non-nuclear signatory states to the treaty to develop nuclear energy at their own pace, subject to international inspection, was compromised by the Zangger Committee. Set up in 1971, this was an ad hoc group of those states in a position to manufacture and export dangerous activities in the Baruch sense (now, in more euphemistic times, 'sensitive' stood in for 'dangerous'). Its remit was to look into the possibility of restricting such exports. These states were themselves regarded as safe because they were either already nuclear weapons states or non-nuclear states with little motivation to go nuclear. In the beginning this was wholly innocent and fully in line with the NPT itself (Article 3) and designed to clarify what sub-paragraph 2 of this Article meant for nuclear exporting states with its reference to the export of equipment capable of producing enriched uranium or plutonium, and the necessity for safeguards in the form of IAEA inspections to be attached to such transfers. The Zangger Committee did not change character until after the Indian demonstration nuclear test of 1974, and the oil supply crisis of the time, which was widely expected to stimulate a new wave of interest in nuclear energy throughout the world (mistakenly, in the end), when it became the London Exporters' Club and then the NSG. In the beginning, although nothing to do with the IAEA (the body charged with inspecting national nuclear programmes under the NPT), and rather too secretive, the NSG supplemented the NPT without breaching the core philosophy of the NPT of devolved control. Where it did arouse early suspicions in the rest of the world was in its potential – as a suppliers' group – to become a sort of economic cartel in the supply of peaceful nuclear energy equipment and material. US policy was to have the NSG ratify a rule that exports of any on a list (the so-called trigger list) of sensitive materials and activities to states that had *not* signed the NPT would be permitted only if the recipient states agreed to have ongoing IAEA inspections made, not only of what they had just purchased from the NSG member, as was standard practice, but also of all their nuclear activities ('full-scope safeguards'). In this the USA was not entirely successful. The NSG gave up regular meetings of all its member states after 1977 (when it last met as the London Club, and not meeting again as a whole until 1991), with European supplier states resisting full-scope safeguards until 1992, on the grounds that importing states (e.g. India and Pakistan) that disliked the policy would turn to domestic or black market international sources of the technology instead, and nothing of their programmes would be inspected. However, since the end of the Cold War, and the discovery of the extent of Iraq's secret nuclear programme after the 1991 Gulf War, the old Acheson–Lilienthal idea that states or at any rate certain states simply could not be trusted with sensitive activities, however much inspection there was and whether or not (we should now say) they were party to the NPT, has returned. The freedom of North Korea or Iran – both party to the treaty – to pursue nuclear energy projects of their own choosing, subject to international inspection, has been circumscribed by US-backed attempts with varying degrees of international support to deny these states access to sensitive activities and projects. And even the vexed Baruch notion of severe punishment for states offending against non-proliferation norms arguably found expression in the 2003 US-led invasion of Iraq.

The Baruch Plan also prefigured the debate as to which nuclear energy-related activities were to be deemed sensitive and which safe. The Plan insisted there was a difference, but conceded that the dividing line could not be drawn with complete certainty. Is the production of heavy water 'dangerous' in the Baruch sense? At the time of Baruch, heavy water was widely seen as almost essential as a moderator for nuclear power plants fuelled using natural uranium, but since then such power plants have become widely perceived as commercially unattractive sources of electrical power and are now more closely associated with the production of weapons-grade plutonium. Heavy water has simply become less safe or more sensitive over time. Indeed, the designation 'weapons-grade' itself suggests that plutonium is safer in some forms than in others. The US Clinton administration felt North Korea to be a better member state of the NPT for its having agreed, under pressure, to base its nuclear power programme on light-water reactors rather than on heavy-water types (under the 1994 Agreed Framework). Light-water reactors when run normally produce plutonium containing a relatively high proportion of the unwanted isotope plutonium-240, which makes its use in bombs more difficult. But the US Carter administration was earlier more purist about plutonium and drew Baruch's dividing line in a different place. It sought to have the separation of all plutonium from used nuclear fuel from commercial reactors to be classified as a sensitive activity, which it was willing to see the USA itself abandon. It sponsored an international initiative (the INFCE programme, which reported in 1980[5]) to test support for its views regarding the separation of plutonium and its belief that it was too sensitive and that there was no commercial justification anywhere for extracting it from spent fuel. In spite of Washington making Baruch-like noises about a willingness to sponsor an international bank of nuclear fuel to assuage countries that felt a need for plutonium to supplement their meagre reserves of uranium fuel, little was achieved in the face of European scepticism.

The Baruch Plan can also be credited with putting back on the international agenda a subject that had lain essentially dormant since the 1920s. In spite of the fact, perhaps surprising in retrospect, that chemical and biological weapons had not been employed by either side in the course of the recently ended world war, even if most of the warring states fully anticipated they would be used, Baruch in effect drew attention to the futility of expecting states to abandon interest in the military uses of nuclear energy if nothing was done about the proliferation of other weapons of mass destruction (to use modern terminology). Subsequently, attempts to control the spread of nuclear weapons have been accompanied, often in different forums and operating at different tempi, by attempts to control, indeed to the point of banning entirely, chemical and biological weapons. The Chemical Weapons Convention, which bans the manufacture, possession and use of chemical weapons, was negotiated in 1994. The Biological Weapons Convention, which entered into force in 1975, aimed to do the same for biological weapons but contained no provision for inspection at all and is widely seen, except perhaps in the USA itself, as requiring modification in this respect. And since 1985, ballistic and other guided missiles beyond battlefield range have been assigned a *de facto* status as new weapons of mass destruction, with their proliferation subject to control by the Missile Technology Control Regime (MTCR), which is to missiles what the NSG is to nuclear technology, with the difference that the MTCR does without the equivalent of the NPT (and the moral authority that goes with it).

Atoms for Peace

The failure of the Baruch Plan as practical politics and the setting in of the Cold War, with the first Soviet nuclear test in 1949 and the Soviet-abetted invasion of South Korea by the North in the following year, saw US anti-proliferation policies temporarily retreat to what could be done without international agreement – namely domestic measures. These were not new: they had already been enshrined in the McMahon Act of 1946. Secrecy, fortified by the probability that a failure to guard the 'secrets' of the wartime bomb programme well enough had contributed to the early success of the Soviet bomb programme via the machinations of the British physicist and Soviet spy Klaus Fuchs, became the chief defence against the emergence of new nuclear states.

But the end of the Korean War and the death of Stalin, together with signs from the new leadership in Moscow that they were keen to see some easing in East–West relations,[6] plus a realisation that secrecy was a dwindling asset with the UK elbowing its way into the nuclear club in 1952, saw the Eisenhower administration take a new anti-proliferation initiative at the end of 1953. The initiative became known as Atoms for Peace and was presented by Eisenhower in a speech to the UN General Assembly (see Appendix B). It was much more modest than the Baruch Plan, but borrowed a key idea from it. This was the creation of an international atomic energy body – to be called the International Atomic Energy Agency – whose task was to bring under its wing (i.e. under international control) what Baruch had called 'dangerous' materials, while at the same time promoting the peaceful uses of nuclear energy internationally. In fact, Atoms for Peace included natural uranium as well as the fissionable materials enriched uranium and plutonium within the materials stockpile to be put under international control. The materials themselves were to be contributed by those states acknowledged to be in possession of national stocks, with donations to be made slowly and piecemeal at first but at a rising rate. These states obviously included the three nuclear powers of the day. The new agency, with such materials at its disposal, would become the competent authority for making available, especially to less developed countries, the then still undoubted commercial benefits of nuclear energy. Like Baruch, Eisenhower aimed to tackle both existing and potential nuclear weapons, but adopted an incremental approach. The progressive transfer to international control of fissionable materials, the raw materials of not only atomic weapons but also of the newer thermonuclear weapons too, would at a minimum slow down the rate of accumulation of nuclear weapons by the already acknowledged nuclear states and perhaps remove an arms-race-driven stimulus to that accumulation as well. And, presumably (Eisenhower's speech was brief, at least in its substantive elements, with details supposed to be filled in later as a result of discussions between those principally involved), Atoms for Peace would do something to prevent the production of sensitive materials elsewhere by making them available from central stocks in support of approved nuclear energy projects in various parts of the world. Production that was nonetheless undertaken at a national level would presumably announce itself at some point before completion and would be difficult to explain away on grounds that it was part of a programme of economic development.

Eisenhower felt that his proposals had the edge over Baruch in that the question of safeguarding national nuclear activities against the diversion of materials to weapons programmes, using international inspection, did not arise, or at least not very acutely. He saw the requirement for inspection as one reason for Baruch's failure, because of the 'irritations and mutual suspicions' setting up such a scheme would inflict on the states involved (not for Acheson's reason that it could not be relied on).

While the Baruch Plan, as we maintain, can be thought of as a blueprint for future US anti-proliferation policy, its immediate practical impact was virtually zero. A possible exception was that its failure to have an impact in the sense of actually establishing a system of international control of nuclear energy removed any doubts in the UK about proceeding on a national basis to develop nuclear weapons. Atoms for Peace on the other hand did leave a tangible legacy, but one that has been widely regarded as counter-productive.[7] Critics seem more or less to have taken their cue from the original private Soviet criticism of Atoms for Peace, that sharing peaceful nuclear technology would only increase the world's ability to make bombs.[8] The basis for this judgement arises from the nature of the legacy. The International Atomic Energy Agency mooted by Eisenhower was indeed set up, and came into formal existence in 1957 as an agency of the UN and based in Vienna. In addition, steps were indeed taken to make the economic and developmental benefits of nuclear energy more widely available on a global scale, by both the USA and the USSR. However, no agreement was reached on the mooted contributions of fissile materials to the Agency, and the dissemination of nuclear technology for peaceful purposes around the world became a matter of the USA and the USSR acting unilaterally and often competitively in the pursuit of Cold War objectives, with the Vienna Agency virtually redundant (and the Soviets nothing daunted by their own warning of the dangers of dissemination, especially with regard to their close ally at the time, the People's Republic of China). This meant that half of Eisenhower's scheme was realised, in that many countries were given, at low cost, 'hands-on' experience of nuclear technology, usually in the form of a donated small nuclear research reactor of some kind, too small to produce plutonium at the sort of rate normally necessary to support a weapons programme. But this was the polar opposite of the old 'secrecy' policy, and introduced many countries to practical and theoretical aspects of nuclear technology years ahead of what might have otherwise been the case. Moreover, the other half of Eisenhower's proposal, the international pool of fissile materials, which promised the placing of sensitive activities and materials under international control and which might have defused most of the actual proliferation dangers arising from the widespread dissemination of nuclear technology that was under way, as we have seen, got almost nowhere. Vestiges of it can be seen, however, in the statute of the IAEA, where it is granted the right to ask governments to place in its safe-keeping deposits of plutonium (in separated form) and enriched uranium to prevent national stockpiling of these dangerous materials.[9] This right has so far never been exercised, but has reappeared on the agenda of the Agency in the context of its possibly acquiring responsibility for safeguarding surplus fissile material emerging in Russia and the USA, with the ending of the Cold War.

But as with all things associated with the Eisenhower presidency, maybe a little revisionism is in order, even for Atoms for Peace.

To begin with, concerning the problem of then current weapons stockpiles, the Eisenhower plan for limiting access by nuclear states to fissile materials via a system of deposits of such materials placed in a central store was quickly developed by the Americans into an idea for a monitored halt to production of such materials for military purposes – the so-called 'fissile material cut-off' proposal. This proposal remains alive in the run-up to the 2005 review conference of the NPT. It was essentially an updating of the disarmament part of the Baruch Plan to allow for a fundamental change in circumstances in the 10 years since the Plan had been presented. The build-up of nuclear weapons stockpiles over that period, mainly in the USA and the USSR, meant that proposals for total nuclear disarmament along Baruch lines, however they were to be phased in, faced a new problem. What was to prevent a state with nuclear weapons holding back and concealing a small number while offering up the rest? No amount of inspection, however intrusive, could be certain of uncovering the hidden weapons. The original cut-off proposal recognises this difficulty and envisages (at least tacitly) that complete nuclear disarmament should not be aimed for, but that instead some low level of nuclear weapons could be retained by agreement, but with a ban on this number being added to. Verifying this ban would be comparatively simple, since while concealing complete weapons may be easy, concealing complete places for the production of new fissile material is less so. We return to this question again when we consider the modern version of the cut-off proposal.

Secondly, the dissemination under Atoms for Peace of basic nuclear technology throughout the world by the combined but neither coordinated nor regulated efforts of the USA and the USSR pre-empted at least some purely national programmes, over which the USA or other external powers would otherwise have had very little control. As it was, countries receiving US nuclear technology under Atoms for Peace would normally need to refer back to the USA for supplies of fuel or replacement components. Consequently, this would allow the USA indirectly to determine how far the technology was being used for peaceful purposes and how far not, with an opportunity to do something about it in the latter case. Where the recipient states concerned were so far behind in nuclear technology in terms of domestic expertise that pre-emption of possible national programmes could hardly apply, the transferred technology would wither on the vine (as happened in the case of nuclear facilities transferred to Indonesia by the USSR). It would only rarely be the case that the technology transferred initiated a flurry of interest in nuclear programmes that would not otherwise have occurred, or not for years. Admittedly, this opportunity to contain proliferation by the back door will have been true only for the USA. It is less clear that the Soviets at this stage (or indeed at any later stage) had any very firm views either way about the dangers of nuclear spread, or for that matter France or other developed states that were now taking an interest in nuclear technology for themselves, for peaceful or other purposes, and were standing ready to enter the export market.

Finally, it can also be said of Atoms for Peace that in certain circumstances there can be something self-limiting about nuclear spread. A state that was anxious about its security in a conventional setting, while nonetheless enjoying a position of relative strength with regard to its regional rivals, might capitalise on this strength to develop its own nuclear weapons. It would be less likely to do this, or less likely to do it openly at least, if it believed that even its weaker rivals might be able simply to follow suit by building on the technology that had been transferred to them under Atoms for Peace.[10] This would be a devolved version (in weaker form, it is true) of the recessed deterrence that the USA would have possessed in a world where the Baruch Plan had actually been implemented.

The Partial Test Ban Treaty and the Nuclear Non-proliferation Treaty

The false dawn of the possibility of US–Soviet cooperation on the problem of nuclear spread that accompanied the death of Stalin and encouraged Eisenhower to make his Atoms for Peace proposal was succeeded by a decade of superpower arms racing and a period when, under Eisenhower, national US security policy in particular became increasingly nuclear-orientated. Neither feature did anything to reduce interest in nuclear weapons in the rest of the world.

The Cuban missile crisis of 1962 marked the starting point of a shift in the direction of superpower relations towards a cautious search for agreements to slacken the pace of the nuclear arms race, which culminated 10 years later in the ABM Treaty of 1972 and a bilateral negotiated freeze on further numerical additions to their respective stocks of offensive weapons. In a different way it also triggered the first search among a set of regional powers for a way to formalise and secure their detachment from the nuclear states system, with a call from Brazil at the UN actually during the Cuban missile crisis for the establishment of a nuclear-free zone for Latin America (see Chapter 4).

The first fruit of this new era in superpower relations – the era of detente – was the Partial Test Ban Treaty (PTBT) of 1963,[11] which neatly combined the sort of parallel restrictions on the nuclear states and non-nuclear states that had been a feature of both the Baruch Plan and Atoms for Peace, but in a new way. The treaty required of signatory states that they conduct all nuclear test explosions in future several hundred feet below the surface of the earth. This not only confined radioactive releases to the territory of the states concerned but also created a double hurdle in front of the acquisition of nuclear weapons. It was a hurdle for the established nuclear states in that further testing of new designs of bomb would be made inconvenient by the need to carry the tests out below ground – perhaps an insurmountable hurdle to the testing of new bombs above a certain size.[12] And it was a hurdle for potential new nuclear states in that an already problematical thing, technically speaking – their first nuclear test – would be made more problematical. At the same time, it avoided the need for the inspections Eisenhower had decried, by relying on nationally owned remote sensing techniques to detect violations. Ordinary atmospheric or seawater sampling – techniques within the competence of a large number of states – would detect the presence of any unusual amount of radioactivity. And satellite reconnaissance – at the time a US–Soviet duopoly – would pick up the characteristic double flashes of light coming from any test, anywhere, that was carried out in the atmosphere.

The treaty had an interesting international reception. It attracted signatures from almost every state of significance apart from France and China, which in the former case was pursuing active national test programmes and in the latter case was very close to doing so. India and Israel (together with all other Middle Eastern states) were among immediate subscribers to the treaty, as was virtually every state within the spheres of influence of either of the superpowers. The appeal of the treaty to a country like India, which was outside these orbits, was threefold. Partly it was to do with the absence of inspection provisions, which India tended to see as a sort of paternalistic neo-colonialism (as with the Baruch Plan). Partly it was the absence of discrimination in the terms of the treaty, which formally applied equally to nuclear and non-nuclear states alike. And thirdly, if it did wish to conduct a test, it could do so, perhaps with difficulty, inside the treaty. The treaty did not go further than it did and aim to halt underground tests too, ostensibly (but see Chapter 6) because of the technical claim that such tests could not always be reliably detected from the outside and that therefore an inspection scheme would be necessary to permit on-site verification of whether any suspect seismic activity was the result of a test or merely an earthquake. And ever since Atoms for Peace, US policy had betrayed a sensitivity to the capacity for inspection provisions to create difficulties for arms control treaties, even if the broadminded or at least diplomatic Eisenhower line that this was a universal problem had been subsequently modified for propaganda purposes in the West to make it seem as something that was a real problem only for the Soviets, with their closed society.

Apart from the matter of inspections, the treaty was a departure from the Baruch and Atoms for Peace tradition in that it made no attempt to link the question of nuclear spread with the uptake of nuclear energy for peaceful purposes. But the continued progress in detente saw a return to something like Baruch first principles with the negotiation of the NPT in 1968.[13] The treaty was negotiated bilaterally across the East–West divide, but with input from comparatively disinterested states in Cold War terms such as India and Brazil, in the forum of the Geneva Eighteen Nation Disarmament Committee.

While there had hardly been an explosion of interest in the peaceful uses of nuclear energy outside the territories of the acknowledged nuclear states themselves (now five, with France and China), by 1968 this was widely anticipated and it did occur, briefly, in the following decade of rapidly increasing oil prices. The NPT aimed to fill two of the key roles Baruch had assigned to his Plan. The idea of a central international monopoly of sensitive activities and materials was almost entirely given up, but the IAEA, under the treaty, was to be given powers to control and inspect all nuclear activities outside the territories of the nuclear weapons states themselves and to ensure that these remained purely peaceful. And these same nuclear weapons states, and other states competent in the peaceful applications of nuclear energy, were assigned the duty of fostering these peaceful applications worldwide. The other important theme of the Baruch Plan, which foresaw those already possessing and manufacturing nuclear weapons abandoning the practice and disarming themselves of them, also featured in the treaty but slightly less prominently (Article 6).[14] In addition, in tacit acknowledgement that the disarmament provisions of Article 6 were unlikely to be enacted in the near future, or, in case they were, to stop up a possible loophole, the NPT was also a non-dissemination treaty in that it prominently (Article 1) required nuclear states to abstain from transferring nuclear weapons to the control of any other state and that states should abstain from acquiring nuclear weapons in this manner. A parallel ban on lending *assistance* to other states in the acquisition of nuclear weapons was weaker, in that only non-nuclear recipients were placed within its ambit.

The NPT was initially received less well than the PTBT in two sectors. Like the PTBT, it left China and France cold, but since the main thrust of the treaty (*pace* Article 6) was directed at states currently non-nuclear, the Chinese and French attitudes had little practical effect. Of more significance was the attitude of non-nuclear states, both within and without the developed world, where it met with more suspicion than had been the case with the PTBT. The reason for this was certainly connected with the event that made the negotiation of the NPT possible in the first place – the period of detente in superpower relations. This made states on the Western side of the divide, at least, less immediately inclined to fall in behind the US position. West Germany and Italy did not ratify the treaty until 1975, and Japan not until 1976; Spain did not accede to the treaty until 1987. Even Australia withheld ratification until 1973. (Appendix C includes a table showing the dates of accession of all parties to the NPT.)

The opposition of West Germany and Japan was worded in terms that indirectly validated the assumption behind the treaty that worldwide interest in the application of nuclear energy for peaceful purposes was about to rise. Both countries were concerned that while their chief competitors in the global export market for peaceful applications of nuclear technology, as nuclear weapons states, were not obliged to submit their own commercial nuclear activities and especially their working prototypes of new kinds of nuclear installations to IAEA inspections, they, as non-nuclear states, were. They complained that, as a result, they would be put at a trade disadvantage through the commercially sensitive information concerning their peaceful nuclear programmes for home and export being put at risk of compromise by the periodic visits of IAEA inspectors from abroad.

Two 'patches' were applied to the treaty to deal with this problem. One was a system of voluntary inspections agreed between the IAEA and the nuclear states behind the treaty, whereby certain nuclear installations in the USA, the UK and the USSR which were not explicitly connected with their own nuclear weapons programmes would receive IAEA inspections. This represented a genuine advance on the original treaty, even if there was some slowness in the negotiation of these arrangements, especially on the Soviet side. The Soviets ratified such an agreement with the IAEA in 1985, and China in 1988. The USA had formally agreed in 1980 to submit certain of its nuclear activities to IAEA inspection (preceded by Britain in 1976 and followed by France in 1981). The designation of which US activities were to be covered by the agreement was to be entirely a matter for the US government, even if Washington conceded that, within the field of activity it opened to the IAEA, it would be reasonable for the Agency to concentrate on facilities of the more modern and hence commercially more sensitive kinds. If the original complaints of Germany and Japan seemed to validate Eisenhower's point in Atoms for Peace about inspections creating suspicions between states, this solution showed that by actually extending inspections this suspicion could be reduced. Further, in this particular instance, the initial actions by the three nuclear states behind the treaty had the bonus effect of encouraging France and China – at the time not even signatories of the treaty – to take steps to bring themselves into line with the other nuclear states.

The second patch showed the same could also apply in reverse – reducing inspection could increase suspicions. West Germany, along with other member states of the EU (in modern terminology) was a member state of Euratom (see Chapter 4), which was a sort of cross between the NPT (on a regional basis for EU states only) and a nuclear-free zone (of the sort that had entered into force in 1968 for Latin America). West Germany (and other EU non-nuclear states) obtained the concession that the inspections of its nuclear installations it was already required to submit to under Euratom could do service for inspections under the NPT. Its keenness to work through Euratom derived from the fact that Euratom inspection was automatically carried out on the commercial nuclear activities of *all* members of the EU, with no special privileges for the nuclear states, except that they (France and, eventually, the UK) were allowed to screen off specifically military activities. The point was conceded, but only after long negotiations and with the proviso that the IAEA validate Euratom inspection procedures (see Chapter 4).

This in itself need not have been a problem in principle, since the NPT (Article 3) specifically permits states to negotiate inspection arrangements with the IAEA as groups if so desired. But the difficulties experienced in practice in harmonising Euratom and Agency inspection procedures (for instance Euratom rules permit inspectors to be nationals of the state whose facilities they inspect) have created suspicion elsewhere. And they have prevented the establishment of a useful model for comparable arrangements in other parts of the globe, since some of the schemes used by the IAEA to validate Euratom procedures – for example the permanent joint inspection teams at large sensitive facilities such as the British reactor fuel reprocessing facility at Sellafield in north-west England – appear to absorb a disproportionately large fraction of total IAEA inspection resources.[15]

The difficulties over Euratom were early evidence of what was to become a discernible fault line running through relations between the USA and Western Europe concerning the NPT and related arrangements. The reason for this is that while the period of East–West detente was essentially over by 1979, and its ending put *bilateral* arms control between the superpowers under a cloud, the same was not true of the NPT. The deterioration in superpower relations did not extend to the NPT, possibly because it was so important to the USA that it strived to prevent this happening, possibly helped by the fact that the Soviets were never able to take a strong view on the subject. At any rate, US non-proliferation policy was never challenged by the Soviets. Correspondingly, this gave an unusual licence to US allies to take issue with the USA over non-proliferation matters without seeming to give aid and comfort to the Soviets, even as the Cold War entered its second phase. But fundamentally the transatlantic problems arose and have never quite vanished because the cooperation between these states required for the NPT to work clashed with the competition between states in their eagerness to market nuclear technology for peaceful purposes worldwide. Economic competition between Western Europe and the USA was a fact of life in the way that economic competition between the USSR and the USA was not. Of course, those states sharing responsibility for the creation and policing of a relatively non-nuclear world were almost certain to disagree over how to apportion the costs of this enterprise, direct and indirect, between them. Their joint endeavours were vulnerable to free riding, as each sought to pass the costs of policing to the others.

An ostensibly equivalent IAEA validation of Japan's domestic inspection arrangements was also agreed, the Japanese equivalent of Euratom being a Japanese national nuclear inspectorate held to be independent of the Japanese government. Again, the reproducibility of such an arrangement elsewhere and its usefulness as a precedent are doubtful. For one thing, comparatively few societies are pluralistic enough to make the notion of an independent national nuclear inspectorate half-way credible. Only Japan's unique status as a country 'allergic' to nuclear weapons prevented the deal with the IAEA being seen as the sort of special treatment likely to arouse international suspicions that Japan was essentially inspecting itself. And yet there is nothing to suggest that it has not been effective (except perhaps that Japanese standards of safety at its nuclear plants may not be up to the international norms that the IAEA also promotes) and, unlike the Euratom arrangements, it is plainly comparatively economical in its use of scarce IAEA inspection resources.[16]

The bargains

It is misleading to think of the NPT solely in terms of the original and tacit Baruch bargain (now made explicit under Article 6 of the treaty): namely, if non-nuclear states curb their interest in acquiring nuclear weapons, this will be reciprocated by states already possessing them giving them up (and in that order). This did not prevent an alleged failure by the nuclear states to meet their end of that bargain becoming the rallying cry for discontent with the treaty at its 2000 review conference. (On the review conferences, see the section 'Bargains barometer', below.)

The network of bargains necessary to achieve Baruch-like ends in a world with a much more widely disseminated expertise in peaceful and military nuclear technology than was the case in 1946 must be correspondingly more complex. Like all worthwhile arms control treaties the NPT stands in constant risk of failure and this risk is represented by the degree of tension that exists in the structure of bargains that lies behind it.

Very simply, to take the Baruch bargain first: nuclear weapons states that are party to the treaty might meet their end of it by substantial though partial acts of disarmament, but total nuclear disarmament must be ruled out, whatever Article 6 says, for two reasons: first, because of the impossible demands it would make on verification, already referred

US policy on non-proliferation and the NPT 141

to; and secondly, because it would eat into the tacit bargain that says, since the nuclear weapons states behind the treaty could cope with a laissez-faire world of unrestricted nuclear proliferation better than most other states, their signature to the treaty must come with special privileges attached to reflect this fact. And the most obvious privilege is that they be allowed to retain some nuclear weapons.

Again, consider the Article 4 bargain, which in effect says non-nuclear states party to the treaty and in good standing can acquire any sort of nuclear facility they believe to be necessary for their commercial nuclear programmes, conditional on inspection by the Vienna Agency of course. The implication is that where states decide to have nothing to do with the treaty, they lose this access. The bargain is under tension in two ways. First, states that resisted treaty membership were never entirely denied such access. It is true that they were expected to accept inspection, but this was normally much less extensive (if sometimes more intrusive) than the inspections faced by treaty members. We have seen that US efforts to improve the bargain within the NSG by pushing for full-scope safeguards were thwarted for almost 20 years by the main European nuclear exporters. But the NSG meant formal French adhesion to a non-proliferation instrument (namely the NSG) at a time when France was outside the NPT itself and therefore theoretically unbound by any of its provisions. The USA followed up its pressure within the NSG with further domestic legislation that also tended to improve the bargain. The Nuclear Nonproliferation Act was passed by Congress in 1978 and bound the USA as an individual nuclear exporter by what the NSG refused to be bound by – namely not to supply nuclear material or technology to any country unless *all* its nuclear activities are under IAEA safeguards or equivalent. This provision of the Act, and the further provision that any country with a plutonium separation (i.e. fuel reprocessing) plant operating outside the context of full-scope safeguards would have its supply of US civil and military aid terminated, would cease to apply only in circumstances where US national security interests became paramount.

The second source of tension is more direct. The old Baruch theme that certain commercial nuclear activities are simply too 'dangerous' to be disseminated, with whatever safeguards, has never left US thinking. Thus the Carter administration reiterated its belief that fuel reprocessing was too 'sensitive' an activity to be allowed to happen anywhere, inspected or uninspected, even if it failed to convince its European NSG partners of this. It accompanied this proposal by a slightly weaker call in the same vein for a ban on all export of uranium enrichment technology. Had the USA succeeded here, the Article 4 bargain would have been weakened again, since it would have implied that even membership of the NPT in good standing would not have allowed a state full access to civilian nuclear technology.[17] And to show that the Baruch Plan is even now not forgotten, the George W. Bush administration returned to the fray in 2004 with its proposal tightly to circumscribe access to the twin technologies of plutonium separation and uranium enrichment, more or less along old Carter lines, if more diplomatically worded.

Article 4 is central to the NPT in as far as it is part of the package of incentives binding states to the treaty, but it is also to do with security directly, if tacitly. The treaty depends not only on its centralised aspects (namely the big powers behind it acting to enforce its provisions) but on its decentralised aspects too. Some non-nuclear states stay that way because they anticipate that acquisition of nuclear weapons by them would trigger compensating acquisition of the same by their immediate rivals. Any state would be likely to get timely warning of weapons development from the inspection activities of the IAEA. Article 4 plays a part in making this example of recessed deterrence work.

The treaty also has or has attached to it specific (and explicit) security bargains. In 1968, the USA, the USSR and the UK promoted a so-called tripartite resolution,[18] wherein each asserted its intention to seek immediate Security Council action (with themselves in the vanguard) to provide assistance to any non-nuclear weapons state party to the NPT that was being made subject to nuclear aggression or nuclear threats. This class of undertaking has come to be known as a 'positive security assurance'. For this bargain to have been tension-free, it should have carried a rider indicating that such a security assurance was strictly limited to states that had signed the NPT *and* were in good standing within it. But such an exclusion was plainly not practical politics (with Cuba a *de jure* and India a *de facto* ally of the USSR at the time and Pakistan and Israel *de facto* allies of the USA).

Ten years later, in 1978, as part of the Carter administration's rather crude drive to improve the NPT, the USA issued a new security assurance, but in the so-called 'negative' format. This said that the USA would not use its nuclear weapons against any non-nuclear party to the NPT or comparable arrangement (a reference to the Latin American nuclear-free zone) unless the USA (or one of its allies) was facing an attack by such a state in concert with a nuclear weapons state. And the same assurance was reaffirmed in 1982,[19] after superpower relations had unmistakably begun to deteriorate once more.

This negative security assurance had two effects. The more obvious was to increase the scope for nuclear-free zones, which had already been given a boost by Article 7 of the NPT. Here it can be seen as yet another form of recessed deterrence. In any non-arbitrary regional grouping or security complex of states where there were no nuclear weapons and no affiliations with nuclear states, then the USA was saying that it could itself do without nuclear weapons even in its warlike dealings with such countries and hence, it must be presumed, would be able to avoid the need for any forward basing of such weapons. But if other nuclear states could not similarly deny themselves, then all assurances were off.

The specific reaffirmation of the pledge in 1982 is probably a clue that this new security assurance had another beneficial effect on non-proliferation objectives, in this case with respect to US allies specifically. But the significance of this was greater than it might seem. Before detente had become established, the USA had encountered enormous difficulties in satisfying its NATO allies of the credibility of its nuclear guarantee while at the same time restricting their national access to nuclear weapons or control over them. The USA was eventually successful in its minimum goal of restricting European NATO interest in national nuclear weapons programmes to the UK and France, but failed in its more ambitious goal of absorbing these small independent nuclear forces within a larger multilateral framework involving the bulk of NATO states under US aegis (waspishly attacked by the British Wilson government as promoting the very nuclear proliferation it was ostensibly designed to counter). With the formal alliance structures put under pressure again by the revival of the Cold War in the 1980s and a modernisation of the East–West nuclear balance in Europe, the pledge could be read as a new signal to US allies that they could rely on the US nuclear umbrella, and therefore made a useful adjunct to the NPT as detente began to evaporate.

The condition of the bargains

The natural condition of the treaty bargains is tension. Tension over the Article 6 bargain remains undiminished, as most recently exemplified at the 2000 treaty review conference. It is difficult to see this situation changing, since the problem here is at heart about the very useful pretence, on the one hand, that states are sovereignly equal and the hard fact of the matter, on the other, that some states are more powerful than others.

The Article 4 bargain, as we have seen, remains subject to the strains imposed by periodic US-led reversion to the Baruch idea that some peaceful nuclear activities are inherently too dangerous to be allowed to disseminate globally. These strains tend to be eased a little by the slightly more relaxed position on this matter taken by the big European states behind the treaty. On the other hand, time has not been kind to the bargain. The promise of even untrammelled transfers of peaceful nuclear technology has simply become less attractive to non-nuclear states, as the commercial applications of nuclear energy have come to be increasingly questioned on both simple economic and environmental grounds. In 2002 more new generating capacity was installed worldwide in the form of wind power than in the form of nuclear. This diminishing attractiveness is an almost universal phenomenon, outside France and to a lesser extent Japan, and while it could be a temporary thing capable of being thrown into reverse by some new crisis over the supply of fossil fuels, for as long as it remains a fact it not only hurts the Article 4 bargain but also reduces the opportunity for the nuclear states to recycle, as nuclear fuel, nuclear weapons they have discarded as a result of agreements reached since the end of the Cold War.[20]

The explicit security bargains are in better shape. The positive assurance bargain that the nuclear powers would act, via the UN Security Council, to assist a non-nuclear member state of the treaty facing nuclear aggression or threat of such was flawed from the start, since it was not offered exclusively to states inside the NPT. It was also flawed in that, before the ending of the Cold War, the Security Council rarely found enough unanimity among its permanent members for it to sanction military action of any kind. Plainly the bargain has improved since it was struck: first, the UN Security Council is less hampered by the operation of the veto than hitherto; and secondly, the number of states not party to the NPT had shrunk to three by 2004 (India, Israel and Pakistan). The second half of the security bargain related to negative security assurances issued by the USA in 1978 and reiterated in 1982. This was an undertaking for 'no first use' of nuclear weapons by the USA, unless it or its allies were attacked by a nuclear state or a state allied to such. In one sense, the value of this has diminished over time. It was directed largely at Cold War allies of the USA (most of them, of course, NPT parties) that might have begun to have doubts about US nuclear guarantees at a period when the will of the USA to intervene militarily on behalf of allies had begun to be questioned as a result of its domestic retrenchment on military expenditure following the Vietnam War. On the other hand, the undertaking retains some force in Asia, and its beneficial effect on nuclear-free zones will be felt both within and outside Latin America as new nuclear-free zones have emerged in Africa and elsewhere. But US attitudes during the 1991 Gulf War will have raised doubts about the continued trustworthiness of the old pledge when the USA seemed to have threatened Iraq – a state party to the NPT – with nuclear retaliation should Iraq have employed chemical or biological weapons against US forces. And these doubts will not have been quietened by the subsequent US 'nuclear posture' review of 1993–94, in which an ongoing role for US nuclear weapons (after the Cold War) was explicitly identified as a way of offsetting chemical and biological weapons in the hands of US enemies. Baruch's warning about chemical and biological weapons and the consequences of a failure to place them under international control comes to mind.

The tacit, decentralised security bargain has probably strengthened over time as, under the aegis of the NPT or otherwise, states have gradually accumulated more knowledge and technical expertise in nuclear matters since the bargain was first struck. The inspection procedures of the IAEA and their capacity to produce timely warnings are not perfect but the tendency has been for corrective steps to be taken whenever shortcomings have come to light.

Bargains barometer: the review conferences

Just as we should anticipate tension in the treaty's underlying structure as a result of the bargains described above, so we might expect tension to be characteristic of the quinquennial review conferences of treaty parties, which started in 1975. Of course, the actual language in which tensions are expressed at the review conferences is not precisely the language we have used above. As the number of signatories to the NPT has grown, complaints about its functioning have tended to concentrate on the Article 6 question, and the failure of the nuclear powers to live up to this bargain. That there has been a substantial degree of nuclear disarmament since 1990 is not denied, but the rider is usually added that the current nuclear stockpiles of the nuclear states within the treaty should be compared with what they were in 1970, when the treaty came into force, and not with some arbitrary high point of the nuclear arms race during the Cold War. The complaints are usually distilled into calls for a *qualitative* sign of new thinking on this matter, perhaps as being intrinsically less reversible than a *quantitative* one, and less privately bilateral. The failure of the Comprehensive Test Ban Treaty (CTBT) to be ratified by the US Senate (see Chapter 6) was very badly received at the ensuing (2000) review conference.

While the review conferences mean something and should be taken seriously by the treaty's sponsors, it is also true that states with *real* complaints about the treaty, to the extent that they are contemplating leaving it and acquiring nuclear weapons for themselves, are unlikely to be heard there. The complaints that are voiced at the conferences are likely to be made by states with no such intentions, and are hence unlikely to provoke an immediate response. So these forums are to some extent theatrical, with participating states making points often as much for home consumption as anything else. In other words, maintaining the effectiveness of the treaty and, which comes to the same thing, keeping its inherent tensions within bounds should not mean the USA or any other of the sponsoring states listening to the complaints made at the review conferences and then acting mechanically on them. A measured and intelligent response is what is needed. And the ability of the sponsoring states to be measured in their response is enhanced by the fact that an agreed position involving the few acknowledged nuclear powers ought to be easier to arrive at and maintain than an agreed position for the dozens of non-nuclear states.

New directions in US policy

The ending of the Cold War, and the Gulf War of 1991 and its aftermath, had an effect on US non-proliferation policy, both on existing trends and tendencies and in more radical directions. Earlier assessments of the direction of US policy in this chapter have had the benefit of historical perspective, which cannot exert the same benign influence over the interpretation of more recent developments. These earlier assessments have also benefited from, and leant credence to, the point made at the start of the chapter, that the Baruch Plan was a serviceable template for the understanding of US non-proliferation policy. And it is with this same assumption that we approach more recent events.

The chief effect of the aftermath of the 1991 Gulf War on US policy was a return to the Baruch blueprint in two respects: the first to do with sensitive technologies, the second counter-proliferation. Both through the NSG and unilaterally, the USA reaffirmed that some nuclear technologies were simply too sensitive to be made available to certain states and should be retained exclusively in the hands of other states (i.e. those seen as safe), admittedly not quite under the international control Baruch had wanted. But US policy demonstrated two old failings. One, arguably, was the refocusing on plutonium and the other, connectedly, was a failure quite to carry with it its natural allies in the attempt to curb nuclear spread.

US policy with respect to North Korea and later Iran concentrated on the supply of nuclear power reactors to both states from Russia. The North Korean reactors were of old design and better at producing weapons-grade plutonium than modern designs (see Chapter 1). And in this case both the recipient (from the US perspective) and the technology might be deemed sensitive. Further, obtaining international support for taking a restrictive attitude to North Korean plans was relatively straightforward. Japan, South Korea and the EU countries all pulled in the same direction as the United States. In the case of Iran, the reactors concerned are of a light-water type and not very suitable for producing weapons-grade plutonium and hence not in themselves unambiguously sensitive. But the old question of where to draw the line between sensitive and non-sensitive facilities was answered differently by the USA and by the EU states (not for the first time), as the latter saw nothing wrong in principle with the Iranian reactor programme.

Counter-proliferation

The most dramatic turn in US policy – triggered by the discoveries in Iraq – came in 1993, in a speech by the then US Secretary of State for Defense, Les Aspin. In it, he championed the idea of counter-proliferation, indicating specifically that it meant measures to equip US armed forces in such a way as to enable the USA to employ force in pursuit of its objectives against states that had already obtained nuclear weapons or other weapons of mass destruction (chemical and biological). An uncontentious example of what Aspin seemed to be saying would be defensive measures against regional attacks by ballistic missiles on US or allied targets, since ballistic missiles would normally carry warheads of a mass-destruction type. Since the outrages of 11 September 2001, the development of defences against ballistic missile attack has been taken further, to include defence of the continental USA, and the adjustment of the 1972 ABM Treaty foreseen as necessary by Aspin has occurred, in the crudest way imaginable: in 2001 the USA withdrew from the ABM Treaty.

In the context of non-proliferation policies, the direct effect of these proposals on the network of NPT bargains at first sight would seem to be benign. US forces equipped in this manner would be in a better position to employ armed force on behalf of the positive security assurances the USA has given to states facing nuclear threats, to say nothing of reassuring its allies in a similar position. In both cases this would reinforce nuclear abstinence. And the warm reception given to Aspin's proposals by US allies in NATO and particularly its nuclear allies, the UK and France, adds to the benign effect. But if the threatening state in question already has or is suspected of having nuclear weapons, the possession of missile defences by the USA or its allies is apt to suggest what the mooted possession of such defences in the Cold War context did, namely, an incentive to strike quickly and preventively at the threatening state's nuclear infrastructure, perhaps using conventional munitions, the better to cope with retaliation using the ragged forces that would (at worst) survive such a preventive attack. So indirectly, but not out of keeping with later interpretations of Aspin's remarks, something like the old Baruch idea of punishment for states that violated non-proliferation rules seemed to be making a reappearance.

However counter-proliferation is interpreted, the very name of the initiative suggests that the USA was expecting proliferation to occur (even if Aspin rather conflated different sorts of proliferation – nuclear, chemical and biological as well as missiles) and that the USA correspondingly had lost faith in the powers of existing multilateral constraints, including the NPT. And if the USA had doubts about the value of the NPT, why should other states believe any different? And specifically in terms of the Article 6 bargain, the counter-proliferation initiative hardly suggests a reduction in US interest in nuclear weapons for itself, but quite possibly the reverse: in the circumstances envisaged, of the USA using force against a state with at most very few nuclear weapons and specifically directed against these same weapons and their means of manufacture, nuclear weapons will be centre-stage and nuclear deterrence need not apply.[21]

The conflation of chemical and biological weapons with nuclear as weapons of mass destruction in US thinking was taken further in the Clinton administration's 'nuclear posture' review, in which the justification for the retention of considerable stocks of nuclear weapons by the USA after the Cold War included the claim that they were necessary to offset holdings of chemical and biological weapons by other states. The irony in relation to the Baruch Plan here is obvious, as it speaks of the futility of looking to curb states' interest in nuclear weapons if nothing is done about chemical and biological weapons. Fifty years later, the same judgement was being made, but this time against a background where safeguards in the form of arms control treaties against the spread of chemical and biological weapons were either now in place or in the process of being erected. US scepticism concerning the efficacy of such treaties was later to be confirmed by the ambiguous support given by the USA to the 1997 Chemical Weapons Convention. Even if US ratification was not withheld, the USA has refused to use the Convention's challenge inspection provisions to pursue its claims concerning alleged on-going chemical weapons programmes on the territories of certain signatory states. Moreover, the George W. Bush administration has taken a hostile stand to the updating of the 1972 Biological Weapons Convention, designed to equip a rather unsatisfactory ban on the manufacture and possession of these weapons with a system of inspection. The reason for this hostility is not a US wish to retain possession of such weapons for itself: it has no plans to retain stocks of either class of weapon. The stated reason is a lack of confidence that any practicable inspection system would work. Official US shows of scepticism concerning the utility of arms control measures with regard to these two classes of weapon then translate into a justification for the retention of stocks of nuclear weapons and a new problem for the Article 6 bargain.[22]

While Aspin quite specifically sought to involve allies in NATO in the project of counter-proliferation, and equally specifically spoke of complementing non-proliferation rather than replacing it, counter-proliferation could be counter-productive in one particular sense. Rousseau's old warning that in politics the strong can never be strong enough to get their own way unless the exercise of that strength is legitimised would seem to mean in the context of non-proliferation that a multilateral use of force mediated through the UN Security Council, as suggested by the Baruch Plan, forms the only sustainable basis for counter-proliferation.

In practice, the implementation of counter-proliferation has been patchy. In 1994, rather than counter-proliferation, more traditional diplomatic methods were used in the case of North Korea. In 1998 US cruise missiles with conventional warheads were launched against a suspected chemical weapons plant in Sudan, and against similar facilities in Iraq, including biological weapons and missile production plants. The Sudan strike seems to have been based on misleading intelligence. Henry Sokolski quotes US Army General Zinni,[23] in charge of the strikes on Iraqi targets in the period between the two Gulf wars, as doubting in public the good they could do, given the ease with which chemical and biological weapons production could be restarted (there were at this time no functioning Iraqi nuclear targets, as allied forces had bombed and fortuitously entombed the 5 MW reactor during the Gulf War in 1991 and the uranium enrichment plants had been dismantled[24]). The experience of the US-led coalition in the occupation of Iraq after the 2003 war and the difficulties experienced by their small army of inspectors in finding evidence of the existence of chemical and biological weapons plant reinforces Zinni's scepticism from a different perspective. Unfindable targets are difficult to bomb. If Baruch was right about the futility of looking to curb the spread of nuclear weapons if nothing is done about chemical and biological weapons, doing something about the latter does not seem to be a job for counter-proliferation, unless it means an all-out invasion of the state suspected of possessing such weapons (accompanied by the overthrow of its government and the country's subsequent internal political and economic reconstruction along lines more acceptable to the USA). The aftermath of the virtually unilateral 2003 invasion of Iraq by the USA, where military success has proved very hard to translate into political success, reinforces Rousseau's warning.

What can be taken as unmistakably remaining of counter-proliferation in US thinking (as of 2005) had received only a brief formal notification in the Aspin speech, where it was referred to as 'border/perimeter' control. In effect this has come to mean a reinforcement of the NSG and parallel approaches to controlling exports of sensitive materials relating to weapons of mass destruction by physically intercepting their shipment (by land, sea or air). Suspected shipments of such materials found to be in contravention of NSG guidelines, for example, are to be intercepted and impounded. An example of what may be intended was seen on 9 December 2002, when Spanish forces, acting on information supplied by US military intelligence, intercepted a ship, the *So San*, in the Arabian Sea transporting Scud ballistic missiles of North Korean origin. When it was discovered that Yemen was the importing country and not Iraq, the shipment was allowed to proceed. Even more multilaterally, in October 2003, the German-registered vessel *BBC China* bound for Libya from Malaysia with centrifuge parts on board was diverted to Italy. This allowed US and British authorities to approach the Malaysian government concerning the activities there of a company run by B.S.A. Tahir, who turned out to be an associate of A.Q. Khan (see below). Other instances may have occurred but, as we have seen, secrecy in all matters to do with controlling exports of sensitive materials is not unusual.

With hindsight, counter-proliferation, in as much as it was a departure from the norms of the NPT, reached its high point with the Aspin speech. The George W. Bush administration thereafter gradually steered a course, unsteady at times, back in the direction of more traditional policies, even, as we saw in Chapter 1, in the particularly trying case of North Korea.

Bush and proliferation

In May 2003 US President George W. Bush announced the Proliferation Security Initiative, and spelt out what was intended by the interdiction scheme. It is a retreat from counter-proliferation in that it aims to be a multilateral effort, like the NSG, and arguably simply an extension of existing export control arrangements. It certainly extends the reach of the controls to exporting states that are not members of the NSG. There seems to be a US recognition of the unfeasibility of not involving a large number of other states from the start, in that powers for example to stop and search ships on the high seas will have to be applied for through the machinery of the UN.[25] It is also in a sense a logical step forward from counter-proliferation in that, since 11 September 2001, non-state groupings' access to weapons of mass destruction has moved up the US non-proliferation agenda, and such groupings do not present targets in the same way as states do, but are in general even more dependent than states on obtaining sensitive materials from outside.

The Bush Proliferation Security Initiative received a warm welcome from NSG members, including Russia and China.

A fuller statement of the position of the Bush administration came in February 2004, when a virtual total retreat from counter-proliferation was confirmed. Bush's National Defense University speech contained seven proposals,[26] three of which were explicitly about strengthening the IAEA, three of which were tactical responses to the emerging 'democratisation' of nuclear proliferation, and the other, at least as important, was about new restrictions on the transfer of nuclear technologies even to NPT signatories in good standing.

Emerging details concerning the cases of two individual nuclear traders – Abdul Qadeer Khan in Pakistan and Karl-Heinz Schaab in Germany, probably (certainly in Schaab's case) acting illegally in terms of their national laws – prompted a renewed call for the Proliferation Security Initiative to be as vigilant in the matter of rogue individuals and companies as in the matter of states implicated in the nuclear black market. Khan, a Pakistani government scientist but one-time employee of a Dutch supplier to Urenco, a metallurgist by training and, indeed, the father of the Pakistan bomb, became personally implicated in the transfer of centrifuges for uranium enrichment to Iran, North Korea and

Libya, with the transactions lubricated via the involvement of traders in Malaysia. Schaab, a German citizen and a former employee of MAN, a supplier company to the German branch of Urenco, sold advanced centrifuge technology to Iraq, via dealers in Singapore, in direct defiance of German law. Khan's legal position is less clear, as is the legal situation in Malaysia and Singapore. The speech also reiterated an earlier Bush proposal (made to the UN at the end of 2003) that states should criminalise proliferative activities where they do not already do so. The speech's third proposal on the democratisation cum black market issue was to extend the principle of the Nunn–Lugar Act of 1991, which sought to help weapons scientists in the former Soviet Union find acceptable alternative employment, to scientists in Iraq and Libya. This proposal was coupled with the promise of aid to states that were willing to abandon research reactors fuelled with highly enriched uranium (such a reactor featured in an unsuccessful last-ditch attempt by Iraq to acquire a bomb before the 1991 war closed in).

The three proposals concerned with the IAEA were of a piece with the broad multilateral tone of the rest of the speech. Bush proposed that only states that had signed up to the Additional Protocol, and the additional safeguards provisions entailed, should be allowed to import nuclear equipment for their peaceful programmes. This is a logical extension of the old US insistence on full-scope safeguards for all nuclear transfers within the context of the treaty, to cover the fact that the scope of safeguards has now been extended under the Additional Protocol. The other two proposals directed at the IAEA concerned the structure of the Agency itself. One advanced the idea of a new special committee of the Agency specifically dedicated to safeguards, with a view to a more speedy determination of where a breach may have occurred and appropriate reaction to it. The Agency already takes safeguards extremely seriously and the head of the safeguards department has the rank of Deputy Director General of the organisation, so the implications of this proposal are not entirely clear. The second structural proposal concerned the IAEA Board of Governors: Bush asked that the membership of states under suspicion of having violated safeguards be suspended. He also suggested that the same should apply to membership of the proposed new special safeguards committee. At a minimum it may be said that these proposals added something to the sanctions facing potential violators of the terms of the NPT.

Perhaps the single most important proposal in the speech concerned a new prohibition on sales of nuclear technology even to states in good standing with respect to the treaty. Bush proposed that the nuclear supplier states (formally, the now 40-strong NSG) should not transfer equipment or technology for plutonium separation or uranium enrichment to any state not already possessing large-scale facilities for engaging in either activity. This is a more liberal and less bullying version of the old Carter proposal. In one respect, the practical significance of this proposal is slight. Plutonium separation even on an industrial scale is not a very difficult technique to master and will be well within the domestic technical competence of many states that have so far shown no practical interest in it. On the other hand, a secret plant, however acquired, will not normally be easy to conceal. Moreover, concerning uranium enrichment methods, NSG states have for 30 years or more operated a tacit moratorium on precisely what the USA now wants explicitly banned. One unwanted effect of this moratorium has been to push such trading underground and onto the black market. But the Bush proposal goes further and supplements the moratorium in an important respect. He prefaced his proposal for a formal export ban with a call for the same exporting states to ensure that importing countries nonetheless have 'reliable access at reasonable cost' to fuel supplies for their reactors. This access will be conditional on the importing states having nothing to do with reprocessing or enrichment for themselves and presumably will also be conditional on them being in good standing with respect to the NPT as a whole.

The chief difficulty with this proposal, or at least its first half, is that it very openly offends against the spirit and the letter of the promise of unrestricted access to commercial nuclear technology of Article 4 of the NPT, and the bargain this embodies, in a way that the tacit moratorium and the rather twilit operations of the NSG never quite did historically. This Article 4 difficulty pertains essentially to the uranium enrichment part of the Bush proposal, in as much as the freedom to separate plutonium for commercial purposes is considerably less valued than was once the case, with the continuing ascendancy of the light-water reactor and the huge difficulties encountered in making a practical proposition of reactors fuelled by plutonium alone (fast-breeder reactors). The strong resurgence of interest in uranium enrichment in France and Japan (both now turning to the centrifuge method), at one time chief proponents of plutonium-fuelled reactors, is evidence of this. But the very importance of the light-water reactor and its requirement for lightly enriched uranium as fuel underlines the need for access to enriched uranium to assure continuity of fuel supplies for states dependent on a modern reactor network for their electrical power supply (hence the developments in France and Japan). Moreover, this commercial demand for enriched uranium has stimulated interest in uranium mining states in attempting to meet this demand directly, by exporting uranium not in its raw state but in the 'value-added' lightly enriched form. Thus Australia, Brazil and South Africa now all take the possibility of industrial-scale uranium enrichment facilities for themselves very seriously.

So, the first difficulty with the new US proposal is where to draw the line between states that qualify as already possessing large-scale enrichment facilities and the rest, which will be cut off from trade in enrichment technology and equipment. France obviously meets the criterion but Japan less clearly so. At least the proposal recognises that there is a legitimate demand for lightly enriched uranium, and is much less crude than the Carter administration's proposal that all plutonium separation should be stopped (in spite of its rider that there should be an international pool of alternative fuel made available). The parallel Bush plan, that there should be guaranteed fuel supplies for reactor-operating states in good standing, echoes the Carter idea but overlooks the problem of the states than mine and export uranium.

Operationalising the Bush proposals

That there are envisaged to be certain states permitted to engage in exchange of materials and technology connected to enrichment is itself suggestive of how the idea might be operationalised. Clusters of such states could become multinational providers of enriched uranium. This is a partial step back towards the old Baruch ideal of international control of all dangerous nuclear materials and activities. In practical terms, the potential for large-scale operation would suggest a cheaper product than an importing state could hope to produce domestically and a multinational character reduces the chance that supplies could be denied on political grounds far removed from proliferation issues. Ideally, what may be needed, in small numbers globally, is a cross between the French inspired Eurodif and the European uranium enrichment consortium Urenco, incorporating the best features of each.[27]

Eurodif involves shared governance of an enrichment collective originally based on France at the centre. France houses the large gas diffusion plants (now becoming obsolescent – see Chapter 1) that do the enriching and keeps the technology (relating to the barrier materials through which the uranium hexafluoride diffuses at rates dependent on its isotopic composition) to itself. However, there are four other states with a financial stake in the company and a call on the enrichment services provided. These are Belgium, Iran, Italy and Spain. The supply and price guarantees originally implied were plainly insufficient to keep the Iranian revolutionary government as firmly behind Eurodif as its predecessor had been (it does not follow that this was for reasons to do with a planned Iranian bomb programme). On the other hand, the model of developed states and developing states being part of the same system with a tight central grip on the key technologies has promising aspects. If its failings have been of a negative kind (failing to divert Iran away from exploring domestic enrichment options), those of Urenco, another possible model, have (as we have seen) been more obtrusive. Under Urenco the three participating states (the UK, the Netherlands and Germany) have shared the technology and in turn passed it downwards, partly at least, to their national chains of suppliers. In allowing this to happen the participating governments have multiplied the statistical probability of leaks occurring, and there are two known instances – Khan and the Netherlands, and Schaab and Germany. On the other hand, because the technology was not solely Germany's to transfer, Urenco interposed itself successfully to block a Brazilian request in 1975 to import a fully functioning centrifuge-based enrichment plant from Germany (in return for privileged German access to its uranium ore).

Ideally, the multinational enrichment arrangements ought to include at least one major supplier of uranium ore, and while it is natural to look for regionality in their composition (e.g. there could be arrangements for the Americas, for Europe and for the Far East/Oceania) this need not be applied rigorously. But getting the balance of IAEA inspection right for such multinational arrangements will not necessarily be simple. There is a need to avoid both under-inspection (or the perception of it), especially where participating states include nuclear weapons states, whose nuclear plant is only voluntarily safeguarded (the NPT being silent on this particular matter), and over-inspection, where states might already be inspected under regional safeguards arrangements, as apply in Latin America and historically in the EU. More positively, the two important regional safeguards organisations – Euratom in the EU and the ABACC in Latin America – have both shown an encouraging flexibility in dealing with the new demands on their relationship with the IAEA as it phases in the Additional Protocol.

One difference between the Bush proposals for clamping down on plutonium separation and uranium enrichment and Carter's earlier proposals is that the former pay greater attention to the sensibilities of other leading states and their economic investment in nuclear power. Some extension of the same multilateralism to address the concerns of other, smaller states in the NPT could help offset the perceived damage done to the Article 4 bargain, which has been made worse, surely, by the apparent targeting of concessions with respect to this bargain to some states (the bigger powers with existing large-scale plant for plutonium separation or uranium enrichment) but not to others, which make up the bulk of signatories of the treaty.

Article 6

We have seen that the treaty reflects a network of bargains and it seems obvious that an adverse shift in the terms of one bargain might be compensated for by a favourable shift in the terms of another. In spite of the somewhat artificial testing of opinion within the bulk of non-nuclear treaty states represented by the review conferences, there seems little doubt that a concession by the nuclear powers on the Article 6 question would add to the stability of the treaty overall. And there are only two realistic concessions on the table, so to say, that are sufficiently well advanced to have a chance of maturing in the near future. One is the coming into force of the CTBT, though this has been held up by the egregious refusal of the USA to ratify it. The other is the Fissile Material Cut-off Treaty (see below), oppositely held up by the refusal of Russia and China to accept it without special concessions for themselves. The CTBT is looked at in Chapter 6.

The Cut-off Treaty is a classical piece of unfinished business from the Baruch and Eisenhower eras – an agreement verified by the IAEA that involves the nuclear weapons states in ending their production of fissile material (highly enriched uranium and plutonium) for weapons purposes. According to Pierre Goldschmidt, writing in 2000 as head of the IAEA safeguards department, the Fissile Material Cut-off Treaty should be understood as only the central panel of a triptych of arrangements, bearing a strong similarity to the proposals originally put forward under Atoms for Peace by Eisenhower.[28] The essential point of the triptych is to enforce, through IAEA inspection of an appropriate kind, the permanence of the nuclear disarmament that has occurred and is scheduled to occur, chiefly in Russia and the USA since the end of the Cold War, which has been found so unimpressive by treaty review conferences, perhaps because of its informal, bilateral and reversible nature. Thus the three panels of the triptych are the IAEA's involvement in or responsibility for: first, taking and keeping out of circulation weapons found by their owners to be surplus to strategic requirements; secondly, ensuring that there is no future production of fissile material for weapons purposes (by submitting *all* plutonium and uranium enrichment plants in the ownership of the treaty nuclear powers to the same schedule of inspection as is met with currently by the non-nuclear signatories of the NPT); and thirdly, conducting a grand audit to ensure that all fissile material ever produced in each of the nuclear powers is equal to the amount used for weapons purposes, plus the amount blended down into nuclear fuel, plus the amount exported less the amount imported. It has to be understood, however, that it is essential for the nuclear states involved, contrary to a literal reading of Article 6, to retain a minimum stockpile of actual nuclear weapons, to allow for the fact that the IAEA will be able to account for fissile materials only within certain error margins. Even in the most modern designs of nuclear reactor, plutonium production rates will vary in the short term with different refuelling schedules, since operators often have to 'feel for' optimum performance by fine tuning the enrichment of the uranium in the fuel elements. Furthermore, very large plutonium separation or uranium enrichment plants seldom see an exact balance in the short term between materials in and materials out, owing to unsuspected and unpredictable variations in the efficiency of the process in question. While in the long run there will be a balance, in the mean time hundreds of kilograms of fissile material can go innocently missing. The possibility that states could take advantage of this phenomenon quickly to reacquire a nuclear stockpile argues against complete disarmament. And even without this so-called MUF problem, complete disarmament would still be a mistake because errors would be inevitable in the IAEA historical audit of fissile materials produced and consumed within nuclear states. In the case of the USA or Russia, total production will have been in the hundreds of tonnes. The IAEA will never be able to say that it can account for the exact whereabouts of all the fissile material produced. It is the well known statistical problem of the difference between two very large numbers, when neither can be known with precision. Suppose the IAEA can verify the amount of fissile material produced to 99.9 per cent and the amount used to 99.9 per cent (much better accuracy than can normally be achieved in practice). If we have 100,000 kg produced then the difference between the two figures could be 200 kg or 10–20 bombs' worth. Thus adherence to a complete nuclear disarmament treaty could not be verified as 20 bombs might have been secretly retained. If the disarmament treaty permitted the retention of, say, 1,000 bombs by either side the possibility that one side might actually have 1,020 is an insignificant problem by comparison.

The first panel of the triptych, according to Goldschmidt, is the one where most progress has already been made. Under the so-called Trilateral Initiative, in 1996 the USA and Russia with IAEA involvement began to develop a framework for the permanent storage and/or recycling as nuclear fuel of surplus plutonium and enriched uranium coming from dismantled nuclear warheads, to be verified by the IAEA. In 2002, the parties concerned announced that the exploratory work was complete, including technical solutions to the problem of allowing inspectors to verify fissile materials configured for military purposes without compromising military secrecy. Some questions remain unanswered, perhaps notably whether the stored materials are to be put under international 'ownership' as well as international supervision (the recycling of such materials to peaceful purposes on a global scale, also proposed by Eisenhower, is now clearly an excessively neat solution to an untidy problem).

The second panel of the triptych is the Fissile Material Cut-off Treaty, designed to halt all new production of fissile material for weapons purposes. This would involve, in effect, as we have seen, the full-blooded extension to the nuclear weapons states of the sort of safeguards already faced by non-nuclear weapons states with extensive nuclear facilities. The negotiation of this treaty is held up within the multilateral Conference on Disarmament (the forum in which the NPT itself was finally negotiated) by Russian and Chinese insistence on tying progress here to US self-restraint in the development of space-based technologies for defence against ballistic missile attack. In fact, all five original nuclear weapons states have moratoriums in place concerning production of fissile material for warlike purposes.

Notes

1 *A Report on the International Control of Atomic Energy*, prepared for the Secretary of State's Committee on Atomic Energy (Washington, DC, US Government Printing Office, 16 March 1946).
2 Dean Acheson, *Present at the Creation: My Years in the State Department* (New York, W.W. Norton and Co., 1969), pp. 150–6.
3 Bertrand Russell, *Common Sense and Nuclear Warfare* (London, George Allen and Unwin, 1959), p. 89.
4 Henry D. Sokolski, *Best of Intentions: America's Campaign against Strategic Weapons Proliferation* (Westport, CT, Praeger, 2001), credits Baruch with an insistence on international controls *tout court*, but it seems clear that the Baruch Plan differed from the Acheson–Lilienthal report in taking a relatively liberal view of the possibility that national controls, with inspection, would also have a part to play.
5 *International Nuclear Fuel Cycle Evaluation*, reports 1–8 of INFCE Working Groups (Vienna, IAEA, 1980).
6 The transitional Malenkov government had made specific proposals to the USA for talks on atomic energy and disarmament in March 1953. See Rosemary J. Foot, 'Nuclear coercion and the ending of the Korean conflict', *International Security*, Vol. 13, No. 3, winter 1988–89, p. 109.
7 By commentators as far apart in time as Leonard Beaton, *Must the Bomb Spread?* (Harmondsworth, Penguin, 1966), and Sokolski, *Best of Intentions*, and by most – I dare say all – commentators in between. But a recent analyst, in the course of a virulent attack on Atoms for Peace and on the character of Baruch for good measure, cannot resist entirely awarding Eisenhower a few points for effort. See Leonard Weiss, 'Atoms for Peace', *Bulletin of the Atomic Scientists*, Vol. 59, No. 6, November/December 2003, pp. 34–44.
8 Sokolski, *Best of Intentions*, p. 30.
9 The statute of the IAEA, Article 12, A5, says the Agency shall have the right 'to require deposit with the Agency of any excess of special fissionable materials [plutonium and enriched uranium] recovered or produced as a by-product over what is needed for [reactor fuelling or research purposes] to prevent stock-piling of these materials'.
10 See for example George H. Quester, 'Preventing proliferation', in George H. Quester (ed.), *Nuclear Proliferation: Breaking the Chain* (Madison, WI, University of Wisconsin Press, 1981), p. 240.
11 Formally, the Treaty Banning Nuclear Weapon Tests in the Atmosphere, in Outer Space and Under Water, opened for signature and in force in 1963.

12 Prior to the treaty, bombs as large as 60 megatonnes (thermonuclear bombs of this kind were at least as large relative to atomic bombs of the Hiroshima type as atomic bombs were to conventional bombs) had been exploded in atmospheric tests. After the treaty, no such enormous bombs were tested anywhere, with 1 megatonne becoming a *de facto* ceiling.
13 Formally, the Treaty on the Non-Proliferation of Nuclear Weapons, opened for signature in 1968 and in force from 1970.
14 An unfortunate feature of Article 6 is that it includes a stipulation that work towards nuclear disarmament should be accompanied by work towards general and complete disarmament, the very same proposal that the USSR had put up in 1946 as an alternative to the Baruch Plan and which has never quite lost its taint of cynicism when appended to more realistic (because more modest) proposals.
15 See David Fischer, 'International safeguards', in David Fischer, Paul Szasz and Jozef Goldblat (eds), *Safeguarding the Atom: A Critical Appraisal* (London, Taylor and Francis for the Stockholm International Peace Research Institute, 1985), pp. 70–3.
16 But only up to a point. IAEA rules under classical safeguards essentially mean that inspection follows flows of nuclear fuel and related materials (uranium ore excepted, flows of which are merely notified to the IAEA by the importer/exporter NPT member state). Japan has a large nuclear energy industry, as, still, does Germany, so that between them, in spite of the shielding they had negotiated for themselves from IAEA inspectors, they traditionally accounted in round figures for 50 per cent of the IAEA inspection effort, measured by cost. The voluntary inspections of the nuclear weapons states add a further 10 per cent, and the inspections of Canada, a state which has a big and awkward nuclear energy programme (awkward from the point of view of non-proliferation because it is based on heavy-water reactors), and for which no inspection privileges of any kind exist, another 10 per cent. So about 5 per cent of the member states of the NPT have historically absorbed 70 per cent of the inspection effort. See David Fischer, *Towards 1995: The Prospects for Ending the Proliferation of Nuclear Weapons* (Aldershot, Dartmouth Publishing Co. for the United Nations Institute for Disarmament Research, 1993), pp. 66–9.
17 It is true that the US meant that this ban on reprocessing (i.e. plutonium separation) should apply to itself and other states advanced in nuclear technology too, but this would not have applied to the production of plutonium for military purposes by the USA or any of the other nuclear weapons states.
18 UN Security Council Resolution 255, 1968.
19 See *Arms Control and Disarmament Agreements: Texts and Histories of the Negotiations* (Washington, DC, US Arms Control and Disarmament Agency, 1990), p. 94.
20 It is less clear that depressed demand for nuclear power hurts the NPT overall, since it dampens down the eternal struggle between, in the economic plane, competitiveness among states in the marketing and export of nuclear equipment and, in the strategic plane, cooperativeness to restrict global access to nuclear weaponry.

21 For a slightly more extreme version of this same point see James J. Wirtz, 'Counterproliferation, conventional counterforce and nuclear war', *Journal of Strategic Studies*, Vol. 23, No. 1, 2000, pp. 5–20.
22 See Janne E. Nolan, *An Elusive Consensus: Nuclear Weapons and American Security after the Cold War* (Washington, DC, Brookings Press, 1999), p. 97.
23 Sokolski, *Best of Intentions*, p. 96.
24 The entombment of the reactor by bombing, which was loaded with fuel and operational, unlike the Iraqi Osirak reactor bombed by Israel in 1981, was simply lucky. Had it instead been set on fire, radioactive fallout in its vicinity and further afield might have reached dangerous levels.
25 See the interview given by John Bolton, US Undersecretary of State for Arms Control and International Security, to *Arms Control Today*, 4 November 2003.
26 See www.whitehouse.gov/news/releases/2004/02/print/20040211-4.html (last accessed 13 April 2005). The headline of the web text of the speech, 'President Announces New Measures to Counter the Threat of WMD', is slightly misleading in that the substance of the speech is about nuclear proliferation.
27 For a pioneering study of multinational nuclear fuel suppliers and their potential contribution to non-proliferation, see Lawrence Scheinman, 'Multinational alternatives and nuclear non-proliferation', *International Organization*, Vol. 35, No. 1, winter 1981, pp. 77–102, reprinted with updated prefatory remarks in *Disarmament Diplomacy*, Issue 76, March/April 2004. See also the website www.acronym.org.uk/textonly/dd/dd76/76ls.htm (last accessed 13 April 2005).
28 Pierre Goldschmidt, 'IAEA safeguards: evolution or revolution?', keynote speech, Institute for Nuclear Materials Management, 41st Annual Meeting, July 2000.

6

Bargaining for test ban treaties

The earliest specific international arrangement, at least indirectly, to restrict the spread of nuclear weapons is the PTBT of 1963. The treaty bans the testing of all nuclear explosive devices anywhere except underground, and only then when the radioactive debris from the explosion is contained wholly within the borders of the state responsible. The negotiation of the treaty – originally designed to be a comprehensive ban on all nuclear testing – began essentially in 1955, when the Soviets unbundled such an agreement from a general and complete disarmament package, starting thereby an unpicking of the all-or-nothing position on arms control and disarmament they had taken over the Baruch Plan, vestiges of which remain in the wording of Article 6 of the NPT. After further jockeying, discussion of a test ban became, on the surface at least, an international argument over how adherence to it could be verified. It was quickly appreciated that a comprehensive ban covering all tests would need each state to concede powers to a body of inspectors to visit sites within the territory of signatories in those cases where the nature of a suspicious event recorded outside the territory could not be established by remote sensing methods. As Eisenhower had complained in his Atoms for Peace speech, intrusive verification created suspicion between states. And in this case even neutral inspectors would be on occasions visiting the weapons test sites (or former sites) of the big powers and in a position to acquire sensitive information concerning the details of their bomb programmes.

It gradually became established that only tests carried out below ground would require on-site intrusive inspection to clear up those cases where remote sensors – seismometers – could not be relied on to say

Bargaining for test ban treaties

definitively that the seismic event they had registered was not a test explosion. The very large numbers of small earthquakes in any one year within a large territory such as that of the USSR or USA meant that there was too much background noise for seismometers reliably to pick out the test of a comparatively small nuclear device. Remote detection of nuclear explosions carried out in any other medium was not thought to present a difficulty. International scientific investigation into the problems presented by earthquakes, involving technical experts from all the nuclear powers at the time, reached a degree of consensus boding well for political agreement, in 1958. They stipulated that 170–180 land control posts and 10 ship-borne ones would be needed for a comprehensive ban, as well as aircraft over-flights and some provision for on-site inspections. But, in the end, on-site inspections proved to be a sticking point, with the Soviets insisting on a maximum annual quota of three and the USA anxious for at least seven.

In 1963 three of the nuclear powers (the USSR, the USA and the UK) agreed a test ban, but only for tests other than those carried out underground and for which no inspection arrangements were necessary at all, with each signatory relying on purely national means to monitor the adherence of the rest to the agreement. France and China remained outside the treaty – although they acted as if bound by its provisions from 1974 and 1980 onwards, respectively – but almost every member state of the UN signed up to it.

As a check to nuclear proliferation, the treaty erected obstacles to new powers entering the nuclear club by requiring them to master the technology of testing weapons underground. At the time this was believed to be a difficult art. Also, the amount then publicly known about the design of nuclear weapons was small enough to make it very improbable that any state could build nuclear weapons without going through the process of testing, even if it wished to. In addition, the treaty paid attention to the importance of a balance of obligation between its signatories.

The nuclear weapons states lost the option to test their weapons in the atmosphere, oceans or outer space, something they had not always been reluctant to explore when free to do so. Were the weapons ever to be used in war, it would be in these media and not or only very exceptionally underground. The radioactive pollution of the atmosphere as a result of the test programmes carried out before 1963, particularly in the northern hemisphere and in the western Pacific, had added to domestic pressure on Western governments, at least, to do something about testing. It was also believed, somewhat optimistically, that even a partial ban would slow down the pace of development of new weapon types and the nuclear arms race generally. It was further thought, rightly, that the treaty would make the testing of extremely large nuclear bombs, such as those tested in the atmosphere by the USA and the USSR during the 1950s and 1960s, impossible. And finally, there was nothing in the verification arrangements favouring the nuclear over the non-nuclear signatories, even if verification was largely in the hands of the nuclear powers themselves, with their mutual antipathy the only guarantee that violations would be made public. Verification of a comprehensive ban, curiously, would be more 'democratic', in that a large number of states could become host to seismometers or set up their own seismic detection centres. Detecting a nuclear explosion in space or high in the atmosphere, on the other hand, was a much more specialised business.

But just as importantly, without being widely perceived at the time, the PTBT amounted to a sustainable bargain. If every state derived some benefit from a brake being applied to nuclear testing, those states that had the best chance of surviving in a completely anarchic world – the most powerful states in other words – could expect privileges in exchange for signing up to an arrangement that sought to make the world slightly less anarchic and slightly more rule-governed. Or to put it differently, those states whose signatures to a test ban treaty were essential for it to have a chance of succeeding could and would expect in exchange for their signatures something more than the run of states whose signatures were less important. And the privilege granted to the nuclear powers was a freedom to carry on testing nuclear weapons.

Bargaining

Bargaining is touched upon in Chapter 5 and bargaining theory has something to add to the understanding of arms control, even if David Kreps discouragingly introduces his chapter on the deficiencies of game theory by concentrating on aspects of the theory of bargaining.[1]

Arms control normally attempts to create a situation which is an improvement for all parties over the *status quo ante*. Thus all states benefit from the creation of a world where there are few nuclear weapons as opposed to one where there are many. The difference between the two worlds in bargaining terms is the surplus created by successful bargaining over the matter at hand. The art of bargaining is about securing the surplus and at the same time as large a share of it for your own side of the bargaining table as possible.

Bargaining theory at least establishes that the share of the bargaining surplus between two (or more) bargainers depends on two things. One is the relative bargaining power of the bargainers (which we look at below) and the other is their respective 'backstop' positions, that is to say, where they are placed in the event that there is a failure to reach a bargain. So, other things being equal, the side with the greater bargaining power will normally obtain the greater share of the surplus created by a successful striking of a bargain. And in addition, other things being equal, the side with the stronger backstop position or that is better at manoeuvring its backstop position upwards will also get a greater share of the surplus. As an example, if, along with Avinash Dixit and Susan Skeath,[2] we use 'patience' as an index of bargaining power (in the sense that being in a hurry for an agreement weakens bargaining power), this has sometimes been to the detriment of the USA in international negotiations. In arms control negotiations there have certainly been occasions when the USA has been hurried by the prospect of upcoming elections in that country. And this, in turn, has been reflected in a drift away from the ideal of bipartisanship in making foreign policy. On the other hand, the separation of powers in that country and the presence of well organised political lobbies give its negotiators considerable scope to present a possibly inflated version of its minimum backstop position, with negotiators saying to their opposite numbers that the Congress in its present mood, for example, would prefer no agreement to the one being proposed at the bargaining table. The relative monolithicity enjoyed during the Cold War by the Soviet Union was not always an advantage.

This is not to say that the pluralist US system is always an advantage. Sometimes the tail is allowed to wag the dog. US weapons laboratories in the 1950s and 1960s virtually invented the concept of the peaceful nuclear explosion to give them a private escape route in the eventuality that a comprehensive test ban would soon be signed. In the event it was not, but peaceful nuclear explosions lived on (in the abstract mainly, although the Soviet Union went on to carry out a few massive earth-moving projects) to complicate the making of arms control treaties ever since. The negative attitude of the US weapons laboratories to test bans has not disappeared and remains a factor in delaying US Senate ratification of the CTBT negotiated in 1996.

In the case of a ban on nuclear testing, analysis is complicated by the fact that the bargain to be struck was at least double headed: there was a bargain to be struck in 1963 in Cold War terms between the nuclear superpowers; and there was also a bargain to be struck between the nuclear weapons states themselves and the rest of the world. There was also a third, intermediate category of states, comprising France and China, which were well along in the process of actually becoming nuclear weapons states (France had begun testing in 1960 and China was to begin in 1964). Bargaining theory cautiously proposes that bargaining where there are more than two participants and bargaining over more than one thing at a time can be easier than it may seem to an innocent eye.

The actual text of the PTBT[3] makes a brief reference in its preamble to putting 'an end to the armaments race' but makes no allusion to the anti-proliferation aspects of the treaty, choosing to highlight its contribution to the reduction of radioactive pollution of the physical environment. It does, however, identify itself as constituting a step along the way to a complete ban on testing.

To take the bargain between the superpowers first, the surplus to be created was a slowing down of the arms race between them. In game theory terms, a nuclear arms race can be characterised by a repeated prisoner's dilemma game or (more optimistically) an assurance game,[4] where in either case the difference between the payoffs for a cooperative outcome to the game and the laissez-faire outcome of non-cooperative arms racing is the surplus (see Chapter 2). The surplus is net of the costs, after the agreement is reached, involved in policing it – detecting violations of the agreement which can otherwise be expected in the prisoner's dilemma interpretation, and reacting to them. It was eventually agreed that policing a comprehensive ban on testing would require each side to accept a certain amount of on-site inspection to decide cases where a seismic reading taken outside the territory of the state concerned was ambiguous as to whether the source of the disturbance detected was an earthquake or a small underground nuclear test explosion. Disagreement remained about how much was likely to be necessary, with the Soviets (as we have seen) willing to concede up to three per year and the USA with the UK insisting on a minimum of seven.

During negotiations, while the USSR was unable to do anything about the one-sided ability of the USA to manipulate upwards its backstop position, the Soviet programmes of particularly large atmospheric tests weakened Western negotiators' backstop positions (i.e. their situation in the event of no agreement being reached) in general by threatening, in effect, ever-increasing radioactive pollution of the northern hemisphere should an agreement not be reached. Public opinion – a political factor in the West in a way that did not apply to Moscow – had already become highly exercised on this matter. Indeed, the same factor increased the impatience of Western negotiators for an agreement which they could present to their increasingly impatient electorates. The year 1963 was one before both a general election in the UK and a presidential election in the USA. In fact, this impatience for an agreement was signalled by long voluntary moratoria on testing, which the Soviets responded to in kind just to the degree necessary to keep impatience for something more permanent from cooling.

Ultimately, agreement was reached in the aftermath of the Cuban missile crisis, which in terms of the present treatment's emphasis on bargaining considerably enlarged the surplus to be bargained over, in the sense that the potential costs of an unrestrained arms race had been underlined and brought home to both parties. The same event saw the first moves towards the creation of a nuclear-free region of the world in the form of the Latin American nuclear-free zone (see Chapter 4).

Bargaining for test ban treaties

Why East–West agreement stopped short of a comprehensive test ban needs to be explained in three parts. One is in connection with the prisoner's dilemma nature of the creation of the surplus. A relatively small surplus that is easy to secure into the indefinite future is preferred to a relatively large surplus that might prove vulnerable to unilateral defection, especially since successful experience in securing the small surplus will increase (or not) confidence that the larger surplus may be secured later. The second is the US backstop. Without a comprehensive ban, the USA would still be able to proof-test its existing stock of nuclear weapons (in other words, validate the shelf-life of weapons built five or ten years previously) and, less clearly at the time and therefore perhaps only with some difficulty, develop new weapons, and thereby underpin US confidence in the capacity of its nuclear forces. Throughout the entire Cold War period the USA was, on average, more reliant on nuclear weapons than was the USSR, partly for geopolitical reasons and partly because of its networks of alliances. Correspondingly, a US agreement to a comprehensive ban could well have needed a further 'sweetener', at the expense of the USSR, possibly in the form of a comparatively high degree of on-site inspection, which would be of more value to the USA, as an open, pluralist society, than to the secretive USSR. The final explanation connects explicitly with the anti-nuclear proliferation element of the treaty and the second of the two bargains referred to above. This element was in the air at the time of negotiation of the PTBT but is nowhere mentioned explicitly in the text. However, five years later, the preamble of the NPT strongly implied a connection between the goals of that treaty and further progress towards reaching a comprehensive ban on all nuclear testing.

A comprehensive ban on testing in 1963 as an anti-proliferation device would have been unequal in its effects on nuclear and non-nuclear signatories. The former would have been far better placed to tolerate a collapse of the arrangement, and presumably a burst of new nuclear powers appearing, than would the average non-nuclear state. Or, in bargaining parlance, the stronger backstop position of the nuclear states in the event of no bargain being struck meant that they would get the better part of the bargain or the greater share of the surplus. A comprehensive ban would have left the nuclear states still in possession of their nuclear weapons and insurance, for themselves principally, against the collapse of the whole.

A partial test ban was, at the time, seen as being almost as effective as a comprehensive ban in lowering the probability of the appearance of new nuclear powers, but at the same time meant an even greater share of the surplus for the nuclear weapons states. Under a partial ban, as we have seen, proof-testing and even the development of new kinds of nuclear weapons would not have been absolutely ruled out for states already in possession of nuclear weapons. In fact this loophole subsequently proved to be rather large, allowing an almost unrestricted programme of nuclear testing by the nuclear weapons states to continue, with the only practical restriction being on the size of the device tested.

Threshold Test Ban Treaty

A formal bilateral agreement – the Threshold Test Ban Treaty (TTBT) – between the two superpowers to restrict all underground tests to a maximum yield of 150 kilotonnes (i.e. equivalent to 150,000 tonnes of TNT) was reached in 1974. Combined with the Peaceful Nuclear Explosions (PNE) Treaty agreed in 1976 it ensured that no underground nuclear explosions carried out for peaceful purposes should be a weapon test in disguise.[5] Article 5 of the NPT had explicitly identified the use of nuclear explosives for peaceful purposes (e.g. large earth-moving projects) as a legitimate activity. The difficulty with this was that it almost amounted to an invitation to states to test a nuclear weapon underground and to claim that it was really a test or use of a nuclear earth-moving device, since the safeguards against this happening as laid out in Article 5 were vague. In fact, India described its first nuclear test explosion, carried out underground in 1974, as that of a peaceful device, admittedly to general scepticism.

Other multilateral implications of what were formally bilateral treaties included the fact that they constituted a further cautious step in the direction of a comprehensive ban on nuclear testing. The limit of 150 kilotonnes was itself a very slight concession to the non-nuclear states, since the military usefulness of individual weapons above this size had come to seem doubtful, except in so far as reliance on heavily concreted silos to protect land-based retaliatory forces (ICBMs) could be compromised by an attacker employing ultra-high-yield warheads designed to destroy such forces before they could be used. But the TTBT contained provisions asking that test sites be geographically delimited and that geological (principally seismic) information relating to these sites should be shared between the two parties. More, the sister PNE Treaty made provision for on-site inspection of these to verify that the TTBT was not being breached when a large explosion was claimed to have constituted – as perhaps in canal digging – a chain of simultaneously or near simultaneously detonated peaceful nuclear explosions.

Both treaties were presented to the US Senate for advice and consent to ratification in mid-1976 (a presidential election year) but fell at this particular hurdle, no doubt connected with the changed party alignment of the new President, Jimmy Carter. However, they were resurrected in 1990 and ratified by the year's end. But very extensive amendments and additions had been made in the interim to the TTBT's verification procedures (the original treaty protocol dealing with this question was one-page long; the 1990 version of the same ran to 100 pages) and analogous although briefer amendments had been made to the PNE Treaty protocol. The changes made the verification procedures much more intrusive than before. On-site inspection became a feature of both treaties and a new inspection technique midway between seismic monitoring (which was retained, with refinements) and the on-site presence of inspectors was introduced in the form of hydrodynamic yield measurement. This is accomplished by a mechanical device placed in the ground near the site of the actual explosion; it produces an accurate, independent reading of the yield by measuring the heaving of the ground in the vicinity of the explosion. This plainly needs at a minimum the passive cooperation of the inspected party. And the Soviets' new willingness to contemplate such intrusive measures indicates that they were probably themselves now in a hurry, to mend fences with the outside world while they got on with implementing far-reaching internal reforms. Of course, the latter did not go entirely to plan.

The 1990 treaties retained the core text of the mid-1970s originals and the TTBT refers in its preamble to an intention to proceed to a comprehensive test ban and speaks of the NPT in supportive language, without allowing itself to be drawn on any further connection between the two.

The ratification of the twin treaties was imminent during the 1990 review conference of the NPT but this made no difference to complaints by non-nuclear states at the conference, led by Mexico, concerning the failure of the nuclear states to make real progress towards their own nuclear disarmament, symbolised by what the Mexicans alleged was a particular lack of progress on the question of a comprehensive test ban. The US delegate at the conference cited the relative progress made on nuclear disarmament from the high point of the arms race, if not relative to 1970 (the year of the entering into force of the NPT and used as a benchmark by the Mexicans). In 1970 the total numbers of strategic nuclear warheads were 4,652 for the United States and 2,700 for the Soviet Union.[6] In 1989, respective, comparable totals were 14,530 and 12,403[7] (and by 2003, 5,974 and 5,436[8]). The US delegate also referred to the upcoming ratification of the twin TTBT and PNE Treaty but was unwilling to envisage a complete ban. The end result was the failure of the review conference to agree a final document, and this was not to be the last time that the outcome of a review conference falsified the predictions, optimistic and pessimistic, made beforehand.

The next review conference, scheduled for 1995, was seen as especially significant by the USA and others, in as much as it would authorise or not the indefinite extension of the NPT (originally projected to have a finite life of 25 years). This added considerably to the bargaining position of Mexico and the rest of the non-aligned group pressing for a comprehensive ban on testing. The nuclear weapons states, including the USA, were keen to see the NPT extended indefinitely. Their backstop position should there not be a comprehensive test ban agreement had been made worse by the implied non-aligned threat of 'no test ban, no NPT extension'. At the 1995 conference, the nuclear states promised a comprehensive test ban treaty by 1996 (negotiations for which had begun at Geneva in 1994, following on from a US moratorium on all testing and on research and development with respect to new nuclear weapons announced in 1992, the latter of course completely unverifiable). The CTBT was indeed agreed and opened for signature in 1996, which was also a presidential election year in the USA.

Comprehensive Test Ban Treaty

This treaty, which is to be of unlimited duration, bans all nuclear explosions, including all peaceful nuclear explosions, although a loophole for the latter was created within the context of the treaty's provision for decennial test ban review conferences, at which a request for a peaceful nuclear explosion could be made. US weapons laboratories were no longer pushing to have the option for peaceful nuclear explosions kept open by the USA, interest in which, real or feigned, had moved away to Brazil and India.

Though it does not appear in the text of the treaty or in the protocols,[9] which are themselves very long and comparable in this respect to the TTBT, an understanding was reached between the nuclear weapons powers that the ban on all nuclear explosions would extend downwards to include so-called hydronuclear tests. These involve the initiation of a test nuclear explosion in the usual way, that is, through the assembly or creation of a critical mass of fissile material, but the 'burning' of the mass is designed to be almost immediately interrupted, before any appreciable amount of energy has been released, beyond that of the chemical explosion normally required to create the critical mass in the first place (see Chapter 1). This is done in the presence of various recording instruments, including X-ray cameras, which register whether the initiation process has been successful. It is difficult to see how this understanding is to be policed in the context of any of the verification techniques designed to accompany the treaty. The one rather slight possibility is through the risk of a hydronuclear test going wrong, which is possible either when a new device is being tested or when an old device is being proof-tested, probably for safety, and there being a much larger release of energy than anticipated. For this reason, such tests are field tests and not laboratory tests. A release of energy equivalent to around 100 tonnes of TNT would have a distinct risk of being detected by the treaty's monitoring system

Bargaining for test ban treaties 169

(even a yield as low as one tonne may be detected when the circumstances for seismic readings are especially favourable).

It seems clear, on the other hand, that while hydronuclear testing may be of some value to established nuclear powers (the USA has conducted dozens of such tests in the past),[10] it would be of little use to inexperienced nuclear weapons states.

Hydrodynamic experiments, however, are permitted. Here there is no release of nuclear energy at all and no risk of any, since the critical mass is simulated in the form of a ball of lead or similar heavy but innocuous metal. Such experiments allow many aspects of a fission explosion (thermonuclear weapons will normally contain two fission critical masses), bar the explosion itself, to be tested. These exceptions, together with the freedom to simulate nuclear test explosions using computers, might be thought of as unstated privileges for the more advanced nuclear weapons states behind the treaty.

The CTBT has three important planks. One is the minimum grouping of 44 states to be assembled behind the treaty before it can enter into force. This includes all the nuclear weapons states, with the rest made up of those states thought to have a certain minimum of expertise in nuclear energy technology and that were member states of the Conference on Disarmament in 1996. Another is the provision for an Executive Council of the treaty, comprising 51 member states, to be elected, on a regional basis chiefly, from the treaty membership as a whole. The treaty membership as a whole, in turn, comprises the Comprehensive Nuclear-Test-Ban Treaty Organization. And the third is the International Monitoring System. This is comprises 321 technical centres throughout the world. Of these, 170 are seismometer stations and 11 are sea-based hydroacoustic stations. These may be compared with the verification requirements laid down in 1958: 170–180 land control posts and 10 ship-borne ones. The CTBT also stipulates 80 stations for the detection of radioactive materials in the atmosphere, and 60 listening stations for the low-pitched sound likely to rumble around the atmosphere generated by the upward thump of an underground test. As in 1958, all of this has to be supplemented by on-site inspections to clear up doubtful cases where a low-yield nuclear test – either of a small device or of a device deliberately muffled by being exploded in an artificial or natural cavity – could not be distinguished, using remote sensors alone, from an earthquake. But instead of an annual quota of such inspections, the principle of challenge inspections was adopted. A treaty party can present evidence to the Executive Council gathered from the monitoring system or elsewhere that a test explosion may have been carried out. The Council can authorise the sending of an inspection team to the site of the suspicious event. In the event of confirmation of the suspicion, the offending state is then reported to the Security Council.

Senate rejection

The US Senate refused ratification of the CTBT in 1999. In terms of the present treatment, the reasons for the Senate's failure to ratify may be described partly as a mismatch between the privileges enshrined in the treaty for the USA and what might have been expected given its overall bargaining position. In other words, the CTBT as proposed is too democratic, from its verification arrangements upwards, and pays too little attention to the power position of the USA. Secondly, and more accidentally as a consequence of the party politicisation of the making of arms control treaties in the USA, an incumbent president trying to use an arms control treaty for electoral purposes (and of course Clinton was not the first to do so) is not normally going to find a Congress controlled by the opposite party a willing accomplice.

On the question of privileges, three aspects seemed especially to trouble the Senate. One concerned verification. Here the USA and countries like it with an open society will nearly always find themselves underprivileged inside arms control agreements. It will, on average, have to work harder to determine whether other states are abiding by the terms of the treaty in question than other states will need to work to ascertain that it is abiding by the treaty terms. Any treaty violation by the USA is likely to be reported in the *New York Times* at least as soon as it may be detected by any international monitoring system. And doubts that the monitoring system attached to the CTBT would work very well in those parts of the world where it was the only safeguard (where politics was less pluralist than in the USA) were heightened by contemporary developments in Iraq, Iran and North Korea. All three were parties to the NPT but Iraq had definitely deceived the IAEA inspectors by establishing a secret bomb programme based on enriched uranium. And North Korea and Iran were at the very least strongly suspected at the time of the Senate hearings into the CTBT of having done something similar, even if in the case of North Korea wrong-doing had been first detected by the Vienna Agency inspectors themselves. Moreover, challenge inspections as embodied in the treaty were proving yet again that Eisenhower's old warning that intrusive verification breeds suspicion between states had lost none of its force. Cast-iron safeguards against challenge inspections being employed against the USA for essentially trivial reasons might have been expected in an ideal treaty. Lastly, the ending of the Cold War meant that the one-sided gains coming the way of the USA as a result of any arms control agreement that permitted US inspectors to visit strategically interesting parts of Soviet territory had themselves virtually evaporated.

Another privilege aspect, not unrelated to verification issues, concerned the machinery of governance of the CTBT. Here the problem for the Senate was simply that no privilege seemed to be apparent at all. Up to a point, the governance of the CTBT was modelled on the lines of the UN itself. There is the Conference of all parties, perhaps the equivalent of the General Assembly of the UN. And there is the Executive Council, perhaps the equivalent of the Security Council (but proportionately larger). But unlike the Security Council there is no in-built guarantee within the Executive Council that no binding vote could be made which put the USA in the minority (faint echoes here of the Baruch Plan, if in mirror image). Assurances by the Clinton administration that in practice this was a virtual impossibility cut little ice with the Senate.

The third aspect of privilege concerns the important issue of how the USA (and the other nuclear states) is to ensure the safety and viability of its nuclear stockpiles and prove new designs of nuclear weapon if all testing is prohibited (except hydrodynamic and computer-simulated testing). In this matter, thoughtful opinion within the Senate will have been torn. A complete ban on testing means that states must make do with 'virtual testing' or actual hydrodynamic tests. All of this amounts to a very considerable privilege for the USA, since of all states it has the most experience at virtual testing and far and away the most highly developed computer facilities as applied to such matters. Compared with a restricted test ban, which might have allowed the nuclear weapons states a small number of actual tests annually and which seems at an early stage of the CTBT negotiations to have been a possibility, the relative privilege for the USA of the comprehensive ban is clearly greater – all the more so, we might think, as the relative importance of nuclear weapons to US security (relative to conventional weapons and relative to the situation among the other nuclear weapons states) has declined sharply since the ending of the Cold War.

What will have caused opinion within the Senate to be torn on this matter was technical evidence from the weapons laboratories as of 1999 that wholly satisfactory computer simulations of nuclear tests were still several years away from being perfected (and progress in this matter, unlike progress on every other front of information technology, has subsequently been slow). This leaves open the possibility that the treaty, possibly in a somewhat emended form, can be resubmitted to the Senate at a later date, as with the TTBT and PNE Treaty. The emendations, which one would hope need not be so lengthy as in the aforementioned instances, to meet the mood of some future Senate, can only be guessed at, but the constitutional arrangements of the Executive Council seem an obvious place to start. These could kill two birds with one stone – satisfy the *amour propre* of the USA that its power position should be recognised in the procedures of the Council, and in such as way as to ensure that challenge inspections are not issued against the USA for what the latter might deem to be specious reasons.

This relatively optimistic assessment of the future of the CTBT is encouraged by the fact that the USA continues to abide (as of 2005) by its 1992 moratorium on nuclear testing, even if it looks set to abandon its parallel undertaking not to carry out research into new types of nuclear warhead.

Notes

1 David M. Kreps, *Game Theory and Economic Modelling* (Oxford, Clarendon Press, 1990).
2 Avinash Dixit and Susan Skeath, *Games of Strategy* (New York, W.W. Norton and Co., 1999), pp. 537–41.
3 The full text of the PTBT is available at www.state.gov/t/ac/trt/4797.htm (last accessed 5 May 2005).
4 See, respectively, Ian Bellany, 'An analogy for arms control', *International Security*, Vol. 6, No. 3, winter 1981/82, and Robert Jervis, 'Cooperation under the security dilemma', *World Politics*, Vol. 30, 1978, pp. 167–214.
5 The full texts of the PNE Treaty (Treaty on Underground Nuclear Explosions for Peaceful Purposes) and the TTBT (Treaty on the Limitation of Underground Nuclear Weapon Tests) are available at www.armscontrol.org/documents/pnet.asp and www.armscontrol.org/documents/ttbt.asp, respectively (last accessed 5 May 2005).
6 Defined as deliverable onto the territory of the respective opposing superpower using delivery systems based on the superpower home territory, or by means of long-range sea-based missiles. *The Military Balance 1970–1971* (London, Institute for Strategic Studies, 1970), p. 89.
7 *The Military Balance 1989–1990* (London, Brasseys for the International Institute for Strategic Studies, 1989), p. 212.
8 *The Military Balance 2003–2004* (Oxford, Oxford University Press for the International Institute for Strategic Studies, 2003), p. 229. These figures still exceed the 1970 figures and all the more so since they are not calculated on a comparable basis. Under so-called START accounting rules, bombers which may have previously carried 10 gravity bombs were now to be counted as carrying only one, and sea-launched ballistic missiles are counted as carrying the number of warheads they are deployed as carrying and not, as previously, the number they are capable of carrying. Nonetheless, a large part of the reduction from 1989 is real.
9 The full text of the Comprehensive Test Ban Treaty and its Protocols is available at www.state.gov/www/global/arms/treaties/ctbt/ctbt1.html (last accessed 5 May 2005).
10 Richard L. Garwin, 'Final review of the Comprehensive Nuclear Test Ban Treaty', hearing before the Committee on Foreign Relations, United States Senate, 106th Congress, 1st Session, 7 October 1999 (Washington, DC, US Government Printing Office, 2000), p. 112.

Appendix A
The Baruch Plan

My Fellow Members of the United Nations Atomic Energy Commission, and My Fellow Citizens of the World:

We are here to make a choice between the quick and the dead. That is our business.

Behind the black portent of the new atomic age lies a hope which, seized upon with faith, can work our salvation. If we fail, then we have damned every man to be the slave of Fear. Let us not deceive ourselves: We must elect World Peace or World Destruction.

Science has torn from nature a secret so vast in its potentialities that our minds cower from the terror it creates. Yet terror is not enough to inhibit the use of the atomic bomb. The terror created by weapons has never stopped man from employing them. For each new weapon a defense has been produced, in time. But now we face a condition in which adequate defense does not exist.

Science, which gave us this dread power, shows that it *can* be made a giant help to humanity, but science does *not* show us how to prevent its baleful use. So we have been appointed to obviate that peril by finding a meeting of the minds and the hearts of our peoples. Only in the will of mankind lies the answer.

It is to express this will and make it effective that we have been assembled. We must provide the mechanism to assure that atomic energy is used for peaceful purposes and preclude its use in war. To that end, we must provide immediate, swift, and sure punishment of those who violate the agreements that are reached by the nations. Penalization is essential if peace is to be more than a feverish interlude between wars. And, too, the United Nations can prescribe individual responsibility and punishment on the principles applied at Nuremberg by the Union of Soviet Socialist Republics, the United Kingdom, France and the United States – a formula certain to benefit the world's future.

Presented to the United Nations Atomic Energy Commission, 14 June 1946.

In this crisis, we represent not only our governments but, in a larger way, we represent the peoples of the world. We must remember that the peoples do not belong to the governments but that the governments belong to the peoples. We must answer their demands; we must answer the world's longing for peace and security.

In that desire the United States shares ardently and hopefully. The search of science for the absolute weapon has reached fruition in this country. But she stands ready to proscribe and destroy this instrument – to lift its use from death to life – if the world will join in a pact to that end.

In our success lies the promise of a new life, freed from the heart-stopping fears that now beset the world. The beginning of victory for the great ideals for which millions have bled and died lies in building a workable plan. Now we approach fulfillment of the aspirations of mankind. At the end of the road lies the fairer, better, surer life we crave and mean to have.

Only by a lasting peace are liberties and democracies strengthened and deepened. War is their enemy. And it will not do to believe that any of us can escape war's devastation. Victor, vanquished, and neutrals alike are affected physically, economically and morally.

Against the degradation of war we can erect a safeguard. That is the guerdon for which we reach. Within the scope for the formula we outline here there will be found, to [i.e. by] those who seek it, the essential elements of our purpose. Others will see only emptiness. Each of us carries his own mirror in which is reflected hope – or determined desperation – courage or cowardice.

There is a famine throughout the world today. It starves men's bodies. But there is a greater famine – the hunger of men's spirit. That starvation can be cured by the conquest of fear, and the substitution of hope, from which springs faith – faith in each other, faith that we want to work together toward salvation, and determination that those who threaten the peace and safety shall be punished.

The peoples of these democracies gathered here have a particular concern with our answer, for their peoples hate war. They will have a heavy exaction to make of those who fail to provide an escape. They are not afraid of an internationalism that protects; they are unwilling to be fobbed off by mouthings about narrow sovereignty, which is today's phrase for yesterday's isolation.

The basis of a sound foreign policy, in this new age, for all the nations here gathered, is that anything that happens, no matter where or how, which menaces the peace of the world, or the economic stability, concerns each and all of us.

That roughly, may be said to be the central theme of the United Nations. It is with that thought we begin consideration of the most important subject that can engage mankind – life itself.

Let there be no quibbling about the duty and the responsibility of this group and of the governments we represent. I was moved, in the afternoon of my life, to add my effort to gain the world's quest, by the broad mandate under which we were created. The resolution of the General Assembly, passed January 24, 1946 in London reads:

Section V. Terms of References of the Commission

The Commission shall proceed with the utmost despatch and enquire into all phases of the problem, and make such recommendations from time to time with

The Baruch Plan

respect to them as it finds possible. In particular the Commission shall make specific proposals:

(a) For extending between all nations the exchange of basic scientific information for peaceful ends;
(b) For control of atomic energy to the extent necessary to ensure its use only for peaceful purposes;
(c) For the elimination from national armaments of atomic weapons and of all other major weapons adaptable to mass destruction;
(d) For effective safeguards by way of inspection and other means to protect complying States against the hazards of violations and evasions.

The work of the Commission should proceed by separate stages, the successful completion of each of which will develop the necessary confidence of the world before the next stage is undertaken....

Our mandate rests, in text and spirit, upon the outcome of the Conference in Moscow of Messrs Molotov of the Union of Soviet Socialist Republics, Bevin of the United Kingdom, and Byrnes of the United States of America. The three Foreign Ministers on December 27, 1945 proposed the establishment of this body.

Their action was animated by a preceding conference in Washington on November 15, 1945, when the President of the United States, associated with Mr Attlee, Prime Minister of the United Kingdom, and Mr Mackenzie King, Prime Minister of Canada, stated that international control of the whole field of atomic energy was immediately essential. They proposed the formation of this body. In examining that source, the Agreed Declaration, it will be found that the fathers of the concept recognized the final means of world salvation – the abolition of war. Solemnly they wrote:

> We are aware that the only complete protection for the civilized world from the destructive use of scientific knowledge lies in the prevention of war. No system of safeguards that can be devised will of itself provide an effective guarantee against production of atomic weapons by a nation bent on aggression. Nor can we ignore the possibility of the development of other weapons, or of new methods of warfare, which may constitute as great a threat to civilization as the military use of atomic energy.

Through the historical approach I have outlined, we find ourselves here to test if man can produce, through his will and faith, the miracle of peace, just as he has, through science and skill, the miracle of the atom.

The United States proposes the creation of an International Atomic Development Authority, to which should be entrusted all phases of the development and use of atomic energy, starting with the raw material and including:

1. Managerial control or ownership of all atomic-energy activities potentially dangerous to world security.
2. Power to control, inspect, and license all other atomic activities.
3. The duty of fostering the beneficial uses of atomic energy.
4. Research and development responsibilities of an affirmative character intended to put the Authority in the forefront of atomic knowledge and thus to enable it to comprehend, and therefore to detect, misuse of atomic energy. To be

effective, the Authority must itself be the world's leader in the field of atomic knowledge and development and thus supplement its legal authority with the great power inherent in possession of leadership in knowledge.

I offer this as a basis for beginning our discussion.

But I think the peoples we serve would not believe – and without faith nothing counts – that a treaty, merely outlawing possession or use of the atomic bomb, constitutes effective fulfillment of the instructions to this Commission. Previous failures have been recorded in trying the method of simple renunciation, unsupported by effective guaranties of security and armament limitation. No one would have faith in that approach alone.

Now, if ever, is the time to act for the common good. Public opinion supports a world movement toward security. If I read the signs aright, the peoples want a program not composed merely of pious thoughts but of enforceable sanctions – an international law with teeth in it.

We of this nation, desirous of helping to bring peace to the world and realizing the heavy obligations upon us arising from our possession of the means of producing the bomb and from the fact that it is part of our armament, are prepared to make our full contribution toward effective control of atomic energy.

When an adequate system for control of atomic energy, including the renunciation of the bomb as a weapon, has been agreed upon and put into effective operation and condign punishments set up for violations of the rules of control which are to be stigmatized as international crimes, we propose that:

1. Manufacture of atomic bombs shall stop;
2. Existing bombs shall be disposed of pursuant to the terms of the treaty; and
3. The Authority shall be in possession of full information as to the know-how for the production of atomic energy.

Let me repeat, so as to avoid misunderstanding: My country is ready to make its full contribution toward the end we seek, subject of course to our constitutional processes and to an adequate system of control becoming fully effective, as we finally work it out.

Now as to violations: In the agreement, penalties of as serious a nature as the nations may wish and as immediate and certain in their execution as possible should be fixed for:

1. Illegal possession or use of an atomic bomb;
2. Illegal possession, or separation, of atomic material suitable for use in an atomic bomb;
3. Seizure of any plant or other property belonging to or licensed by the Authority;
4. Willful interference with the activities of the Authority;
5. Creation or operation of dangerous projects in a manner contrary to, or in the absence of, a license granted by the international control body.

It would be a deception, to which I am unwilling to lend myself, were I not to say to you and to our peoples that the matter of punishment lies at the very heart of our present security system. It might as well be admitted, here and now, that the subject goes straight to the veto power contained in the Charter of the

The Baruch Plan

United Nations so far as it relates to the field of atomic energy. The Charter permits penalization only by concurrence of each of the five great powers – the Union of Soviet Socialist Republics, the United Kingdom, China, France, and the United States.

I want to make very plain that I am concerned here with the veto power only as it affects this particular problem. There must be no veto to protect those who violate their solemn agreements not to develop or use atomic energy for destructive purposes.

The bomb does not wait upon debate. To delay may be to die. The time between violation and preventive action or punishment would be all too short for extended discussion as to the course to be followed.

As matters now stand several years may be necessary for another country to produce a bomb, *de novo*. However, once the basic information is generally known, and the Authority has established producing plants for peaceful purposes in the several countries, an illegal seizure of such a plant might permit a malevolent nation to produce a bomb in 12 months, and if preceded by secret preparation and necessary facilities perhaps even in a much shorter time. The time required – the advance warning given of the possible use of a bomb – can only be generally estimated but obviously will depend upon many factors, including the success with which the Authority has been able to introduce elements of safety in the design of its plants and the degree to which illegal and secret preparation for the military use of atomic energy will have been eliminated. Presumably no nation would think of starting a war with only one bomb.

This shows how imperative speed is in detecting and penalizing violations.

The process of prevention and penalization – a problem of profound statecraft – is, as I read it, implicit in the Moscow statement, signed by the Union of Soviet Socialist Republics, the United States and the United Kingdom a few months ago.

But before a country is ready to relinquish any winning weapons it must have more than words to reassure it. It must have a guarantee of safety, not only against the offenders in the atomic area but against the illegal users of other weapons – bacteriological, biological, gas – perhaps – why not! – against war itself.

In the elimination of war lies our solution, for only then will nations cease to compete with one another in the production and use of dread 'secret' weapons which are evaluated solely by their capacity to kill. This devilish program takes us back not merely to the Dark Ages but from cosmos to chaos. If we succeed in finding a suitable way to control atomic weapons, it is reasonable to hope that we may also preclude the use of other weapons adaptable to mass destruction. When a man learns to say 'A' he can, if he chooses, learn the rest of the alphabet too.

Let this be anchored in our minds: Peace is never long preserved by weight of metal or by an armament race. Peace can be made tranquil and secure only by understanding and agreement fortified by sanctions. We must embrace international cooperation or international disintegration.

Science has taught us how to put the atom to work. But to make it work for good instead of for evil lies in the domain dealing with the principles of human duty. We are now facing a problem more of ethics than of physics.

The solution will require apparent sacrifice in pride and in position, but better pain as the price of peace than death as the price of war.

I now submit the following measures as representing the fundamental features of a plan which would give effect to certain of the conclusions with [sic] I have epitomized.

1. *General.* The Authority should set up a thorough plan for control of the field of atomic energy, through various forms of ownership, dominion, licenses, operation, inspection, research, and management by competent personnel. After this is provided for, there should be as little interference as may be with the economic plans and the present private, corporate and state relationships in the several countries involved.
2. *Raw Materials.* The Authority should have as one of its earliest purposes to obtain and maintain complete and accurate information on world supplies of uranium and thorium and to bring them under its dominion. The precise pattern of control for various types of deposits of such materials will have to depend upon the geological, mining, refining and economic facts involved in different situations.

    The Authority should conduct continuous surveys so that it will have the most complete knowledge of the world geology of uranium and thorium. Only after all current information on world sources of uranium and thorium is known to us all can equitable plans be made for their production, refining, and distribution.
3. *Primary Production Plants.* The Authority should exercise complete managerial control of the production of fissionable materials in dangerous quantities and must own and control the product of these plants.
4. *Atomic Explosives.* The Authority should be given sole and exclusive right to conduct research in the field of atomic explosives. Research activities in the field of atomic explosives are essential in order that the Authority may keep in the forefront of knowledge in the field of atomic energy and fulfill the objective of preventing illicit manufacture of bombs. Only by maintaining its position as the best-informed agency will the Authority be able to determine the line between intrinsically dangerous and non-dangerous activities.
5. *Strategic Distribution of Activities and Materials.* The activities entrusted exclusively to the Authority because they are intrinsically dangerous to security should be distributed throughout the world. Similarly, stockpiles of raw materials and fissionable materials should not be centralized.
6. *Non-Dangerous Activities.* A function of the Authority should be promotion of the peacetime benefits of atomic energy.

    Atomic research (except in explosives), the use of research reactors, the production of radioactive tracers by means of non-dangerous reactors, the use of such tracers, and to some extent the production of power should be open to nations and their citizens under reasonable licensing arrangements from the Authority. Denatured materials, whose use we know also requires suitable safeguards, should be furnished for such purposes by the Authority under lease or other arrangement. Denaturing seems to have been overestimated by the public as a safety measure.
7. *Definition of Dangerous and Non-Dangerous Activities.* Although a reasonable dividing line can be drawn between dangerous and non-dangerous activities, it is not hard and fast. Provision should, therefore, be made to

assure constant re-examination of the questions and to permit revision of the dividing line as changing conditions and new discoveries may require.
8. *Operations of Dangerous Activities.* Any plant dealing with uranium or thorium after it once reaches the potential of dangerous use must be not only subject to the most rigorous and competent inspection by the Authority, but its actual operation shall be under the management, supervision, and control of the Authority.
9. *Inspection.* By assigning intrinsically dangerous activities exclusively to the Authority, the difficulties of inspection are reduced. If the Authority is the only agency which may lawfully conduct dangerous activities, then visible operation by others than the Authority will constitute an unambiguous danger signal. Inspection will also occur in connection with the licensing functions of the Authority.
10. *Freedom of Access.* Adequate ingress and egress for all qualified representatives of the Authority must be assured. Many of the inspection activities of the Authority should grow out of, and be incidental to, its other functions. Important measures of inspection will be associated with the tight control of raw materials, for this is a keystone of the plan. The continuing activities of prospecting, survey, and research in relation to raw materials will be designed not only to serve the affirmative development functions of the Authority but also to assure that no surreptitious operations are conducted in the raw-materials field by nations or their citizens.
11. *Personnel.* The personnel of the Authority should be recruited on a basis of proven competence but also so far as possible on an international basis.
12. *Progress by Stages.* A primary step in the creation of the system of control is the setting forth, in comprehensive terms, of the functions, responsibilities, powers, and limitations of the Authority. Once a charter for the Authority has been adopted, the Authority and the system of control for which it will be responsible will require time to become fully organized and effective. The plan of control will, therefore, have to come into effect in successive stages. These should be specifically fixed in the charter or means should be otherwise set forth in the charter for transitions from one stage to another, as contemplated in the resolution of the United Nations Assembly which created this Commission.
13. *Disclosures.* In the deliberations of the United Nations Commission on Atomic Energy, the United States is prepared to make available the information essential to a reasonable understanding of the proposals which it advocates. Further disclosures must be dependent, in the interests of all, upon the effective ratification of the treaty. When the Authority is actually created, the United States will join the other nations in making available the further information essential to that organization for the performance of its functions. As the successive stages of international control are reached, the United States will be prepared to yield, to the extent required by each stage, national control of activities in this field to the Authority.
14. *International Control.* There will be questions about the extent of control to be allowed to national bodies, when the Authority is established. Purely national authorities for control and development of atomic energy should to the extent necessary for the effective operation of the Authority be

subordinate to it. This is neither an endorsement nor a disapproval of the creation of national authorities. The Commission should evolve a clear demarcation of the scope of duties and responsibilities of such national authorities.

And now I end. I have submitted an outline for present discussion. Our consideration will be broadened by the criticism of the United States proposals and by the plans of the other nations, which, it is to be hoped, will be submitted at their early convenience. I and my associates of the United States Delegation will make available to each member of this body books and pamphlets, including the Acheson–Lilienthal report, recently made by the United States Department of State, and the McMahon Committee Monograph No. I entitled 'Essential Information on Atomic Energy' relating to the McMahon Bill recently passed by the United States Senate, which may prove of value in assessing the situation.

All of us are consecrated to making an end of gloom and hopelessness. It will not be an easy job. The way is long and thorny, but supremely worth traveling. All of us want to stand erect, with our faces to the sun, instead of being forced to burrow into the earth, like rats.

The pattern of salvation must be worked out by all for all.

The light at the end of the tunnel is dim, but our path seems to grow brighter as we actually begin our journey. We cannot yet light the way to the end. However, we hope the suggestions of my Government will be illuminating.

Let us keep in mind the exhortation of Abraham Lincoln, whose words, uttered at a moment of shattering national peril, form a complete text for our deliberation. I quote, paraphrasing slightly:

> We cannot escape history. We of this meeting will be remembered in spite of ourselves. No personal significance or insignificance can spare one or another of us. The fiery trial through which we are passing will light us down in honor or dishonor to the latest generation.
>
> We say we are for Peace. The world will not forget that we say this. We know how to save Peace. The world knows that we do. We, even we here, hold the power and have the responsibility.
>
> We shall nobly save, or meanly lose, the last, best hope of earth. The way is plain, peaceful, generous, just – a way which, if followed, the world will forever applaud.

My thanks for your attention.

Appendix B
Atoms for Peace

Madame President, Members of the General Assembly:

When Secretary General Hammarskjold's invitation to address this General Assembly reached me in Bermuda, I was just beginning a series of conferences with the Prime Ministers and Foreign Ministers of Great Britain and of France. Our subject was some of the problems that beset our world.

During the remainder of the Bermuda Conference, I had constantly in mind that ahead of me lay a great honor. That honor is mine today as I stand here, privileged to address the General Assembly of the United Nations.

At the same time that I appreciate the distinction of addressing you, I have a sense of exhilaration as I look upon this Assembly.

Never before in history has so much hope for so many people been gathered together in a single organization. Your deliberations and decisions during these somber years have already realized part of those hopes.

But the great test and the great accomplishments still lie ahead. And in the confident expectation of those accomplishments, I would use the office which, for the time being, I hold, to assure you that the Government of the United States will remain steadfast in its support of this body. This we shall do in the conviction that you will provide a great share of the wisdom, the courage, and the faith which can bring to this world lasting peace for all nations, and happiness and well-being for all men.

Clearly, it would not be fitting for me to take this occasion to present to you a unilateral American report on Bermuda. Nevertheless, I assure you that in our deliberations on that lovely island we sought to invoke those same great concepts of universal peace and human dignity which are so clearly etched in your Charter.

This address was given by US President Dwight D. Eisenhower before the General Assembly of the United Nations, 8 December 1953.

Neither would it be a measure of this great opportunity merely to recite, however hopefully, pious platitudes.

I therefore decided that this occasion warranted my saying to you some of the things that have been on the minds and hearts of my legislative and executive associates and on mine for a great many months – thoughts I had originally planned to say primarily to the American people.

I know that the American people share my deep belief that if a danger exists in the world, it is a danger shared by all – and equally, that if hope exists in the mind of one nation, that hope should be shared by all.

Finally, if there is to be advanced any proposal designed to ease even by the smallest measure the tensions of today's world, what more appropriate audience could there be than the members of the General Assembly of the United Nations?

I feel impelled to speak today in a language that in a sense is new – one which I, who have spent so much of my life in the military profession, would have preferred never to use.

That new language is the language of atomic warfare.

The atomic age has moved forward at such a pace that every citizen of the world should have some comprehension, at least in comparative terms, of the extent of this development of the utmost significance to every one of us. Clearly, if the people of the world are to conduct an intelligent search for peace, they must be armed with the significant facts of today's existence.

My recital of atomic danger and power is necessarily stated in United States terms, for these are the only incontrovertible facts that I know. I need hardly point out to this Assembly, however, that this subject is global, not merely national in character.

On July 16, 1945, the United States set off the world's first atomic explosion. Since that date in 1945, the United States of America has conducted 42 test explosions.

Atomic bombs today are more than 25 times as powerful as the weapons with which the atomic age dawned, while hydrogen weapons are in the ranges of millions of tons of TNT equivalent.

Today, the United States' stockpile of atomic weapons, which, of course, increases daily, exceeds by many times the explosive equivalent of the total of all bombs and all shells that came from every plane and every gun in every theatre of war in all of the years of World War II.

A single air group, whether afloat or land-based, can now deliver to any reachable target a destructive cargo exceeding in power all the bombs that fell on Britain in all of World War II.

In size and variety, the development of atomic weapons has been no less remarkable. The development has been such that atomic weapons have virtually achieved conventional status within our armed services. In the United States, the Army, the Navy, the Air Force, and the Marine Corps are all capable of putting this weapon to military use.

But the dread secret, and the fearful engines of atomic might, are not ours alone.

In the first place, the secret is possessed by our friends and allies, Great Britain and Canada, whose scientific genius made a tremendous contribution to our original discoveries, and the designs of atomic bombs.

Atoms for Peace

The secret is also known by the Soviet Union.

The Soviet Union has informed us that, over recent years, it has devoted extensive resources to atomic weapons. During this period, the Soviet Union has exploded a series of atomic devices, including at least one involving thermonuclear reactions.

If at one time the United States possessed what might have been called a monopoly of atomic power, that monopoly ceased to exist several years ago. Therefore, although our earlier start has permitted us to accumulate what is today a great quantitative advantage, the atomic realities of today comprehend two facts of even greater significance.

First, the knowledge now possessed by several nations will eventually be shared by others – possibly all others.

Second, even a vast superiority in numbers of weapons, and a consequent capability of devastating retaliation, is no preventive, of itself, against the fearful material damage and toll of human lives that would be inflicted by surprise aggression.

The free world, at least dimly aware of these facts, has naturally embarked on a large program of warning and defense systems. That program will be accelerated and expanded.

But let no one think that the expenditure of vast sums for weapons and systems of defense can guarantee absolute safety for the cities and citizens of any nation. The awful arithmetic of the atomic bomb does not permit any such easy solution. Even against the most powerful defense, an aggressor in possession of the effective minimum number of atomic bombs for a surprise attack could probably place a sufficient number of his bombs on the chosen targets to cause hideous damage.

Should such an atomic attack be launched against the United States, our reactions would be swift and resolute. But for me to say that the defense capabilities of the United States are such that they could inflict terrible losses upon an aggressor – for me to say that the retaliation capabilities of the United States are so great that such an aggressor's land would be laid waste – all this, while fact, is not the true expression of the purpose and the hope of the United States.

To pause there would be to confirm the hopeless finality of a belief that two atomic colossi are doomed malevolently to eye each other indefinitely across a trembling world. To stop there would be to accept helplessly the probability of civilization destroyed – the annihilation of the irreplaceable heritage of mankind handed down to us generation from generation – and the condemnation of mankind to begin all over again the age-old struggle upward from savagery toward decency, and right, and justice.

Surely no sane member of the human race could discover victory in such desolation. Could anyone wish his name to be coupled by history with such human degradation and destruction?

Occasional pages of history do record the faces of the 'Great Destroyers' but the whole book of history reveals mankind's never-ending quest for peace, and mankind's God-given capacity to build.

It is with the book of history, and not with isolated pages, that the United States will ever wish to be identified. My country wants to be constructive, not destructive. It wants agreement, not wars, among nations. It wants itself to live in freedom, and in the confidence that the people of every other nation enjoy equally the right of choosing their own way of life.

So my country's purpose is to help us move out of the dark chamber of horrors into the light, to find a way by which the minds of men, the hopes of men, the souls of men everywhere, can move forward toward peace and happiness and well-being.

In this quest, I know that we must not lack patience.

I know that in a world divided, such as ours today, salvation cannot be attained by one dramatic act.

I know that many steps will have to be taken over many months before the world can look at itself one day and truly realize that a new climate of mutually peaceful confidence is abroad in the world.

But I know, above all else, that we must start to take these steps – now.

The United States and its allies, Great Britain and France, have over the past months tried to take some of these steps. Let no one say that we shun the conference table.

On the record has long stood the request of the United States, Great Britain, and France to negotiate with the Soviet Union the problems of a divided Germany.

On that record has long stood the request of the same three nations to negotiate the problems of Korea.

Most recently, we have received from the Soviet Union what is in effect an expression of willingness to hold a Four Power meeting. Along with our allies, Great Britain and France, we were pleased to see that this note did not contain the unacceptable preconditions previously put forward.

As you already know from our joint Bermuda communiqué, the United States, Great Britain, and France have agreed promptly to meet with the Soviet Union.

The Government of the United States approaches this conference with hopeful sincerity. We will bend every effort of our minds to the single purpose of emerging from that conference with tangible results toward peace – the only true way of lessening international tension.

We never have, we never will, propose or suggest that the Soviet Union surrender what is rightfully theirs.

We will never say that the people of Russia are an enemy with whom we have no desire ever to deal or mingle in friendly and fruitful relationship.

On the contrary, we hope that this coming Conference may initiate a relationship with the Soviet Union which will eventually bring about a free inter-mingling of the peoples of the east and of the west – the one sure, human way of developing the understanding required for confident and peaceful relations.

Instead of the discontent which is now settling upon Eastern Germany, occupied Austria, and countries of Eastern Europe, we seek a harmonious family of free European nations, with none a threat to the other, and least of all a threat to the peoples of Russia.

Beyond the turmoil and strife and misery of Asia, we seek peaceful opportunity for these peoples to develop their natural resources and to elevate their lives.

These are not idle works or shallow visions. Behind them lies a story of nations lately come to independence, not as a result of war, but through free grant or peaceful negotiation. There is a record, already written, of assistance gladly given by nations of the west to needy peoples, and to those suffering the temporary effects of famine, drought, and natural disaster.

These are deeds of peace. They speak more loudly than promises or protestations of peaceful intent.

But I do not wish to rest either upon the reiteration of past proposals or the restatement of past deeds. The gravity of the time is such that every new avenue of peace, no matter how dimly discernible, should be explored.

There is at least one new avenue of peace which has not yet been well explored – an avenue now laid out by the General Assembly of the United Nations.

In its resolution of November 18th, 1953 this General Assembly suggested – and I quote – 'that the Disarmament Commission study the desirability of establishing a sub-committee consisting of representatives of the Powers principally involved, which should seek in private an acceptable solution ... and report on such a solution to the General Assembly and to the Security Council not later than 1 September 1954.'

The United States, heeding the suggestion of the General Assembly of the United Nations, is instantly prepared to meet privately with such other countries as may be 'principally involved,' to seek 'an acceptable solution' to the atomic armaments race which over-shadows not only the peace, but the very life, of the world.

We shall carry into these private or diplomatic talks a new conception.

The United States would seek more than the mere reduction or elimination of atomic materials for military purposes.

It is not enough to take this weapon out of the hands of the soldiers. It must be put into the hands of those who will know how to strip its military casing and adapt it to the arts of peace.

The United States knows that if the fearful trend of atomic military build-up can be reversed, this greatest of destructive forces can be developed into a great boon, for the benefit of all mankind.

The United States knows that peaceful power from atomic energy is no dream of the future. That capability, already proved, is here – now – today. Who can doubt, if the entire body of the world's scientists and engineers had adequate amounts of fissionable material with which to test and develop their ideas, that this capability would rapidly be transformed into universal, efficient, and economic usage.

To hasten the day when fear of the atom will begin to disappear from the minds of people, and the governments of the East and West, there are certain steps that can be taken now.

I therefore make the following proposals:

The Governments principally involved, to the extent permitted by elementary prudence, to begin now and continue to make joint contributions from their stockpiles of normal uranium and fissionable materials to an International Atomic Energy Agency. We would expect that such an agency would be set up under the aegis of the United Nations.

The ratios of contributions, the procedures and other details would properly be within the scope of the 'private conversations' I have referred to earlier.

The United States is prepared to undertake these explorations in good faith.

Any partner of the United States acting in the same good faith will find the United States a not unreasonable or ungenerous associate.

Undoubtedly initial and early contributions to this plan would be small in quantity. However, the proposal has the great virtue that it can be undertaken without the irritations and mutual suspicions incident to any attempt to set up a completely acceptable system of world-wide inspection and control.

The Atomic Energy Agency could be made responsible for the impounding, storage, and protection of the contributed fissionable and other materials. The ingenuity of our scientists will provide special safe conditions under which such a bank of fissionable material can be made essentially immune to surprise seizure.

The more important responsibility of this Atomic Energy Agency would be to devise methods whereby this fissionable material would be allocated to serve the peaceful pursuits of mankind. Experts would be mobilized to apply atomic energy to the needs of agriculture, medicine, and other peaceful activities. A special purpose would be to provide abundant electrical energy in the power-starved areas of the world. Thus the contributing powers would be dedicating some of their strength to serve the needs rather than the fears of mankind.

The United States would be more than willing – it would be proud to take up with others 'principally involved' the development of plans whereby such peaceful use of atomic energy would be expedited.

Of those 'principally involved' the Soviet Union must, of course, be one.

I would be prepared to submit to the Congress of the United States, and with every expectation of approval, any such plan that would:

First – encourage world-wide investigation into the most effective peacetime uses of fissionable material, and with the certainty that they had all the material needed for the conduct of all experiments that were appropriate;

Second – begin to diminish the potential destructive power of the world's atomic stockpiles;

Third – allow all peoples of all nations to see that, in this enlightened age, the great powers of the earth, both of the East and of the West, are interested in human aspirations first, rather than in building up the armaments of war;

Fourth – open up a new channel for peaceful discussion, and initiate at least a new approach to the many difficult problems that must be solved in both private and public conversations, if the world is to shake off the inertia imposed by fear, and is to make positive progress toward peace.

Against the dark background of the atomic bomb, the United States does not wish merely to present strength, but also the desire and the hope for peace.

The coming months will be fraught with fateful decisions. In this Assembly; in the capitals and military headquarters of the world; in the hearts of men everywhere, be they governors, or governed, may they be decisions which will lead this work out of fear and into peace.

To the making of these fateful decisions, the United States pledges before you – and therefore before the world – its determination to help solve the fearful atomic dilemma – to devote its entire heart and mind to find the way by which the miraculous inventiveness of man shall not be dedicated to his death, but consecrated to his life.

I again thank the delegates for the great honor they have done me, in inviting me to appear before them, and in listening to me so courteously. Thank you.

Appendix C
Treaty on the Non-proliferation of Nuclear Weapons

Preamble

The States concluding this Treaty, hereinafter referred to as the 'Parties to the Treaty',
 Considering the devastation that would be visited upon all mankind by a nuclear war and the consequent need to make every effort to avert the danger of such a war and to take measures to safeguard the security of peoples,
 Believing that the proliferation of nuclear weapons would seriously enhance the danger of nuclear war,
 In conformity with resolutions of the United Nations General Assembly calling for the conclusion of an agreement on the prevention of wider dissemination of nuclear weapons,
 Undertaking to cooperate in facilitating the application of International Atomic Energy Agency safeguards on peaceful nuclear activities,
 Expressing their support for research, development and other efforts to further the application, within the framework of the International Atomic Energy Agency safeguards system, of the principle of safeguarding effectively the flow of source and special fissionable materials by use of instruments and other techniques at certain strategic points,
 Affirming the principle that the benefits of peaceful applications of nuclear technology, including any technological by-products which may be derived by nuclear-weapon States from the development of nuclear explosive devices, should

---

Signed at Washington, London and Moscow 1 July 1968. Ratification advised by US Senate 13 March 1969. Ratified by the US President 24 November 1969. US ratification deposited at Washington, London and Moscow 5 March 1970. Proclaimed by the US President 5 March 1970. Entered into force 5 March 1970.

be available for peaceful purposes to all Parties of the Treaty, whether nuclear-weapon or non-nuclear weapon States,

Convinced that, in furtherance of this principle, all Parties to the Treaty are entitled to participate in the fullest possible exchange of scientific information for, and to contribute alone or in cooperation with other States to, the further development of the applications of atomic energy for peaceful purposes,

Declaring their intention to achieve at the earliest possible date the cessation of the nuclear arms race and to undertake effective measures in the direction of nuclear disarmament,

Urging the cooperation of all States in the attainment of this objective,

Recalling the determination expressed by the Parties to the 1963 Treaty banning nuclear weapon tests in the atmosphere, in outer space and under water in its Preamble to seek to achieve the discontinuance of all test explosions of nuclear weapons for all time and to continue negotiations to this end,

Desiring to further the easing of international tension and the strengthening of trust between States in order to facilitate the cessation of the manufacture of nuclear weapons, the liquidation of all their existing stockpiles, and the elimination from national arsenals of nuclear weapons and the means of their delivery pursuant to a Treaty on general and complete disarmament under strict and effective international control,

Recalling that, in accordance with the Charter of the United Nations, States must refrain in their international relations from the threat or use of force against the territorial integrity or political independence of any State, or in any other manner inconsistent with the Purposes of the United Nations, and that the establishment and maintenance of international peace and security are to be promoted with the least diversion for armaments of the world's human and economic resources,

Have agreed as follows:

Article 1

Each nuclear-weapon State Party to the Treaty undertakes not to transfer to any recipient whatsoever nuclear weapons or other nuclear explosive devices or control over such weapons or explosive devices directly, or indirectly; and not in any way to assist, encourage, or induce any non-nuclear weapon State to manufacture or otherwise acquire nuclear weapons or other nuclear explosive devices, or control over such weapons or explosive devices.

Article 2

Each non-nuclear-weapon State Party to the Treaty undertakes not to receive the transfer from any transferor whatsoever of nuclear weapons or other nuclear explosive devices or of control over such weapons or explosive devices directly, or indirectly; not to manufacture or otherwise acquire nuclear weapons or other nuclear explosive devices; and not to seek or receive any assistance in the manufacture of nuclear weapons or other nuclear explosive devices.

The Non-proliferation Treaty

Article 3

1. Each non-nuclear-weapon State Party to the Treaty undertakes to accept safeguards, as set forth in an agreement to be negotiated and concluded with the International Atomic Energy Agency in accordance with the Statute of the International Atomic Energy Agency and the Agency's safeguards system, for the exclusive purpose of verification of the fulfillment of its obligations assumed under this Treaty with a view to preventing diversion of nuclear energy from peaceful uses to nuclear weapons or other nuclear explosive devices. Procedures for the safeguards required by this article shall be followed with respect to source or special fissionable material whether it is being produced, processed or used in any principal nuclear facility or is outside any such facility. The safeguards required by this article shall be applied to all source or special fissionable material in all peaceful nuclear activities within the territory of such State, under its jurisdiction, or carried out under its control anywhere.

2. Each State Party to the Treaty undertakes not to provide: (a) source or special fissionable material, or (b) equipment or material especially designed or prepared for the processing, use or production of special fissionable material, to any non-nuclear-weapon State for peaceful purposes, unless the source or special fissionable material shall be subject to the safeguards required by this article.

3. The safeguards required by this article shall be implemented in a manner designed to comply with Article 4 of this Treaty, and to avoid hampering the economic or technological development of the Parties or international cooperation in the field of peaceful nuclear activities, including the international exchange of nuclear material and equipment for the processing, use or production of nuclear material for peaceful purposes in accordance with the provisions of this article and the principle of safeguarding set forth in the Preamble of the Treaty.

4. Non-nuclear-weapon States Party to the Treaty shall conclude agreements with the International Atomic Energy Agency to meet the requirements of this article either individually or together with other States in accordance with the Statute of the International Atomic Energy Agency. Negotiation of such agreements shall commence within 180 days from the original entry into force of this Treaty. For States depositing their instruments of ratification or accession after the 180-day period, negotiation of such agreements shall commence not later than the date of such deposit. Such agreements shall enter into force not later than eighteen months after the date of initiation of negotiations.

Article 4

1. Nothing in this Treaty shall be interpreted as affecting the inalienable right of all the Parties to the Treaty to develop research, production and use of nuclear energy for peaceful purposes without discrimination and in conformity with articles I and II of this Treaty.

2. All the Parties to the Treaty undertake to facilitate, and have the right to participate in, the fullest possible exchange of equipment, materials and scientific

and technological information for the peaceful uses of nuclear energy. Parties to the Treaty in a position to do so shall also cooperate in contributing alone or together with other States or international organizations to the further development of the applications of nuclear energy for peaceful purposes, especially in the territories of non-nuclear-weapon States Party to the Treaty, with due consideration for the needs of the developing areas of the world.

Article 5

Each party to the Treaty undertakes to take appropriate measures to ensure that, in accordance with this Treaty, under appropriate international observation and through appropriate international procedures, potential benefits from any peaceful applications of nuclear explosions will be made available to non-nuclear-weapon States Party to the Treaty on a nondiscriminatory basis and that the charge to such Parties for the explosive devices used will be as low as possible and exclude any charge for research and development. Non-nuclear-weapon States Party to the Treaty shall be able to obtain such benefits, pursuant to a special international agreement or agreements, through an appropriate international body with adequate representation of non-nuclear-weapon States. Negotiations on this subject shall commence as soon as possible after the Treaty enters into force. Non-nuclear-weapon States Party to the Treaty so desiring may also obtain such benefits pursuant to bilateral agreements.

Article 6

Each of the Parties to the Treaty undertakes to pursue negotiations in good faith on effective measures relating to cessation of the nuclear arms race at an early date and to nuclear disarmament, and on a Treaty on general and complete disarmament under strict and effective international control.

Article 7

Nothing in this Treaty affects the right of any group of States to conclude regional treaties in order to assure the total absence of nuclear weapons in their respective territories.

Article 8

1. Any Party to the Treaty may propose amendments to this Treaty. The text of any proposed amendment shall be submitted to the Depositary Governments which shall circulate it to all Parties to the Treaty. Thereupon, if requested to do so by one-third or more of the Parties to the Treaty, the Depositary Governments shall convene a conference, to which they shall invite all the Parties to the Treaty, to consider such an amendment.

2. Any amendment to this Treaty must be approved by a majority of the votes of all the Parties to the Treaty, including the votes of all nuclear-weapon States Party to the Treaty and all other Parties which, on the date the amendment is circulated, are members of the Board of Governors of the International Atomic Energy Agency. The amendment shall enter into force for each Party that deposits its instrument of ratification of the amendment upon the deposit of such instruments of ratification by a majority of all the Parties, including the instruments of ratification of all nuclear-weapon States Party to the Treaty and all other Parties which, on the date the amendment is circulated, are members of the Board of Governors of the International Atomic Energy Agency. Thereafter, it shall enter into force for any other Party upon the deposit of its instrument of ratification of the amendment.

3. Five years after the entry into force of this Treaty, a conference of Parties to the Treaty shall be held in Geneva, Switzerland, in order to review the operation of this Treaty with a view to assuring that the purposes of the Preamble and the provisions of the Treaty are being realized. At intervals of five years thereafter, a majority of the Parties to the Treaty may obtain, by submitting a proposal to this effect to the Depositary Governments, the convening of further conferences with the same objective of reviewing the operation of the Treaty.

Article 9

1. This Treaty shall be open to all States for signature. Any State which does not sign the Treaty before its entry into force in accordance with paragraph 3 of this article may accede to it at any time.

2. This Treaty shall be subject to ratification by signatory States. Instruments of ratification and instruments of accession shall be deposited with the Governments of the United States of America, the United Kingdom of Great Britain and Northern Ireland and the Union of Soviet Socialist Republics, which are hereby designated the Depositary Governments.

3. This Treaty shall enter into force after its ratification by the States, the Governments of which are designated Depositaries of the Treaty, and forty other States signatory to this Treaty and the deposit of their instruments of ratification. For the purposes of this Treaty, a nuclear-weapon State is one which has manufactured and exploded a nuclear weapon or other nuclear explosive device prior to January 1, 1967.

4. For States whose instruments of ratification or accession are deposited subsequent to the entry into force of this Treaty, it shall enter into force on the date of the deposit of their instruments of ratification or accession.

5. The Depositary Governments shall promptly inform all signatory and acceding States of the date of each signature, the date of deposit of each instrument of ratification or of accession, the date of the entry into force of this Treaty, and the date of receipt of any requests for convening a conference or other notices.

6. This Treaty shall be registered by the Depositary Governments pursuant to article 102 of the Charter of the United Nations.

Article 10

1. Each Party shall in exercising its national sovereignty have the right to withdraw from the Treaty if it decides that extraordinary events, related to the subject matter of this Treaty, have jeopardized the supreme interests of its country. It shall give notice of such withdrawal to all other Parties to the Treaty and to the United Nations Security Council three months in advance. Such notice shall include a statement of the extraordinary events it regards as having jeopardized its supreme interests.

2. Twenty-five years after the entry into force of the Treaty, a conference shall be convened to decide whether the Treaty shall continue in force indefinitely, or shall be extended for an additional fixed period or periods. This decision shall be taken by a majority of the Parties to the Treaty.

Article 11

This Treaty, the English, Russian, French, Spanish and Chinese texts of which are equally authentic, shall be deposited in the archives of the Depositary Governments. Duly certified copies of this Treaty shall be transmitted by the Depositary Governments to the Governments of the signatory and acceding States.

IN WITNESS WHEREOF the undersigned, duly authorized, have signed this Treaty.
DONE in triplicate, at the cities of Washington, London and Moscow, this first day of July one thousand nine hundred and sixty-eight.

Table A.1. Signatories and parties to the Treaty on the Non-proliferation of Nuclear Weapons

Country	Date of signature	Date of ratification	Date of accession (A)/ succession (S)
Afghanistan	1 July 1968	4 February 1970	
Albania			12 September 1990 (A)
Algeria			12 January 1995(A)
Andorra			7 June 1996 (A)
Angola			14 October 1996 (A)
Antigua and Barbuda			17 June 1985 (S)
Argentina			10 February 1995 (A)
Armenia*			15 July 1993 (A)
Australia*	27 February 1970	23 January 1973	
Austria*	1 July 1968	27 June 1969	
Azerbaijan*			22 September 1992 (A)
Bahamas			11 August 1976 (S)
Bahrain			3 November 1988 (A)
Bangladesh*			31 August 1979 (A)
Barbados	1 July 1968	21 February 1980	
Belarus			22 July 1993 (A)
Belgium*	20 August 1968	2 May 1975	
Belize			9 August 1985 (S)
Benin	1 July 1968	31 October 1972	
Bhutan*			23 May 1985 (A)
Bolivia	1 July 1968	26 May 1970	
Bosnia and Herzegovina			15 August 1994 (S)
Botswana	1 July 1968	28 April 1969	
Brazil			18 September 1998 (A)
Brunei			26 March 1985 (A)
Bulgaria*	1 July 1968	5 September 1969	
Burkina Faso*	25 November 1968	3 March 1970	
Burundi			19 March 1971 (A)
Cambodia			2 June 1972 (A)
Cameroon	17 July 1968	8 January 1969	
Canada*	23 July 1968	8 January 1969	
Cape Verde			24 October 1979 (A)
Central African Republic			25 October 1970 (A)
Chad	1 July 1968	10 March 1971	
Chile*			25 May 1995 (A)
China*			9 March 1992 (A)
Colombia	1 July 1968	8 April 1986	
Comoros			4 October 1995 (A)
Congo*			23 October 1978 (A)
Costa Rica	1 July 1968	3 March 1970	
Cote d'Ivoire	1 July 1968	6 March 1973	
Croatia*			29 June 1992 (S)
Cuba*	14 September 2002	4 November 2002	
Cyprus*	1 July 1968	10 February 1970	
Czech Republic*			1 January 1993 (S)

Country	Date of signature	Date of ratification	Date of accession (A)/ succession (S)
Denmark*	1 July 1968	3 January 1969	
Djibouti			16 October 1996 (A)
Dominica			10 August 1984 (S)
Dominican Republic	1 July 1968	24 July 1971	
Ecuador*	9 July 1968	7 March 1969	
Egypt[1]	1 July 1968	26 February 1981	
El Salvador*	1 July 1968	11 July 1972	
Equatorial Guinea			1 November 1984 (A)
Eritrea			3 March 1995 (A)
Estonia			7 January 1992 (A)
Ethiopia	5 September 1968	5 February 1970	
Fiji			14 July 1972 (S)
Finland*	1 July 1968	5 February 1969	
France*			3 August 1992 (A)
FYR Macedonia			12 April 1995 (A)
Gabon			19 February 1974 (A)
Gambia	4 September 1968	12 May 1975	
Georgia*			7 March 1994 (A)
Germany[2]*	28 November 1969	2 May 1975	
Ghana*	1 July 1968	4 May 1970	
Greece*	1 July 1968	11 March 1970	
Grenada			2 September 1975 (S)
Guatemala	26 July 1968	22 September 1970	
Guinea			29 April 1985 (A)
Guinea-Bissau			20 August 1976 (S)
Guyana			19 October 1993 (A)
Haiti	1 July 1968	2 June 1970	
Holy See*[1]			25 February 1971 (A)
Honduras	1 July 1968	16 May 1973	
Hungary*	1 July 1968	27 May 1969	
Iceland*	1 July 1968	18 July 1969	
Indonesia*[1]	2 March 1970	12 July 1979	
Iran	1 July 1968	2 February 1970	
Iraq	1 July 1968	29 October 1969	
Ireland*	1 July 1968	1 July 1968	
Italy*[1]	28 January 1969	2 May 1975	
Jamaica*	14 April 1969	5 March 1970	
Japan*[1]	3 February 1970	8 June 1976	
Jordan*	10 July 1968	11 February 1970	
Kazakhstan			14 February 1994 (A)
Kenya	1 July 1968	11 June 1970	
Kiribati			18 April 1985 (S)
Kuwait*	15 August 1968	17 November 1989	
Kyrgyzstan			5 July 1994 (A)
Laos	1 July 1968	20 February 1970	
Latvia*			31 January 1992 (A)
Lebanon	1 July 1968	15 July 1970	
Lesotho	9 July 1968	20 May 1970	
Liberia	1 July 1968	5 March 1970	
Libya	18 July 1968	26 May 1975	

The Non-proliferation Treaty 195

Country	Date of signature	Date of ratification	Date of accession (A)/ succession (S)
Liechtenstein[1]			20 April 1978 (A)
Lithuania*			23 September 1991 (A)
Luxembourg*	14 August 1968	2 May 1975	
Madagascar*	22 August 1968	8 October 1970	
Malawi			18 February 1986 (S)
Malaysia	1 July 1968	5 March 1970	
Maldive Islands	11 September 1968	7 April 1970	
Mali*	14 July 1969	10 February 1970	
Malta	17 April 1969	6 February 1970	
Marshall Islands			30 January 1995 (A)
Mauritania			26 October 1993 (A)
Mauritius	1 July 1968	8 April 1969	
Mexico[1]	26 July 1968	21 January 1969	
Micronesia			14 April 1995 (A)
Moldova			11 October 1994 (A)
Monaco*			13 March 1995 (A)
Mongolia*	1 July 1968	14 May 1969	
Morocco	1 July 1968	27 November 1970	
Mozambique			4 September 1990 (A)
Myanmar			2 December 1992 (A)
Namibia			2 October 1992 (A)
Nauru			7 June 1982 (A)
Nepal	1 July 1968	5 January 1970	
Netherlands*[3]	20 August 1968	2 May 1975	
New Zealand*	1 July 1968	10 September 1969	
Nicaragua*	1 July 1968	6 March 1973	
Niger			9 October 1992 (A)
Nigeria	1 July 1968	27 September 1968	
North Korea			12 December 1985 (A)
Norway*	1 July 1968	5 February 1969	
Oman			23 January 1997 (A)
Palau			12 April 1995 (A)
Panama*	1 July 1968	13 January 1977	
Papua New Guinea			13 January 1982 (A)
Paraguay*	1 July 1968	4 February 1970	
Peru*	1 July 1968	3 March 1970	
Philippines	1 July 1968	5 October 1972	
Poland*	1 July 1968	12 June 1969	
Portugal*			15 December 1977 (A)
Qatar			3 April 1989 (A)
Romania*	1 July 1968	4 February 1970	
Russia[4]	1 July 1968	5 March 1970	
Rwanda			20 May 1975 (A)
St Kitts and Nevis			22 March 1993 (A)
St Lucia			28 December 1979 (S)
St Vincent and the Grenadines			6 November 1984 (S)
San Marino	1 July 1968	10 August 1970	
Sao Tome and Principe			20 July 1983 (A)
Saudi Arabia			3 October 1988 (A)

Country	Date of signature	Date of ratification	Date of accession (A)/succession (S)
Senegal	1 July 1968	17 December 1970	
Seychelles*			12 March 1985 (A)
Sierra Leone			26 February 1975 (A)
Singapore	5 February 1970	10 March 1976	
Slovakia			1 January 1993 (S)
Slovenia*			7 April 1992 (A)
Solomon Islands			17 June 1981 (S)
Somalia	1 July 1968	5 March 1970	
South Africa*			10 July 1991 (A)
South Korea*	1 July 1968	23 April 1975	
Spain*			5 November 1987 (A)
Sri Lanka	1 July 1968	5 March 1979	
Sudan	24 December 1968	31 October 1973	
Suriname			30 June 1976 (S)
Swaziland	24 June 1969	11 December 1969	
Sweden*	19 August 1968	9 January 1970	
Switzerland[1]*	27 November 1969	9 March 1977	
Syria	1 July 1968	24 September 1969	
Taiwan*[5]	1 July 1968	27 January 1970	
Tajikistan*			17 January 1995 (A)
Tanzania*			31 May 1991 (A)
Thailand			2 December 1972 (A)
Togo	1 July 1968	26 February 1970	
Tonga			7 July 1971 (S)
Trinidad and Tobago	20 August 1968	30 October 1986	
Tunisia	1 July 1968	26 February 1970	
Turkey*[1]	28 January 1969	17 April 1980	
Turkmenistan			29 September 1994 (A)
Tuvalu			19 January 1979 (S)
UAE			26 September 1995 (A)
Uganda			20 October 1982 (A)
UK*[6]	1 July 1968	27 November 1968	
Ukraine			5 December 1994 (A)
Uruguay*	1 July 1968	31 August 1970	
USA	1 July 1968	5 March 1970	
Uzbekistan*			2 May 1992 (A)
Vanuatu			26 August 1995 (A)
Venezuela	1 July 1968	25 September 1975	
Vietnam			14 June 1982 (A)
Western Samoa			17 March 1975 (A)
Yemen[7]	14 November 1968	1 June 1979	
Yugoslavia	10 July 1968	4 March 1970	
Zaire	22 July 1968	4 August 1970	
Zambia			15 May 1991 (A)
Zimbabwe			26 September 1991 (A)

See opposite for notes to Table.

*   An asterisk indicates states for which the Additional Protocol was in force as of early 2005. Iran and Libya have pledged to be bound by the Additional Protocol pending its entry into force for these states.
1   With statement.
2   The former German Democratic Republic, which united with the Federal Republic of Germany on 3 October 1990, had signed the NPT on 1 July 1968 and deposited its instrument of ratification on 31 October 1969.
3   Extended to Netherlands Antilles and Aruba.
4   Russia has given notice that it would continue to exercise the rights and fulfil the obligations of the former Soviet Union arising from the NPT.
5   On 27 January 1970, an instrument of ratification was deposited in the name of the Republic of China. From 1 January 1979, the United States recognised the People's Republic of China as the sole legal government of China. The authorities on Taiwan state that they will continue to abide by the provisions of the Treaty and the United States regards them as bound by the obligations imposed by the Treaty.
6   Extended to Aguilla and territories under the territorial sovereignty of the United Kingdom.
7   The Republic of Yemen resulted from the union of the Yemen Arab Republic and the People's Democratic Republic of Yemen. The table indicates the date of signature and ratification by the People's Democratic Republic of Yemen, which was the first of these two states to become a party to the NPT. The Yemen Arab Republic signed the NPT on 23 September 1968 and deposited its instrument of ratification on 14 May 1986.

Appendix D
Treaty of Tlatelolco documentation and texts

The Treaty of Tlatelolco, opened for signature in 1967, was first amended at a special general conference in July 1990 to attach the phrase 'and the Caribbean' to the title. The Treaty was amended again in May 1991 to replace paragraph 2 of Article 25. The original Treaty paragraph had excluded political entities 'part or all of whose territory' is in dispute with 'an extra-continental country and one or more Latin American States' prior to the opening of signature of the Treaty. This clause effectively excluded Guyana from membership. Belize (formerly British Honduras) attained its independence from the UK in 1981 and became eligible for membership from that date; Guyana gained independence from Britain in 1966, but has ongoing territorial disputes with Venezuela and Suriname.

The amendment replaced the original text with the following: 'The condition of State Party to the Treaty of Tlatelolco shall be restricted to independent states which are situated within the zone of application of the Treaty in accordance with Article 4 of same, and with Paragraph 1 of the present Article, and which were members of the United Nations as of December 10, 1985, as well as the non-autonomous territories mentioned in Document OAS/CER.P, AG/DOC. 1939/85 of November 5, 1985,[1] once they attain their independence.' This amendment, adopted by consensus at the 1991 General Conference, has not yet been ratified by all of the current contracting parties to the Treaty.

The third amending of the Treaty occurred at a special general conference in August 1992, when amendments to Articles 14–16, 19 and 20 were adopted. The most significant of these was a change in Article 16 to designate the IAEA as having the sole authority to conduct special inspections of Tlatelolco parties; the original text gave this authority both to the IAEA and to OPANAL, the Treaty's executive agency. These amendments have not yet been ratified by all of the current contracting parties to the Treaty. The complete text of this third set of amendments is reproduced below.

Article 14

2. The Contracting Parties shall simultaneously transmit to the Agency a copy of the reports sent to the International Atomic Energy Agency in relation to matters subject to the present Treaty which are relevant to the Agency's work.

3. The information provided by the Contracting Parties cannot be divulged or communicated to third parties, totally or partially, by the recipients of the reports except with the express consent of the former.

Article 15

1. At the request of any of the Parties, and with the authorization of the Council, the Secretary General may request any of the Contracting Parties to provide the Agency with complementary or supplementary information regarding any extraordinary fact or circumstance which affects compliance with the present Treaty, explaining the reasons he/they had for such action. The Contracting Parties commit themselves to cooperate quickly and fully with the Secretary General.

2. The Secretary General will immediately inform the Council and the Contracting Parties about such requests and their respective replies.

Article 16

1. The International Atomic Energy Agency has the power of carrying out special inspections in conformity with Article 12 and with the agreements referred to in Article 13 of this Treaty.

2. At the request of any of the Contracting Parties, and following the procedures established under Article 15 of the present Treaty, the Council may submit to the consideration of the International Atomic Energy Agency a requisition that the latter initiate the arrangements required for the carrying out of a special inspection.

3. The Secretary General shall request the General Director of the International Atomic Energy Agency to transmit to him in a timely manner the information sent by the former to the IAEA Board of Governors regarding the conclusion of the said special inspection. The Secretary General shall promptly impart such information to the Council.

4. By the Agency or the Secretary General, the Council shall transmit such information to all of the Contracting Parties.

Article 19

The Agency may conclude agreements with the International Atomic Energy Agency as are authorized by the General Conference and as it considers appropriate to facilitate the efficient operation of the Control System established by this Treaty.

Article 20

1. The Agency may also enter into relations with any international organization or body, especially any which may be established in the future to supervise disarmament or measures for the control of armaments in any party of the world.

2. The Contracting Parties may, when they see fit, request the advice of the Inter-American Nuclear Energy Commission on all technical matters connected with the application of this Treaty with which the Commission is competent to deal under its Statute.

Treaty for the Prohibition of Nuclear Weapons in Latin America

Signed at Mexico City, 14 February 1967; entered into force 22 April 1968.

Preamble

In the name of their peoples and faithfully interpreting their desires and aspirations, the Governments of the States which sign the Treaty for the Prohibition of Nuclear Weapons in Latin America,

Desiring to contribute, so far as lies in their power, towards ending the armaments race, especially in the field of nuclear weapons, and towards strengthening a world at peace, based on the sovereign equality of States, mutual respect and good neighbourliness,

Recalling that the United Nations General Assembly, in its Resolution 808 (IX), adopted unanimously as one of the three points of a coordinated programme of disarmament 'the total prohibition of the use and manufacture of nuclear weapons and weapons of mass destruction of every type,'

Recalling that military denuclearized zones are not an end in themselves but rather a means for achieving general and complete disarmament at a later stage,

Recalling United Nations General Assembly Resolution 1911 (XVIII), which established that the measures that should be agreed upon for the denuclearization of Latin America should be taken 'in the light of the principles of the Charter of the United Nations and of regional agreements,'

Recalling United Nations General Assembly Resolution 2028 (XX), which established the principle of an acceptable balance of mutual responsibilities and duties for the nuclear and non-nuclear powers, and

Recalling that the Charter of the Organization of American States proclaims that it is an essential purpose of the Organization to strengthen the peace and security of the hemisphere,

Convinced:

That the incalculable destructive power of nuclear weapons has made it imperative that the legal prohibition of war should be strictly observed in practice if the survival of civilization and of mankind itself is to be assured,

That nuclear weapons, whose terrible effects are suffered, indiscriminately and inexorably, by military forces and civilian population alike, constitute, through the persistence of the radioactivity they release, an attack on the integrity of the human species and ultimately may even render the whole earth uninhabitable,

That general and complete disarmament under effective international control is a vital matter which all the peoples of the world equally demand,

That the proliferation of nuclear weapons, which seems inevitable unless States, in the exercise of their sovereign rights, impose restrictions on themselves in order to prevent it, would make any agreement on disarmament enormously difficult and would increase the danger of the outbreak of a nuclear conflagration,

That the establishment of militarily denuclearized zones is closely linked with the maintenance of peace and security in the respective regions,

That the military denuclearization of vast geographical zones, adopted by the sovereign decision of the States comprised therein, will exercise a beneficial influence on other regions where similar conditions exist,

That the privileged situation of the signatory States, whose territories are wholly free from nuclear weapons, imposes upon them the inescapable duty of preserving that situation both in their own interest and for the good of mankind,

That the existence of nuclear weapons in any country of Latin America would make it a target for possible nuclear attacks and would inevitably set off, throughout the region, a ruinous race in nuclear weapons which would involve the unjustifiable diversion, for warlike purposes, of the limited resources required for economic and social development,

That the foregoing reasons, together with the traditional peace-loving outlook of Latin America, give rise to an inescapable necessity that nuclear energy should be used in that region exclusively for peaceful purposes, and that the Latin American countries should use their right to the greatest and most equitable possible access to this new source of energy in order to expedite the economic and social development of their peoples,

Convinced finally:

That the military denuclearization of Latin America – being understood to mean the undertaking entered into internationally in this Treaty to keep their territories forever free from nuclear weapons – will constitute a measure which will spare their peoples from the squandering of their limited resources on nuclear armaments and will protect them against possible nuclear attacks on their territories, and will also constitute a significant contribution towards preventing the proliferation of nuclear weapons and a powerful factor for general and complete disarmament, and

That Latin America, faithful to its tradition of universality, must not only endeavour to banish from its homelands the scourge of a nuclear war, but must also strive to promote the well-being and advancement of its peoples, at the same time co-operating in the fulfillment of the ideals of mankind, that is to say, in the consolidation of a permanent peace based on equal rights, economic fairness and social justice for all, in accordance with the principles and purposes set forth in the Charter of the United Nations and in the Charter of the Organization of American States.

Have agreed as follows:

Obligations

Article 1

1. The Contracting Parties hereby undertake to use exclusively for peaceful purposes the nuclear material and facilities which are under their jurisdiction, and to prohibit and prevent in their respective territories:

(a) The testing, use, manufacture, production or acquisition by any means whatsoever of any nuclear weapons, by the Parties themselves, directly or indirectly, on behalf of anyone else or in any other way, and
(b) The receipt, storage, installation, deployment and any form of possession of any nuclear weapons, directly or indirectly, by the Parties themselves, by anyone on their behalf or in any other way.

2. The Contracting Parties also undertake to refrain from engaging in, encouraging or authorizing, directly or indirectly, or in any way participating in the testing, use, manufacture, production, possession or control of any nuclear weapon.

Definition of the Contracting Parties

Article 2

For the purposes of this Treaty, the Contracting Parties are those for whom the Treaty is in force.

Definition of territory

Article 3

For the purposes of this Treaty, the term 'territory' shall include the territorial sea, air space and any other space over which the State exercises sovereignty in accordance with its own legislation.

Zone of application

Article 4

1. The zone of application of this Treaty is the whole of the territories for which the Treaty is in force.

2. Upon fulfillment of the requirements of article 28, paragraph 1, the zone of application of this Treaty shall also be that which is situated in the western hemisphere within the following limits (except the continental part of the territory of the United States of America and its territorial waters): starting at a point located at 35° north latitude, 75° west longitude; from this point directly southward to a point at 30° north latitude, 75° west longitude; from there, directly eastward to a point at 30° north latitude, 50° west longitude; from there, along a loxodromic line to a point at 5° north latitude, 20° west longitude; from there directly southward to a point 60° south latitude, 20° west longitude; from there, directly westward to a point at 60° south latitude, 115° west longitude; from there, directly northward to a point at 0 latitude, 115° west longitude; from there, along a loxodromic line to a point at 35° north latitude, 150° west longitude; from there, directly eastward to a point at 35° north latitude, 75° west longitude.

Definition of nuclear weapons

Article 5

For the purposes of this Treaty, a nuclear weapon is any device which is capable of releasing nuclear energy in an uncontrolled manner and which has a group of characteristics that are appropriate for use for warlike purposes. An instrument that may be used for the transport or propulsion of the device is not included in this definition if it is separable from the device and not an indivisible part thereof.

Meeting of signatories

Article 6

At the request of any of the signatory States or if the Agency established by article 7 should so decide, a meeting of all the signatories may be convoked to consider in common questions which may affect the very essence of this instrument, including possible amendments to it. In either case, the meeting will be convoked by the General Secretary.

Organization

Article 7

1. In order to ensure compliance with the obligations of this Treaty, the Contracting Parties hereby establish an international organization to be known as the 'Agency for the Prohibition of Nuclear Weapons in Latin America,' hereinafter referred to as 'the Agency.' Only the Contracting Parties shall be affected by its decisions.

2. The Agency shall be responsible for the holding of periodic or extraordinary consultations among Member States on matters relating to the purposes, measures and procedures set forth in this Treaty and to the supervision of compliance with the obligations arising therefrom.

3. The Contracting Parties agree to extend to the Agency full and prompt cooperation in accordance with the provisions of this Treaty, of any agreements they may conclude with the Agency and of any agreements the Agency may conclude with any other international organization or body.

4. The headquarters of the Agency shall be in Mexico City.

Organs

Article 8

1. There are hereby established as principal organs of the Agency a General Conference, a Council and a Secretariat.

2. Such subsidiary organs as are considered necessary by the General Conference may be established within the purview of this Treaty.

The General Conference

Article 9

1. The General Conference, the supreme organ of the Agency, shall be composed of all the Contracting Parties; it shall hold regular sessions every two years, and may also hold special sessions whenever this Treaty so provides or, in the opinion of the Council, the circumstances so require.

2. The General Conference:

(a) May consider and decide on any matters or questions covered by this Treaty, within the limits thereof, including those referring to powers and functions of any organ provided for in this Treaty.
(b) Shall establish procedures for the control system to ensure observance of this Treaty in accordance with its provisions.
(c) Shall elect the Members of the Council and the General Secretary.
(d) May remove the General Secretary from office if the proper functioning of the Agency so requires.

Treaty of Tlatelolco

(e) Shall receive and consider the biennial and special reports submitted by the Council and the General Secretary.
(f) Shall initiate and consider studies designed to facilitate the optimum fulfillment of the aims of this Treaty, without prejudice to the power of the General Secretary independently to carry out similar studies for submission to and consideration by the Conference.
(g) Shall be the organ competent to authorize the conclusion of agreements with Governments and other international organizations and bodies.

3. The General Conference shall adopt the Agency's budget and fix the scale of financial contributions to be paid by Member States, taking into account the systems and criteria used for the same purpose by the United Nations.

4. The General Conference shall elect its officers for each session and may establish such subsidiary organs as it deems necessary for the performance of its functions.

5. Each Member of the Agency shall have one vote. The decisions of the General Conference shall be taken by a two-thirds majority of the Members present and voting in the case of matters relating to the control system and measures referred to in article 20, the admission of new Members, the election or removal of the General Secretary, adoption of the budget and matters related thereto. Decisions on other matters, as well as procedural questions and also determination of which questions must be decided by a two-thirds majority, shall be taken by a simple majority of the Members present and voting.

6. The General Conference shall adopt its own rules of procedure.

The Council

Article 10

1. The Council shall be composed of five Members of the Agency elected by the General Conference from among the Contracting Parties, due account being taken of equitable geographic distribution.

2. The Members of the Council shall be elected for a term of four years. However, in the first election three will be elected for two years. Outgoing Members may not be reelected for the following period unless the limited number of States for which the Treaty is in force so requires.

3. Each Member of the Council shall have one representative.

4. The Council shall be so organized as to be able to function continuously.

5. In addition to the functions conferred upon it by this Treaty and to those which may be assigned to it by the General Conference, the Council shall, through the General Secretary, ensure the proper operation of the control system in accordance with the provisions of this Treaty and with the decisions adopted by the General Conference.

6. The Council shall submit an annual report on its work to the General Conference as well as such special reports as it deems necessary or which the General Conference requests of it.

7. The Council shall elect its officers for each session.

8. The decisions of the Council shall be taken by a simple majority of its Members present and voting.

9. The Council shall adopt its own rules of procedure.

The Secretariat

Article 11

1. The Secretariat shall consist of a General Secretary, who shall be the chief administrative officer of the Agency, and of such staff as the Agency may require. The term of office of the General Secretary shall be four years and he may be re-elected for a single additional term. The General Secretary may not be a national of the country in which the Agency has its headquarters. In case the office of General Secretary becomes vacant, a new election shall be held to fill the office for the remainder of the term.

2. The staff of the Secretariat shall be appointed by the General Secretary, in accordance with rules laid down by the General Conference.

3. In addition to the functions conferred upon him by this Treaty and to those which may be assigned to him by the General Conference, the General Secretary shall ensure, as provided by article 10, paragraph 5, the proper operation of the control system established by this Treaty, in accordance with the provisions of the Treaty and the decisions taken by the General Conference.

4. The General Secretary shall act in that capacity in all meetings of the General Conference and of the Council and shall make an annual report to both bodies on the work of the Agency and any special reports requested by the General Conference or the Council or which the General Secretary may deem desirable.

5. The General Secretary shall establish the procedures for distributing to all Contracting Parties information received by the Agency from governmental sources and such information from non-governmental sources as may be of interest to the Agency.

6. In the performance of their duties the General Secretary and the staff shall not seek or receive instructions from any Government or from any other authority external to the Agency and shall refrain from any action which might reflect on their position as international officials responsible only to the Agency; subject to their responsibility to the Agency, they shall not disclose any industrial secrets or other confidential information coming to their knowledge by reason of their official duties in the Agency.

7. Each of the Contracting Parties undertakes to respect the exclusively international character of the responsibilities of the General Secretary and the staff and not to seek to influence them in the discharge of their responsibilities.

Treaty of Tlatelolco

Control system

Article 12

1. For the purpose of verifying compliance with the obligations entered into by the Contracting Parties in accordance with article 1, a control system shall be established which shall be put into effect in accordance with the provisions of articles 13–18 of this Treaty.

2. The control system shall be used in particular for the purpose of verifying:

(a) That devices, services and facilities intended for peaceful uses of nuclear energy are not used in the testing or manufacture of nuclear weapons,
(b) That none of the activities prohibited in article 1 of this Treaty are carried out in the territory of the Contracting Parties with nuclear materials or weapons introduced from abroad, and
(c) That explosions for peaceful purposes are compatible with article 18 of this Treaty.

IAEA safeguards

Article 13

Each Contracting Party shall negotiate multilateral or bilateral agreements with the International Atomic Energy Agency for the application of its safeguards to its nuclear activities. Each Contracting Party shall initiate negotiations within a period of 180 days after the date of the deposit of its instrument of ratification of this Treaty. These agreements shall enter into force, for each Party, not later than eighteen months after the date of the initiation of such negotiations except in case of unforeseen circumstances or *force majeure*.

Reports of the Parties

Article 14

1. The Contracting Parties shall submit to the Agency and to the International Atomic Energy Agency, for their information, semi-annual reports stating that no activity prohibited under this Treaty has occurred in their respective territories.

2. The Contracting Parties shall simultaneously transmit to the Agency a copy of any report they may submit to the International Atomic Energy Agency which relates to matters that are the subject of this Treaty and to the application of safeguards.

3. The Contracting Parties shall also transmit to the Organization of American States, for its information, any reports that may be of interest to it, in accordance with the obligations established by the Inter-American System.

Special reports requested by the General Secretary

Article 15

1. With the authorization of the Council, the General Secretary may request any of the Contracting Parties to provide the Agency with complementary or supplementary information regarding any event or circumstance connected with compliance with this Treaty, explaining his reasons. The Contracting Parties undertake to cooperate promptly and fully with the General Secretary.

2. The General Secretary shall inform the Council and the Contracting Parties forthwith of such requests and of the respective replies.

Special inspections

Article 16

1. The International Atomic Energy Agency and the Council established by this Treaty have the power of carrying out special inspections in the following cases:

(a) In the case of the International Atomic Energy Agency, in accordance with the agreements referred to in article 13 of this Treaty;
(b) In the case of the Council:
   (i) When so requested, the reasons for the request being stated, by any Party which suspects that some activity prohibited by this Treaty has been carried out or is about to be carried out, either in the territory of any other Party or in any other place on such latter Party's behalf, the Council shall immediately arrange for such an inspection in accordance with article 10, paragraph 5.
   (ii) When requested by any Party which has been suspected of or charged with having violated this Treaty, the Council shall immediately arrange for the special inspection requested in accordance with article 10, paragraph 5.

The above requests will be made to the Council through the General Secretary.

2. The costs and expenses of any special inspection carried out under paragraph 1, sub-paragraph (b), sections (i) and (ii) of this article shall be borne by the requesting Party or Parties, except where the Council concludes on the basis of the report on the special inspection that, in view of the circumstances existing in the case, such costs and expenses should be borne by the agency.

3. The General Conference shall formulate the procedures for the organization and execution of the special inspections carried out in accordance with paragraph 1, sub-paragraph (b), sections (i) and (ii) of this article.

4. The Contracting Parties undertake to grant the inspectors carrying out such special inspections full and free access to all places and all information which may be necessary for the performance of their duties and which are directly and

intimately connected with the suspicion of violation of this Treaty. If so requested by the authorities of the Contracting Party in whose territory the inspection is carried out, the inspectors designated by the General Conference shall be accompanied by representatives of said authorities, provided that this does not in any way delay or hinder the work of the inspectors.

5. The Council shall immediately transmit to all the Parties, through the General Secretary, a copy of any report resulting from special inspections.

6. Similarly, the Council shall send through the General Secretary to the Secretary-General of the United Nations, for transmission to the United Nations Security Council and General Assembly, and to the Council of the Organization of American States, for its information, a copy of any report resulting from any special inspection carried out in accordance with paragraph 1, sub-paragraph (b), sections (i) and (ii) of this article.

7. The Council may decide, or any Contracting Party may request, the convening of a special session of the General Conference for the purpose of considering the reports resulting from any special inspection. In such a case, the General Secretary shall take immediate steps to convene the special session requested.

8. The General Conference, convened in special session under this article, may make recommendations to the Contracting Parties and submit reports to the Secretary-General of the United Nations to be transmitted to the United Nations Security Council and the General Assembly.

Use of nuclear energy for peaceful purposes

Article 17

Nothing in the provisions of this Treaty shall prejudice the rights of the Contracting Parties, in conformity with this Treaty, to use nuclear energy for peaceful purposes, in particular for their economic development and social progress.

Explosions for peaceful purposes

Article 18

1. The Contracting Parties may carry out explosions of nuclear devices for peaceful purposes – including explosions which involve devices similar to those used in nuclear weapons – or collaborate with third parties for the same purpose, provided that they do so in accordance with the provisions of this article and the other articles of the Treaty, particularly articles 1 and 5.

2. Contracting Parties intending to carry out, or to cooperate in carrying out, such an explosion shall notify the Agency and the International Atomic Energy Agency, as far in advance as the circumstances require, of the date of the explosion and shall at the same time provide the following information:

(a) The nature of the nuclear device and the source from which it was obtained,
(b) The place and purpose of the planned explosion,
(c) The procedures which will be followed in order to comply with paragraph 3 of this article,
(d) The expected force of the device, and
(e) The fullest possible information on any possible radioactive fall-out that may result from the explosion or explosions, and measures which will be taken to avoid danger to the population, flora, fauna and territories of any other Party or Parties.

3. The General Secretary and the technical personnel designated by the Council and the International Atomic Energy Agency may observe all the preparations, including the explosion of the device, and shall have unrestricted access to any area in the vicinity of the site of the explosion in order to ascertain whether the device and the procedures followed during the explosion are in conformity with the information supplied under paragraph 2 of this article and the other provisions of this Treaty.

4. The Contracting Parties may accept the collaboration of third parties for the purpose set forth in paragraph 1 of the present article, in accordance with paragraphs 2 and 3 thereof.

Relations with other international organizations

Article 19

1. The Agency may conclude such agreements with the International Atomic Energy Agency as are authorized by the General Conference and as it considers likely to facilitate the efficient operation of the control system established by this Treaty.

2. The Agency may also enter into relations with any international organization or body, especially any which may be established in the future to supervise disarmament or measures for the control of armaments in any part of the world.

3. The Contracting Parties may, if they see fit, request the advice of the International American Nuclear Energy Commission on all technical matters connected with the application of this Treaty with which the Commission is competent to deal under its Statute.

Measures in the event of violation of the Treaty

Article 20

1. The General Conference shall take note of all cases in which, in its opinion, any Contracting Party is not complying fully with its obligations under this Treaty

and shall draw the matter to the attention of the Party concerned, making such recommendations as it deems appropriate.

2. If, in its opinion, such non-compliance constitutes a violation of this Treaty which might endanger peace and security, the General Conference shall report thereon simultaneously to the United Nations Security Council and the General Assembly through the Secretary-General of the United Nations, and to the Council of the Organization of American States. The General Conference shall likewise report to the International Atomic Energy Agency for such purposes as are relevant in accordance with its Statute.

United Nations and Organization of American States

Article 21

None of the provisions of this Treaty shall be construed as impairing the rights and obligations of the Parties under the Charter of the United Nations or, in the case of States Members of the Organization of American States, under existing regional treaties.

Privileges and immunities

Article 22

1. The Agency shall enjoy in the territory of each of the Contracting Parties such legal capacity and such privileges and immunities as may be necessary for the exercise of its functions and the fulfillment of its purposes.

2. Representatives of the Contracting Parties accredited to the Agency and officials of the Agency shall similarly enjoy such privileges and immunities as are necessary for the performance of their functions.

3. The Agency may conclude agreements with the Contracting Parties with a view to determining the details of the application of paragraphs 1 and 2 of this article.

Notification of other agreements

Article 23

Once this Treaty has entered into force, the Secretariat shall be notified immediately of any international agreement concluded by any of the Contracting Parties on matters with which this Treaty is concerned; the Secretariat shall register it and notify the other Contracting Parties.

Settlement of disputes

Article 24

Unless the Parties concerned agree on another mode of peaceful settlement, any question or dispute concerning the interpretation or application of this Treaty which is not settled shall be referred to the International Court of Justice with the prior consent of the Parties to the controversy.

Signature

Article 25

1. This Treaty shall be open indefinitely for signature by:
(a) All the Latin American Republics, and
(b) All other sovereign States situated in their entirety south of latitude 35° degrees north in the western hemisphere; and, except as provided in paragraph 2 of this article, all such States which become sovereign, when they have been admitted by the General Conference.

2. The General Conference shall not take any decision regarding the admission of a political entity part or all of whose territory is the subject, prior to the date when this Treaty is opened for signature, of a dispute or claim between an extra-continental country and one or more Latin American States, so long as the dispute has not been settled by peaceful means.

Ratification and deposit

Article 26

1. This Treaty shall be subject to ratification by signatory States in accordance with their respective constitutional procedures.

2. This Treaty and the instruments of ratification shall be deposited with the Government of the Mexican United States, which is hereby designated the Depositary Government.

3. The Depositary Government shall send certified copies of this Treaty to the Governments of signatory States and shall notify them of the deposit of each instrument of ratification.

Reservations

Article 27

This Treaty shall not be subject to reservations.

Entry into force

Article 28

1. Subject to the provisions of paragraph 2 of this article, this Treaty shall enter into force among the States that have ratified it as soon as the following requirements have been met:
   (a) Deposit of the instruments of ratification of this Treaty with the Depositary Government by the Governments of the States mentioned in article 25 which are in existence on the date when this Treaty is opened for signature and which are not affected by the provisions of article 25, paragraph 2;
   (b) Signature and ratification of Additional Protocol I annexed to this Treaty by all extra-continental or continental States having *de jure* or *de facto* international responsibility for territories situated in the zone of application of the Treaty;
   (c) Signature and ratification of the Additional Protocol II annexed to this Treaty by all powers possessing nuclear weapons;
   (d) Conclusion of bilateral or multilateral agreements on the application of Safeguards System of the International Atomic Energy Agency in accordance with article 13 of this Treaty.

2. All signatory States shall have the imprescriptible right to waive, wholly or in part, the requirements laid down in the preceding paragraph. They may do so by means of a declaration which shall be annexed to their respective instrument of ratification and which may be formulated at the time of deposit of the instrument or subsequently. For those States which exercise this right, this Treaty shall enter into force upon deposit of the declaration, or as soon as those requirements have been met which have not been expressly waived.

3. As soon as this Treaty has entered into force in accordance with the provisions of paragraph 2 for eleven States, the Depositary Government shall convene a preliminary meeting of those States in order that the Agency may be set up and commence its work.

4. After the entry into force of this Treaty for all the countries of the zone, the rise of a new power possessing nuclear weapons shall have the effect of suspending the execution of this Treaty for those countries which have ratified it without waiving requirements of paragraph 1, sub-paragraph (c) of this article, and which request such suspension; the Treaty shall remain suspended until the new power, on its own initiative or upon request by the General Conference, ratifies the annexed Additional Protocol II.

Amendments

Article 29

1. Any Contracting Party may propose amendments to this Treaty and shall submit its proposals to the Council through the General Secretary, who shall

transmit them to all the other Contracting Parties and, in addition, to all other signatories in accordance with article 6. The Council, through the General Secretary, shall immediately following the meeting of signatories convene a special session of the General Conference to examine the proposals made, for the adoption of which a two-thirds majority of the Contracting Parties present and voting shall be required.

2. Amendments adopted shall enter into force as soon as the requirements set forth in article 28 of this Treaty have been complied with.

Duration and denunciation

Article 30

1. This Treaty shall be of a permanent nature and shall remain in force indefinitely, but any Party may denounce it by notifying the General Secretary of the Agency if, in the opinion of the denouncing State, there have arisen or may arise circumstances connected with the content of this Treaty or of the annexed Additional Protocols I and II which affect its supreme interests or the peace and security of one or more Contracting Parties.

2. The denunciation shall take effect three months after the delivery to the General Secretary of the Agency of the notification by the Government of the signatory State concerned. The General Secretary shall immediately communicate such notification to the other Contracting Parties and to the Secretary-General of the United Nations for the information of the United Nations Security Council and the General Assembly. He shall also communicate it to the Secretary-General of the Organization of American States.

Authentic texts and registration

Article 31

This Treaty, of which the Spanish, Chinese, English, French, Portuguese and Russian texts are equally authentic, shall be registered by the Depositary Government in accordance with article 102 of the United Nations Charter. The Depositary Government shall notify the Secretary-General of the United Nations of the signatures, ratification and amendments relating to this Treaty and shall communicate them to the Secretary-General of the Organization of American States for its information.

Transitional Article

Denunciation of the declaration referred to article 28, paragraph 2, shall be subject to the same procedures as the denunciation of this Treaty, except that it will take effect on the date of delivery of the respective notification.

IN WITNESS WHEREOF the undersigned Plenipotentiaries, having deposited their full powers, found in good and due form, sign this Treaty on behalf of their respective Governments.

DONE at Mexico, Distrito Federal, on the Fourteenth day of February, one thousand nine hundred and sixty-seven.

Additional Protocol I to the Treaty for the Prohibition of Nuclear Weapons in Latin America

The undersigned Plenipotentiaries, furnished with full powers by their respective Governments,

Convinced that the Treaty for the Prohibition of Nuclear Weapons in Latin America, negotiated and signed in accordance with the recommendations of the General Assembly of the United Nations in Resolution 1911 (XVIII) of 27 November 1963, represents an important step towards ensuring the non-proliferation of nuclear weapons,

Aware that the non-proliferation of nuclear weapons is not an end in itself but, rather, a means of achieving general and complete disarmament at a later stage, and

Desiring to contribute, so far as lies in their power, towards ending the armaments race, especially in the field of nuclear weapons, and towards strengthening a world at peace, based on mutual respect and sovereign equality of States,

Have agreed as follows:

Article 1. To undertake to apply the statute of denuclearization in respect of warlike purposes as defined in articles 1, 3, 5 and 13 of the Treaty for the Prohibition of Nuclear Weapons in Latin America in territories for which, *de jure* or *de facto*, they are internationally responsible and which lie within the limits of the geographical zone established in that Treaty.

Signed by the United States at Washington, DC, 26 May 1977. Ratification advised by the US Senate 13 November 1981. Ratified by the US President 19 November 1981. US ratification deposited at Mexico City 23 November 1981. Proclaimed by the US President 4 December 1981.

Article 2. The duration of this Protocol shall be the same as that of the Treaty for the Prohibition of Nuclear Weapons in Latin America of which this Protocol is an annex, and the provisions regarding ratification and denunciation contained in the Treaty shall be applicable to it.

Article 3. This Protocol shall enter into force, for the States which have ratified it, on the date of the deposit of their respective instruments of ratification.

IN WITNESS WHEREOF the undersigned Plenipotentiaries, having deposited their full powers, found in good and due form, sign this Protocol on behalf of their respective Governments.

Additional Protocol II to the Treaty for the Prohibition of Nuclear Weapons in Latin America

The undersigned Plenipotentiaries, furnished with full powers by their respective Governments,

Convinced that the Treaty for the Prohibition of Nuclear Weapons in Latin America, negotiated and signed in accordance with the recommendations of the General Assembly of the United Nations in Resolution 1911 (XVIII) of 27 November 1963, represents an important step towards ensuring the non-proliferation of nuclear weapons,

Aware that the non-proliferation of nuclear weapons is not an end in itself but, rather, a means of achieving general and complete disarmament at a later stage, and

Desiring to contribute, so far as lies in their power, towards ending the armaments race, especially in the field of nuclear weapons, and towards promoting and strengthening a world at peace, based on mutual respect and sovereign equality of States,

Have agreed as follows:

Article 1. The statute of denuclearization of Latin America in respect or warlike purposes, as defined, delimited and set forth in the Treaty for the Prohibition of Nuclear Weapons in Latin America of which this instrument is an annex, shall be fully respected by the Parties to this Protocol in all its express aims and provisions.

Article 2. The Governments represented by the undersigned Plenipotentiaries undertake, therefore, not to contribute in any way to the performance of acts involving a violation of the obligations of article 1 of the Treaty in the territories to which the Treaty applies in accordance with article 4 thereof.

Article 3. The Governments represented by the undersigned Plenipotentiaries also undertake not to use or threaten to use nuclear weapons against the

---

Signed by the United States at Mexico City 1 April 1968. Ratification advised by the US Senate 19 April 1971. Ratified by the US President 8 May 1971. US ratification deposited at Mexico City 12 May 1971. Proclaimed by the US President 11 June 1971.

Contracting Parties of the Treaty for the Prohibition of Nuclear Weapons in Latin America.

Article 4. The duration of this Protocol shall be the same as that of the Treaty for the Prohibition of Nuclear Weapons in Latin America of which this protocol is an annex, and the definitions of territory and nuclear weapons set forth in articles 3 and 5 of the Treaty shall be applicable to this Protocol, as well as the provisions regarding ratification, reservations, denunciation, authentic texts and registration contained in articles 26, 27, 30 and 31 of the Treaty.

Article 5. This Protocol shall enter into force, for the States which have ratified it, on the date of the deposit of their respective instruments of ratification.

IN WITNESS WHEREOF the undersigned Plenipotentiaries, having deposited their full powers, found in good and due form, sign this Additional Protocol on behalf of their respective Governments.

Proclamation by President Nixon on ratification of Additional Protocol II to the Treaty for the Prohibition of Nuclear Weapons in Latin America

By the President of the United States of America

A Proclamation

Considering that:

Additional Protocol II to the Treaty for the Prohibition of Nuclear Weapons in Latin America, done at the City of Mexico on February 14, 1967, was signed on behalf of the United States of America on April 1, 1968, the text of which Protocol is word for word as follows:

[The text of the Protocol appears here.]

The Senate of the United States of America by its resolution of April 19, 1971, two-thirds of the Senators present concurring, gave its advice and consent to the ratification of Additional Protocol II, with the following understandings and declarations:

I

That the United States Government understands the reference in Article 3 of the Treaty to 'its own legislation' to relate only to such legislation as is compatible with the rules of international law and as involves an exercise of sovereignty consistent with those rules, and accordingly that ratification of Additional Protocol II by the United States Government could not be regarded as implying recognition, for the purposes of this Treaty and its protocols or for any other purpose, of any legislation which did not, in the view of the United States, comply with the relevant rules of international law.

That the United States Government takes note of the Preparatory Commission's interpretation of the Treaty, as set forth in the Final Act, that, governed by the principles and rules of international law, each of the Contracting Parties retains exclusive power and legal competence, unaffected by the terms of the Treaty, to grant or deny non-Contracting Parties transit and transport privileges.

That as regards the undertaking in Article 3 of Protocol II not to use or threaten to use nuclear weapons against the Contracting Parties, the United States Government would have to consider that an armed attack by a Contracting Party, in which it was assisted by a nuclear-weapon state, would be incompatible with the Contracting Party's corresponding obligations under Article I of the Treaty.

II

That the United States Government considers that the technology of making nuclear explosive devices for peaceful purposes is indistinguishable from the technology of making nuclear weapons, and that nuclear weapons and nuclear explosive devices for peaceful purposes are both capable of releasing nuclear energy in an uncontrolled manner and have the common group of characteristics of large amounts of energy generated instantaneously from a compact source. Therefore, the United States Government understands the definition contained in Article 5 of the Treaty as necessarily encompassing all nuclear explosive devices. It is also understood that Articles 1 and 5 restrict accordingly the activities of the Contracting Parties under paragraph 1 of Article 18.

That the United States Government understands that paragraph 4 of Article 18 of the Treaty permits, and that United States adherence to Protocol II will not prevent, collaboration by the United States with Contracting Parties for the purpose of carrying out explosions of nuclear devices for peaceful purposes in a manner consistent with a policy of not contributing to the proliferation of nuclear weapons capabilities. In this connection, the United States Government notes Article V of the Treaty on the Non-Proliferation of Nuclear Weapons, under which it joined in an undertaking to take appropriate measures to ensure that potential benefits of peaceful applications of nuclear explosions would be made available to non-nuclear-weapon states party to that Treaty, and reaffirms its willingness to extend such undertaking, on the same basis, to states precluded by the present Treaty from manufacturing or acquiring any nuclear explosive device.

III

That the United States Government also declares that, although not required by Protocol II, it will act with respect to such territories of Protocol I adherents as are within the geographical area defined in paragraph 2 of Article 4 of the Treaty in the same manner as Protocol II requires it to act with respect to the territories of Contracting Parties.

Treaty of Tlatelolco

The President ratified Additional Protocol II on May 8, 1971, with the above recited understandings and declarations, in pursuance of the advice and consent of the Senate.

It is provided in Article 5 of Additional Protocol II that the Protocol shall enter into force, for the States which have ratified it, on the date of the deposit of their respective instruments of ratification.

The instrument of ratification of the United Kingdom of Great Britain and Northern Ireland was deposited on December 11, 1969 with understandings and a declaration, and the instrument of ratification of the United States of America was deposited on May 12, 1971 with the above recited understandings and declarations.

In accordance with Article 5 of Additional Protocol II, the Protocol entered into force for the United States of America on May 12, 1971, subject to the above recited understandings and declarations.

NOW, THEREFORE, I, Richard Nixon, President of the United States of America, proclaim and make public Additional Protocol II to the Treaty for the Prohibition of Nuclear Weapons in Latin America to the end that it shall be observed and fulfilled with good faith, subject to the above recited understandings and declarations, on and after May 12, 1971 by the United States of America and by the citizens of the United States of America and all other persons subject to the jurisdiction thereof.

IN TESTIMONY WHEREOF, I have signed this proclamation and caused the Seal of the United States of America to be affixed.

DONE at the city of Washington this eleventh day of June in the year of our Lord one thousand nine hundred seventy-one and of the Independence of the United States of America the one hundred ninety-fifth.

[Seal]

Note

1 The Organization of American States' document lists Bermuda, Cayman, Turks and Caicos and British Virgin Islands, Montserrat, Guadeloupe, Martinique, French Guiana, St Pierre, Miquelon, Netherlands Antilles (Aruba, Bonaire, Curaçao, Saba, St Eustatius, St Martin), Greenland, and US Virgin Islands as 'nonautonomous territories' in one sense or another; Anguilla, with ties to the UK, is considered something of special case, more than 'nonautonomous' but less than independent. Greenland is not within the zone of application, and as such would not be eligible for membership should it one day achieve independence from Denmark.

Table A.2. Status of signatures and ratifications of the Treaty for the Prohibition of Nuclear Weapons in Latin America and the Caribbean

Country	Signature	Ratification	Waiver
Antigua and Barbuda	11 October 1983	11 October 1983	11 October 1983
Argentina*	27 September 1967	18 January 1994	18 January 1994
Bahamas	29 November 1976	26 April 1977	26 April 1977
Barbados*	18 October 1968	25 April 1969	25 April 1969
Belize*	14 February 1992	9 November 1994	9 November 1994
Bolivia	14 February 1967	18 February 1969	18 February 1969
Brazil*	9 May 1967	29 January 1968	30 May 1994
Colombia*	14 February 1967	4 August 1972	6 September 1972
Costa Rica*	14 February 1967	25 August 1969	25 August 1969
Chile*	14 February 1967	9 October 1974	18 January 1994
Cuba*	25 March 1995	23 October 2002	23 October 2002
Dominica	2 May 1989	4 June 1993	25 August 1993
Dominican Republic*	28 July 1967	14 June 1968	14 June 1968
Ecuador*	14 February 1967	11 February 1969	11 February 1969
El Salvador*	14 February 1967	22 April 1968	22 April 1968
Grenada*	29 April 1975	20 June 1975	20 June 1975
Guatemala*	14 February 1967	6 February 1970	6 February 1970
Guyana*	16 January 1995	16 January 1995	14 May 1997
Haiti	14 February 1967	23 May 1969	23 May 1969
Honduras	14 February 1967	23 September 1968	23 September 1968
Jamaica*	26 October 1967	26 June 1969	26 June 1969
Mexico*	14 February 1967	20 September 1967	20 September 1967
Nicaragua	15 February 1967	24 October 1968	24 October 1968
Panama*	14 February 1967	11 June 1971	11 June 1971
Paraguay*	26 April 1967	19 March 1969	19 March 1969
Peru*	14 February 1967	4 March 1969	4 March 1969
St Kitts and Nevis	18 February 1994	18 April 1995	14 February 1997
St Lucia	25 August 1992	2 June 1995	2 June 1995
St Vincent and the Grenadines	14 February 1992	14 February 1992	11 May 1992
Suriname*	13 February 1976	10 June 1977	10 June 1977
Trinidad and Tobago	27 June 1967	3 December 1970	27 June 1975
Uruguay*	14 February 1967	20 August 1968	20 August 1968
Venezuela*	14 February 1967	23 March 1970	23 March 1970

*Signifies states that have ratified at least some of the three (1990, 1991 and 1992) amendments to the treaty.

Appendix E

Joint Declaration on the Denuclearization of the Korean Peninsula

South and North Korea,

In order to eliminate the danger of nuclear war through the denuclearization of the Korean peninsula, to create conditions and an environment favourable to peace and the peaceful unification of Korea, and thus to contribute to the peace and security of Asia and the world,

Declare as follows;

1. South and North Korea shall not test, manufacture, produce, receive, possess, store, deploy or use nuclear weapons.

2. South and North Korea shall use nuclear energy solely for peaceful purposes.

3. South and North Korea shall not possess nuclear reprocessing and uranium enrichment facilities.

4. In order to verify the denuclearization of the Korean peninsula, South and North Korea shall conduct inspections of particular subjects chosen by the other side and agreed upon between the two sides, in accordance with the procedures and methods to be determined by the South–North Joint Nuclear Control Commission.

5. In order to implement this joint declaration, South and North Korea shall establish and operate a South–North Joint Nuclear Control Commission within one month of the entry into force of this joint declaration.

Entry into force on 19 February 1992.

6. This joint declaration shall enter into force from the date the South and the North exchange the appropriate instruments following the completion of their respective procedures for bringing it into effect.

Chung Won-shik

Chief Delegate
of the South
delegation to the
South–North
High-Level Negotiations

Prime Minister of the
Republic of Korea

Yon Hyong-muk

Head
of the North
delegation to the
South–North
High-Level Negotiations

Premier of the
Administration Council of
the Democratic People's
Republic of Korea

Index

ABACC *see* Brazilian–Argentine Agency for Accounting and Control of Nuclear Materials
accidental nuclear war, 51, 61–7, 72
Acheson–Lilienthal report, 127, 129, 130, 132
Additional Protocol (to IAEA safeguards agreements), 40, 42, 82, 84, 85, 86, 87, 94–6, 98, 99, 100–1, 115, 123–4, 151, 154
advanced gas-cooled reactor (AGR), 12
AFCONE *see* African Commission on Nuclear Energy
African Commission on Nuclear Energy (AFCONE), 115
African nuclear-free zone, 52, 58, 113, 114–16
Agency for the Prohibition of Nuclear Weapons in Latin America (OPANAL), 109, 111–12, 114, 115, 117
AGR *see* advanced gas-cooled reactor
Agreed Framework (between North Korea and the USA), 33–4, 129
Al Tuwaitha nuclear complex, 28–9
Albright, David, 30
Algeria, 18, 114–15

Antarctic Treaty, 106, 107
Anti-Ballistic Missile Treaty, 107, 135, 147
anti-missile defence, 70, 114, 128, 157
Argentina, 18, 22, 26, 27–8, 43, 58, 108, 109, 110, 112
Aspin, Les, US Secretary of State for Defense, 146, 147–50
Atoms for Peace initiative, 76, 88, 131–5, 155, 160
text, 181–6
see also Eisenhower, President Dwight D.
Attlee, Clement, Prime Minister, 128
Australia, 23, 24, 138, 152
Austria, 64

Baghdadtron, 30
ballistic missiles, 149
Bangkok, Treaty of *see* South East Asian nuclear-free zone
Baruch, Bernard M., 2
Baruch Plan, 126–31, 132, 134, 135, 137, 140, 141, 143, 144, 146, 147, 148, 149, 153, 155, 160, 171
text, 173–80

Belgium, 153
Belize, 112
biological weapons, 41–2, 131, 144, 147, 148, 149
  Convention, 131, 148
Blair, Bruce G., 65
Bolivia, 108
Bracken, Paul, 64
Brams, Steven J., 64
Brazil, 18, 23, 24, 25, 26, 27–8, 43, 58, 108, 109, 110, 112, 152
  peaceful nuclear explosions, 110–11, 154
Brazilian–Argentine Agency for Accounting and Control of Nuclear Materials (ABACC), 111, 113, 154
Bueno de Mesquita, Bruce, 49
Bush, President George W., 100, 107, 142, 148, 150–4
Bushehr (reactor complex), 37
Butler inquiry, 99
Buzan, Barry, 49

caesium-137, 17
calutron, 19, 28, 92
  see also Baghdadtron
Canada, 23, 24, 99
CANDU (reactor), 8, 9, 80
Capenhurst (uranium enrichment plant), 11–12, 27
Carter, President Jimmy, 12–14, 25, 32, 101, 130, 141, 142, 152–4, 166
chemical weapons, 41–2, 131, 144, 147, 148, 149
  Convention, 131, 148
Chernobyl, 16–17
Chile, 108, 109, 111, 112, 113
China, 16, 18, 31, 35, 36, 37, 38, 43, 48, 61, 62, 97, 107, 110, 115, 117, 133, 135, 150, 155, 157, 161, 163
Christopher, Warren, US Secretary of State, 37
Clinton, President Bill, 130, 148, 170–1
Collor de Mello, Fernando, 27

Comprehensive Test Ban Treaty (CTBT), 3, 53, 145, 155, 163–6, 168–72
Conference on Disarmament (UN), 107, 156
Costa Rica, 108
CTBT *see* Comprehensive Test Ban Treaty
Cuba, 48, 108, 109, 112, 113, 135, 164
cut-off (in fissile material production), 107, 134, 155

disarmament, nuclear, difficulties involved in, 155, 156
Dixit, Avinash, 163

Ecuador, 108
Eden, Prime Minister Anthony, 118
Eisenhower, President Dwight D., 132–5, 136, 155–6
ElBaradei, Mohamed, 38, 42
electromagnetic isotope separation (EMIS), 19
Elster, Jon, 49, 51
EMIS *see* electromagnetic isotope separation
environmental swipe, 32, 85, 87, 91, 93, 96
Euratom, 12, 53, 91, 111, 121–4, 138–40, 154
Eurodif, 153
European Union, 101, 121, 123, 124, 146
  Three, 40–1

fast breeder (reactor), 5
Fischer, David, 82, 85
France, 22, 25, 28, 30, 61, 62, 64, 97, 109–10, 116, 121, 135, 137, 141, 143, 147, 152–3, 161, 163
Fuchs, Klaus, 131

Garwin, Richard, 64
gas centrifuge, 20–2, 27, 29, 35–6, 38–40, 42, 97–8, 99, 100, 111, 113, 114–15, 150, 154
  supercritical, 41, 98

Index

gas diffusion, 20–1, 27, 97–8, 111, 153
Germany, 22, 25, 37, 52, 64, 98, 109, 111, 121, 122, 137–8, 149, 150–1, 154
Goldschmidt, Pierre, 155–6
Guyana, 112

heavy water, 8, 38, 80, 130
highly enriched uranium, 2, 18–24, 69, 80, 81, 91, 92, 95, 110, 127, 132, 133, 149, 151, 152, 155
Holland, 22, 98, 109, 150, 154
hot cell, 92, 95
hot line, 63, 65

IAEA *see* International Atomic Energy Agency
India, 1, 18, 42, 48, 52, 61, 65–7, 68, 90, 129, 135, 144, 166
Indonesia, 134
INFCE *see* International Fuel Cycle Evaluation
INFCIRC/66, 81, 90, 94, 95, 96, 101
INFCIRC/153, 39, 81, 83, 90, 93, 94, 101
INFCIRC/193, 122, 123
INFCIRC/540, 94
International Atomic Energy Agency (IAEA), 2, 12, 26, 27, 28, 29, 30, 31–2, 37–40, 42, 69, 76, 78, 81–90, 92, 94, 96, 99, 100, 113, 114, 119–20, 121–4, 132, 133, 138–40, 150–1, 154, 155–6, 170
International Fuel Cycle Evaluation (INFCE), 14, 130
iodine-131, 16–17
Iran, 18, 24, 26, 37–41, 43, 87, 98, 100, 129, 146, 150, 153, 170
  National Council of Resistance of, 37–8
Iraq, 18, 20, 26, 28–31, 37, 43, 82, 87, 90, 91, 92, 94, 95, 97, 98, 99, 101, 129, 144, 146, 149, 151, 153, 170
IRT-5000 (reactor), 29

Israel, 1, 18, 43, 48, 53, 67, 90, 92, 95, 135, 144
Italy, 29, 92, 137, 149, 153

Japan, 22, 28, 52, 137–8, 140, 144, 146, 152–3
Joint Declaration on the Denuclearization of the Korean Peninsula, 52, 119–20
  text, 221–2

Kazakhstan, 97
KEDO *see* Korean Peninsula Energy Development Organisation
Kelly, James, 34
Kendall, Henry W., 65
Kennan, George F., 126, 127, 128
Khan, A.Q., 98, 100, 149, 150–2, 154
Kilgour, D. Marc, 64
Kim Il Sung, 32
Korean Peninsula Energy Development Organisation (KEDO), 33, 34, 119–20
Kreps, David M., 163

laser enrichment (of uranium), 23–4, 37
Latin American nuclear-free zone, 2, 26, 43, 106, 108–13, 135, 144, 164
  parties, 220
  text (including amendments and protocols), 198–219
Libya, 18, 26, 41–2, 43, 87, 97, 98, 114–15, 149, 151
London Exporters' Club, 129

McMahon Act, 128, 131
Magnox (reactor), 8–12, 27, 32–3, 81, 93, 96
Malaysia, 149, 151
Manhattan Project, 11, 19–20, 28
material unaccounted for (MUF), 89, 91, 122, 156
Mexico, 108, 167
Missile Technology Control Regime (MTCR), 131

Mitramas, 29
MTCR *see* Missile Technology Control Regime
MUF *see* material unaccounted for

negative security assurances, 41, 104, 142
Nigeria, 115
No-dong (missile), 33
Non-proliferation Treaty *see* Nuclear Non-proliferation Treaty (NPT)
North Korea, 16, 26, 31–6, 41, 43, 87, 90, 93–4, 95, 97, 101, 119–20, 130, 131, 146, 148, 149, 150, 170
NPT *see* Nuclear Non-proliferation Treaty
NSG *see* Nuclear Suppliers' Group
nuclear bomb, 6–7, 13, 106, 127
nuclear-free zones, 96, 104–6, 108–18
  defence expenditures within, 113, 116–18, 120
Nuclear Nonproliferation Act (USA), 91, 97, 141
Nuclear Non-proliferation Treaty (NPT), 1–4, 18, 26, 28, 31, 37, 40, 67, 114
  as alternative to 'going nuclear', 42–3
  bargains inherent in, 140–5, 152–7
  collective action, 59–61, 76
  disarmament, 160
  IAEA, 76–101
  nuclear-free zones, 104, 109, 111–12, 117, 120–1, 122–4, 138–40
  nuclear testing, 165, 167–8
  origins, 137–8
  parties, 193–7
  peaceful nuclear explosions, 110
  plutonium fuel cycle, 12–14
  review conferences, 90, 91, 145, 155, 167–8
  security assurances, 142–3
  targets of, 52–3
  text 187–92
nuclear reactor, 7–10, 13, 84, 88–9, 96, 115, 149, 151, 155

Nuclear Suppliers' Group (NSG), 90, 91, 95, 101, 129, 131, 141, 149, 150–3
nuclear theft, 67–9

OPANAL *see* Agency for the Prohibition of Nuclear Weapons in Latin America
Osirak (reactor), 30, 90, 92
Outer Space Treaty, 107

Pakistan, 1, 18, 25, 36, 42, 48, 60, 61, 65–7, 68, 97, 98, 129, 144, 150
Partial Test Ban Treaty (PTBT), 135–7, 160–6
Peaceful Nuclear Explosions (PNE) Treaty, 166–7, 171
Pelindaba, Treaty of *see* African nuclear-free zone
plutonium, 2–6, 69, 80, 81, 85, 88, 89, 90, 91, 92, 93, 96, 97, 99, 110, 115, 127, 130, 132, 133, 151–2, 155
PNE Treaty *see* Peaceful Nuclear Explosions Treaty
polonium, 7, 41
positive security assurances, 41, 104, 142
Powell, Colin, US Secretary of State, 35
pressurised water reactor (PWR), 9–12, 15–16, 25, 32, 33, 36, 37, 129, 152
prisoner's dilemma, 54, 55, 57, 70, 71, 73, 164–5
Pritchard, Jack, 34
PTBT *see* Partial Test Ban Treaty
PWR *see* pressurised water reactor

radioactive waste, 14–18, 93, 106, 115
Rapacki Plan, 118–19
Rarotonga, Treaty of *see* South Pacific nuclear-free zone
Reagan, President Ronald, 108, 128
Reykjavik summit, 128
Riker, William, 49
Robles, Garcia, 108

Index

Rousseau, J-J., 148
Russell, Bertrand, 128
Russia, 22, 36, 37, 38, 61, 64, 93, 107, 150, 155, 157
  nuclear warhead totals, 70, 145, 156, 167

safeguards, 12, 22, 31–2, 37, 76–7
  classical, 81–5, 88, 89, 100
  Cut-off Treaty, 156
  full-scope, 13, 90, 101, 129, 151
  integrated, 84, 86, 98, 100
  Karlsruhe doctrine, 83, 88–90, 91–5, 101
Schaab, Karl Heinz, 29, 98, 100, 150–1, 154
Schelling, T.C., 71
Seabed Treaty, 107
Sellafield, 15, 139
  see also Windscale
Singapore, 151
Skeath, Susan, 163
Sokolski, Henry, 149
South Africa, 18, 22, 23, 25, 26, 42, 43, 58, 67, 90, 97, 114, 115, 152
South East Asian nuclear-free zone, 52, 113, 116–18
South Korea, 24, 25, 35, 36, 119–20, 131, 146
South Pacific nuclear-free zone, 2, 113–14, 115
Soviet Union, 20, 29, 48, 51, 58, 59, 62, 63, 97, 110, 117, 122, 128, 131, 133, 134, 138, 151, 160, 161, 163–4
Spain, 137, 149, 153
Stalin, J., 127–8, 131, 135
Stemmler, Bruno, 29
strontium-90, 17
Sudan, 148–9
Sweden, 16

Tahir, B.S.A., 149
terrorism, 69, 150
thermonuclear bomb, 7
thorium, 4, 5
Three Mile Island, 16, 18

Threshold Test Ban Treaty (TTBT), 166–8, 171
Tlatelolco, Treaty of *see* Latin American nuclear-free zone
Trident D5 missile, 65, 68
TTBT *see* Threshold Test Ban Treaty

UK, 58, 59, 61, 62, 64, 65, 68, 97, 98, 109–10, 128, 147, 154, 161, 164
  Magnox reactor, 8–12
uranium, 4, 5, 97, 152, 154
Urenco, 12, 22, 29, 31, 98, 150–1, 153–4
USA, 7, 43, 48, 51, 58, 59, 61, 97, 117
  accidental nuclear war, 62–5
  Additional Protocol, 100–1
  Atoms for Peace, 131, 135
  Baruch Plan, 126–31
  Comprehensive Test Ban Treaty, 155, 163, 170–2
  counter-proliferation, 146–50
  Euratom and Europe, 11–14, 122, 139–40, 143, 146
  Latin American nuclear-free zone, 109–10
  Manhattan Project, 18–20
  North Korea, 32–6
  NPT origins, 137–8
  nuclear testing, 161–72
  nuclear warhead totals, 70, 145, 148, 156, 167
  Nunn–Lugar Act, 151
  peaceful nuclear explosions, 110, 163, 166–7, 168
  pressurised water reactor (PWR), 11–12, 16
  Proliferation Security Initiative, 150
  radiological weapons, 16
  security assurances, 142–4, 147
  weapons laboratories, 163, 168
USSR *see* Soviet Union

Waltz, Kenneth N., 48–51, 53, 57, 58, 59, 66, 73
Wilson, Prime Minister Harold, 143
Windscale, 11, 17

Yemen, 149
Yongbyon nuclear complex, 31, 34, 93

Zangger Committee, 90, 129
Zinni, US Army General, 149

EU authorised representative for GPSR:
Easy Access System Europe, Mustamäe tee 50,
10621 Tallinn, Estonia
gpsr.requests@easproject.com